CW01034329

toni morrison and motherhood

TONI MORRISON

and

MOTHERHOOD

A Politics of the Heart

ANDREA O'REILLY

State University of New York Press

Published by
STATE UNIVERSITY OF NEW YORK PRESS
ALBANY

© 2004 State University of New York

For information, contact
State University of New York Press,
Albany, NY   www.sunypress.edu

Production, Laurie Searl
Marketing, Fran Keneston

Library of Congress Cataloging-in-Publication Data

O'Reilly, Andrea, 1961–
   Toni Morrison and motherhood : a politics of the heart / Andrea O'Reilly.
      p. cm.
   Based on author's thesis (Ph.D.)—York University.
   Includes bibliographical references (p.) and index.
   ISBN 0-7914-6075-4 (alk. paper) — ISBN 0-7914-6076-2 (pbk. : alk. paper)
   1. Morrison, Toni—Characters—Mothers. 2. Domestic fiction, American—History and
criticism. 3. Morrison, Toni—Political and social views. 4. African American families in
literature. 5. African American women in literature. 6. Mother and child in literature. 7.
Motherhood in literature. 8. Mothers in literature. I. Title.

PS3563.O8749Z79 2004
813'.54—dc22
                                                                          2004041739

10   9   8   7   6   5   4   3   2   1

for Terry Conlin

Contents

Preface

Di Brandt begins the prologue to her book *Wild Woman Dancing* (1993) discussing how the birth of her first child in 1976 called into question all that she had learned—or thought she had learned—in her Masters English literature program completed the same year. She writes: "It was like falling into a vacuum, narratively speaking. I realized suddenly, with a shock, that none of the texts I had read so carefully, none of the literary skills I had acquired so diligently as a student of literature, had anything remotely to do with the experience of becoming a mother" (3). Similarly, I first became a mother the same year I completed an Honors B.A. in English and Women's Studies (1984). Two years later I began a Ph.D. in English and gave birth to my second child four months later in December 1986. Twenty-five years old with two children born in under three years and the only mother in my Ph.D. program, I hungered for stories by and about mothers and wondered, as did Brandt, "Where . . . were the mothers, symbolic or otherwise, whom I might have turned to in that moment of loneliness and desperation?" (4). My graduate specialization was in the field of Women's Studies in English, and so I turned to women's literature and feminist theory in search of the absent mother. However, in 1986 little had been published in feminist theory or feminist literary theory on the topic of mothering-motherhood, and what had been written tended to reenact the patriarchal marginalization of motherhood.[1] It would seem that Di Brandt's observation that "the mother has been so largely absent in Western narrative, not because she is unnarratable, but because her subjectivity has been violently, and repeatedly, suppressed" (7) held true for most early feminist thinking on motherhood as well. Fortunately, as a Canadian resident and scholar, the mother-centered works of Canadian women writers Margaret Laurence, Adele Wiseman, and Joy Obasan was known to me. But I longed for more. My quest led me to the "rediscovered" late-eighteenth-century women writers who engaged with the topic of motherhood, in both narrative and essay form, and whose writings gave rise to the ideology of moral motherhood that in turn became the maternal feminism of the suffragist movement of the late nineteenth century. I rationalized that though I did not research directly women's narratives on mothering or feminist thought on motherhood, I did at least study, from a historical perspective, the emergence of the ideology and institution of motherhood. And so my fields of specialization became women's studies in literature and eighteenth-century literature.

All of this changed one cold and snowy night in February 1988. That fall I had signed up for a course on the African American novel and in the second term we moved to black women's fiction. I had tucked my one- and three-year-olds into bed with plans to begin the novel due for next week's class; the novel was Toni Morrison's *Beloved* (1987). I do not remember much from that night except that I finished the book at four in the morning when I should have been sleeping, given that my children would be up in two hours, and realized that I had found the maternal narrative for which I had been searching. In the three weeks that followed, I read all of Morrison's novels and met with my professor of African American literature and asked if she would be my supervisor for a dissertation on mothering and Toni Morrison. She asked me if I was sure, given that such a switch would add time to a Ph.D. already delayed by the birth of my two and soon to be three children. Yes, I was sure.

In the fifteen years that have passed since I first read Morrison, I have been asked on numerous occasions, "Why Morrison?" Or, more specifically, people wondered how I, a woman of English, Scottish, Irish ancestry who grew up in working-class Hamilton in southern Ontario, Canada, got so hooked on Morrison and motherhood. Every time I was asked this question, and even now as I finish this book on Morrison, I find myself at a loss for an explanation. I am a mother, and though my experiences of motherhood differ substantially from those narrated in Morrison, I nonetheless felt more at home in Morrison's maternal world than that of Anglo-American feminist thought. By 1988 when I first read Morrison, I was well versed in seventies and eighties Anglo-American feminist thinking on motherhood and yet never felt a sense of belonging or connection with this body of knowledge. Most of Anglo-American feminist writing on motherhood in 1988, with the notable exceptions of Sara Ruddick and Adrienne Rich, was daughter-centric and approached motherhood only as it had been defined by patriarchal culture. Specifically, it was work women did in the privacy of their homes that had no political import or cultural value and was oppressive to women.[2] While I did motherwork in the home, I also performed what Patricia Hill Collins defines as othermothering and regarded the mothering I did in the home—feminist, antiracist, antihomophobic, anticlassist, anticonsumerist, education-centered childrearing—as a highly political undertaking with profound cultural significance. And while I found (and still find) mothering to be the most difficult work I have ever undertaken, I have never felt oppressed or disempowered by motherhood.[3] Morrison portrays motherhood, in all of its dimensions—motherwork, motherlove, and the motherline—as a political enterprise with social consequences. This made sense to me. And when she remarked in an interview, "There was something so valuable about what happened when one became a mother. For me it was the most liberating thing that ever happened . . ." (1989: interview with Bill Moyers), I could not have agreed more.

When I first read Morrison, I analyzed her portrayals of mothers and motherhood through the lens of Anglo-American feminist thought on motherhood, as there was little published on black motherhood in 1987 and I was not familiar with what was available. However, I quickly realized that the Anglo-American perspective was hopelessly inadequate for an understanding of Morrison's maternal vision. I spent a lot of time piecing together information on black motherhood; a task made easier by the publication of Collins's *Black Feminist Thought* in 1990 and Patricia Bell-Scott's edited anthology *Double Stitch: Black Women Write about Mothers and Daughters* in 1991. As well, Anglo-American feminist thought by the late eighties and certainly by the mid-nineties had called into question the early feminist view that linked motherhood with oppression. In particular, the early Anglo-American feminist paradigm that problematized if not pathologized mother-daughter identification had fallen out of favor and most contemporary Anglo-American feminist theorists, by at least the late eighties, had come to regard mother-daughter connection and closeness as essential for female empowerment. This is of particular relevance to Morrison given her emphasis on the motherline.[4] By the time I came to write this book in 1999, research on black motherhood was far more available to me than it had been in 1988 (though more scholarship in this field is still urgently needed) and I had a far more extensive, diverse, and vibrant Anglo-American feminist tradition on motherhood from which to draw.

The intent of a preface is traditionally to introduce the book's thesis and to outline its format. To this business I now turn. The intent of this book is to read Morrison as a maternal theorist. The first chapter will examine black women's experiences of, and perspectives on motherhood; next it will explore how Morrison, building upon the traditions of black motherhood, defines motherhood as a site of power for black women and describes motherwork as enterprise concerned specifically with the empowerment of children. The remaining five chapters will explore how Morrison's maternal theory is enacted in her seven novels. Morrison, in her rendition of mothering as a political and public enterprise, emerges as a social commentator and political theorist who radically, through her maternal philosophy, reworks, rethinks, and reconfigures the concerns and strategies of African American, and in particular black women's, emancipation in America. In this, Morrison emerges as one of the most important and instructive voices in contemporary debates on race and gender; indeed, a voice that does and should keep you awake at night.

Acknowledgments

In *Song of Solomon* the narrator, commenting upon the importance of other-mothering, says this about Hagar Dead: "She needed what most colored girls needed: a chorus of mamas, grandmamas, aunts, cousins, sisters, neighbors, Sunday school teachers, best girl friends, and what all to give her the strength life demanded of her – and the humor with which to live it" (311). I believe that scholars likewise, need a "chorus of mamas" to think and write well. Fortunately, I have been blessed with a symphony in my life. In the ten plus years I have worked on this book, my chorus of mamas bestowed upon me the strength a writing life demands and the humor with which to live it.

This book is developed from my Ph.D. dissertation. I would first like to thank the many people who aided and sustained me on this part of my journey. In the fall of 1986 when I began my doctoral studies at York University, I had a two-year-old son and was six months pregnant with my second child. Three years later, I gave birth to my third child. After six years of study, I left the program to teach full-time as contract faculty. With three young children and a full-time teaching load, the journey to the completion of my Ph.D. was a long and arduous one. Thankfully, I did not make this journey alone.

I am grateful to the members of my dissertation committee, in particular Leslie Sanders, my supervisor, and Nancy Mandell: Leslie sustained me as a mother-scholar and Nancy showed me the importance of motherhood as an area of scholarship. I am also deeply grateful to Jan Pearson, Graduate Program Assistant in the Department of English: her kindness and wisdom made all the difference. Thanks are also due to the staff at the York University Cooperative daycare who, for over a decade, mothered my children while I wrote about motherhood. I could not have done it without them. As well, I am deeply grateful to my many friends who accompanied me on this journey; they kept me going each and every time I resolved to call it quits. Thanks to the Grad Lounge gang; in particular Dale Hall, Tony Crawford and Michael Collison. Thanks are due to Carol Davison, a dear friend since the early days of my Ph.D., who always asked the right questions and to Jerry Ginsburg for our talks in the hall. I am deeply grateful to Angela Bosco and Linda O'Neill: their friendship made the completion of my dissertation endurable and their generous childcare made it possible. I would also like to thank my extended family, in particular my mother-in-law Lois Conlin who generously provided childcare over the years. I am deeply grateful to my many friends of my Ph.D. years, Chris Cudahy, Terri Urovitz, Karen Bible, and Christy Taylor: our monthly 'meetings' sustained me. Special thanks are due to Siobhan McEwan and Dorothy Liptrot who stood by me during those difficult years, and to my sister Jennifer O'Reilly who, in her kindness and humour, kept me human even as I became an academic.

In 1996, having completed my Ph.D., I turned my attention to developing my dissertation into a book. Special thanks are due to Phil Page who generously agreed to read my thesis and provided me with the praise and instruction needed to develop it into a book. Thank you also to the members of *The Association for Research on Mothering*. My thinking on motherhood was enriched and sustained by this splendid community of scholars. In particular I would like to thank Patrice DiQuinzio for her careful reading of an early draft and Nancy Gerber and Elizabeth Bourque Johnson for giving me encouragement and advice when I needed it the most. Thanks also to my research assistants, Giselle Vincent, Brenda Clews, Amy Saricino, and Roni Hoffman, who not only created order from chaos, but did so with good cheer and kind support. I am also deeply indebted to Randy Chase, who proofread the manuscript and prepared the index: all scholars should have the good fortune of working with someone as talented and dedicated as Randy. I am deeply grateful to my editor James Peltz for his belief in the manuscript, and to Laurie Searl for her skill in turning it into a book. Finally, thank you to my dear friend and colleague at *The Association for Research on Mothering*, Cheryl Dobinson, for always listening when I despaired.

I would like to conclude my acknowledgments with thanks to my family. Thank you to Jean Allan O'Reilly, my mother: she has supported me in every imaginable way and was the first to teach me to believe in myself. Special thanks are due to my toughest critic, my most avid supporter, my closest friend, and my spouse of twenty-one years, Terry Conlin. He has made mothering enjoyable and writing possible; he has enabled me to be both ship and harbor. But most of all I would like to thank my children, Jesse, Erin, and Casey O'Reilly-Conlin. I began my work on Toni Morrison when they were all under the age of five; they are now 19, 17, and 14. They generously shared their childhood with Toni Morrison and accepted, with few complaints, the demands this stranger made on their mother's time and attention. With this book, as with my others, my children have shown the greatest respect for my scholarship and have graciously accepted that books and a computer are a normal part of mothering. The confidence, courage, and compassion that writing this book demanded of me I acquired in mothering my children. To paraphrase Toni Morrison: "My children demanded that I deliver something that somebody can use," and for this I am forever grateful.

chapter one

A Politics of the Heart

Toni Morrison's Theory of Motherhood as a Site of
Power and Motherwork as Concerned with the
Empowerment of Children

MOTHERHOOD IS A CENTRAL THEME in Morrison's fiction and is a topic she returns to time and time again in her many interviews and articles. In her reflections on motherhood, both inside and outside her fiction, Morrison articulates a fully developed theory of African American mothering that is central to her larger political and philosophical stance on black womanhood. Building upon black women's experiences of, and perspectives on motherhood, Morrison develops a view of black motherhood that is, in terms of both maternal identity and role, radically different than the motherhood practised and prescribed in the dominant culture. Morrison defines and positions maternal identity as a site of power for black women. From this position of power black mothers engage in a maternal practice that has as its explicit goal the empowerment of children. This chapter will introduce Morrison's theory of motherhood, what I have termed "A Politics of the Heart." Drawing upon Patricia Hill Collins's standpoint theory, I will detail how the traditions and practices of black mothering give rise to a distinct black maternal perspective on motherhood. The chapter will then examine how Morrison, building from this standpoint on black motherhood, defines black motherhood as a site of power for women. Next, borrowing from Sara Ruddick's model of maternal practice, I will explore how and in which ways Morrison defines motherwork as a political enterprise that assumes as its central aim the empowerment of children. Motherwork, in Morrison, is concerned with how mothers, raising black children in a racist and sexist world, can best protect their children, instruct them in how to protect themselves, challenge racism, and, for daughters, the sexism that seeks to harm them.

PATRICIA HILL COLLINS'S STANDPOINT THEORY

In *Black Feminist Thought: Knowledge, Consciousness, and the Politics of Empowerment,* Patricia Hill Collins writes, "[E]very culture has a worldview that it uses to order and evaluate its own experiences" (10). Black women, Collins goes on to explain,

> fashioned an independent standpoint about the meaning of Black womanhood. These self definitions enabled Black women to use African-derived conceptions of self and community to resist negative evaluations of Black womanhood advanced by dominant groups. In all, Black women's grounding in traditional African-American culture fostered the development of a distinctive African American women's culture. (11)

The black female standpoint develops in opposition to and in resistance against the dominant view or what Collins calls the controlling images of black womanhood. Collins argues that "the dominant ideology of the slave era fostered the creation of four interrelated, socially constructed controlling images of Black womanhood, each reflecting the dominant group's interest in maintaining Black women's subordination" (71). The four controlling images that Collins examines include the mammy, the matriarch, the welfare mother, and the Jezebel. By way of controlling images, as Collins explains, "certain assumed qualities are attached to Black women and [then] used to justify [that] oppression" (7). "From the mammies, Jezebels, and breeder women of slavery," Collins writes, "to the smiling Aunt Jemimas on pancake mix boxes, ubiquitous Black prostitutes, and ever-present welfare mothers of contemporary popular culture, the nexus of negative stereotypical images applied to African-American women has been fundamental to Black women's oppression" (7). Black women, according to Collins, may resist these derogatory stereotypes through the creation of a distinct black female standpoint that is based on black women's own experiences and meanings of womanhood.

The black female standpoint, Collins argues, develops through an interplay between two discourses of knowledge: "the commonplace taken-for granted knowledge" and the "everyday ideas" of black women that are clarified and rearticulated by black women intellectuals or theorists to form a specialized black feminist thought. In turn, as Collins explains, "the consciousness of Black women may be transformed by [this] thought" (20). She elaborates:

> Through the process of rearticulation, Black women intellectuals offer African-American women a different view of themselves and their world from that forwarded by the dominant group. . . . By taking the core themes of a Black women's standpoint and infusing them with new meaning, Black women intellectuals can stimulate a new consciousness that utilizes Black's women's everyday, taken-for granted knowledge. Rather than raising consciousness, Black feminist thought affirms and rearticulates a consciousness that already exists. More, important, this rearticulated consciousness empowers African-American women and stimulates resistance. (31–32)

In other words, the black female standpoint, emerging from black women's everyday experiences and clarified by black feminist theory, not only provides a distinct "angle of vision on self, community and society" but also, in so doing, enables black women to counter and interrupt the dominant discourse of black womanhood.

The formation and articulation of a self-defined standpoint, Collins emphasizes, "is [thus] key to Black women's survival" (26). As Audre Lorde argues, "[I]t is axiomatic that if we do not define ourselves for ourselves, we will be defined by others—for their use and to our detriment" (as quoted in Collins, 21, 1991). However, as Collins emphasizes the importance of self-definition, she recognizes that black women, as an oppressed group, inevitably must struggle to convey this self-definition, positioned as they are at the periphery of the dominant white, male culture. Collins writes: "An oppressed group's experiences may put its members in a position to see things differently, but their lack of control over ideological apparatuses of society makes expressing a self-defined standpoint more difficult" (26). The black female standpoint is thus, in Collins's words, "an independent, viable, yet subjugated knowledge" (13).

Collins's standpoint thesis provides a useful conceptual framework for viewing Morrison as a maternal theorist. To borrow from Collins's paradigm: Morrison is an intellectual who takes the core themes of black motherhood and develops from them a new consciousness of black motherhood that empowers African American women and engenders resistance. Furthermore, Morrison's standpoint on black motherhood challenges, and enables black women to challenge the controlling images of black motherhood, which Collins has defined as the mammy, the matriarch, Jezebel, and the welfare mother. Morrison's standpoint on black motherhood enables black women to resist these negative evaluations of black motherhood by rearticulating the power that is inherent in black women's everyday experiences of motherhood. This rearticulation centers upon a reaffirmation of the traditional roles and beliefs of black motherhood that gives rise to Morrison's theory of hood as a site of power for black women and her theory of motherwork as an enterprise concerned with the empowerment of children. The following section will explore "the commonplace taken-for granted knowledge" and "everyday ideas" of black motherhood from which Morrison develops her theory of motherhood as a "politics of the heart."

AFRICAN AMERICAN WOMANIST THOUGHT ON MOTHERHOOD

"During the early stages of contemporary women's liberation movement," bell hooks writes, "feminist analyses of motherhood reflected the race and class biases of participants" (1984: 133). "Some white, middle class, college educated women argued," hooks continues, that motherhood was:

the locus of women's oppression. Had black women voiced their views on
motherhood, it would not have been named a serious obstacle to our freedom as women. Racism, availability of jobs, lack of skills or education . . .
would have been at the top of the list—but not motherhood. (1984: 133)

Feminist theory on motherhood, as hooks identifies, is racially codified. Drawing upon contemporary womanist[1] thought on black motherhood, I will argue
that there exists a distinct African American tradition of motherhood. Two interrelated themes or perspectives distinguish the African American tradition of
motherhood. First, mothers and motherhood are valued by, and central to
African American culture. Secondly, it is recognized that mothers and mothering
are what make possible the physical and psychological well-being and empowerment of African American people and the larger African American culture. Black
women raise children in a society that is at best indifferent to the needs of black
children and the concerns of black mothers. The focus of black motherhood, in
both practice and thought, is how to preserve, protect, and more generally
empower black children so that they may resist racist practices that seek to harm
them and grow into adulthood whole and complete. For the purpose of this discussion, I employ African Canadian theorists Wanda Thomas Bernard and Candace Bernard's definition of empowerment: "empowerment is naming, analyzing,
and challenging oppression on an individual, collective, and/or structural level.
Empowerment, which occurs through the development of critical consciousness,
is gaining control, exercising choices, and engaging in collective social action"
(46). To fulfill the task of empowering children, mothers must hold power in
African American culture, and mothering likewise must be valued and supported. In turn, African American culture, understanding the importance of
mothering for individual and cultural well-being and empowerment, gives power
to mothers and prominence to the work of mothering. In other words, black
mothers require power to do the important work of mothering and are accorded
power because of the importance of mothering.

The African American tradition of motherhood centers upon the recognition that mothering, in its concern with the physical and psychological well-
being of children and its focus upon the empowerment of children, has cultural
and political import, value, and prominence, and that motherhood, as a consequence, is a site of power for black women. This section will examine this tradition of African American mothering under five interrelated topics: "Othermothering and Community Mothering," "Motherhood as Social Activism and as a
Site of Power," "Matrifocality," "Nurturance as Resistance: Providing a Homeplace," and "The Motherline: Mothers as Cultural Bearers." Next it will examine
this tradition in the context of mothers' relationships with their children. Specifically, this section will consider how daughters seek identification or connection
with their mothers due to the cultural centrality and significance of the mother
role and how this connection gives rise to the daughters' empowerment in
African American culture. Finally, the section will explore how African American

mothers remain, contrary to the normative scripts of mother-son relation, involved in their sons' lives and how this involvement fosters physical survival, psychological well-being, and overall empowerment.

OTHERMOTHERING AND COMMUNITY MOTHERING

Stanlie James, in "Mothering: A Possible Black Feminist Link to Social Transformations" defines othermothering "as acceptance of responsibility for a child not one's own, in an arrangement that may or may not be formal" (45). Othermothers usually care for children. In contrast, community mothers, as Njoki Nathani Wane explains, "take care of the community. These women are typically past their childbearing years" (112). "The role of community mothers," as Arlene Edwards notes, "often evolved from that of being othermothers" (88). James argues that othermothering and community mothering developed from, in Arlene Edwards's words, "West African practices of communal lifestyles and interdependence of communities" (88). Consequently, as Patricia Hill Collins has observed, "[m]othering [in West Africa] was not a privatized nurturing 'occupation' reserved for biological mothers, and the economic support of children was not the exclusive responsibility of men" (1993: 45). Rather, mothering expressed itself as both nurturance and work, and care of children was viewed as the duty of the larger community. Collins argues that these complementary dimensions of mothering and the practice of communal mothering/othermothering give women great influence and status in West African societies. She elaborates:

> First, since they are not dependent on males for economic support and provide much of their own and their children's economic support, women are structurally central to families. Second, the image of the mother is culturally elaborated and valued across diverse West African societies. . . . Finally, while the biological mother-child bond is valued, childcare was a collective responsibility, a situation fostering cooperative, age-stratified, woman centered "mothering" networks. (45)

These West African cultural practices, Collins argues, were retained by enslaved African Americans and gave rise to a distinct tradition of African American motherhood in which the custom of othermothering and community mothering was emphasized and elaborated. Arlene Edwards, in her article "Community Mothering: The Relationship Between Mothering and the Community Work of Black Women," explains:

> The experience of slavery saw the translation of othermothering to new settings, since the care of children was an expected task of enslaved Black women in addition to the field or house duties. . . . [T]he familial instability of slavery engendered the adaptation of communality in the form of fostering children whose parents, particularly mothers, had been sold. This tradition of communality gave rise to the practice of othermothering. The

survival of the concept is inherent to the survival of Black people as a whole . . . since it allowed for the provision of care to extended family and non blood relations. (80)

The practice of othermothering remains central to the African American tradition of motherhood and is regarded as essential for the survival of black people. Bell hooks, in her article "Revolutionary Parenting" (1984), comments:

> Child care is a responsibility that can be shared with other childrearers, with people who do not live with children. This form of parenting is revolutionary in this society because it takes place in opposition to the idea that parents, especially mothers, should be the only childrearers. Many people raised in black communities experienced this type of community-based child care. Black women who had to leave the home and work to help provide for families could not afford to send children to day care centers and such centers did not always exist. They relied on people in their communities to help. Even in families where the mother stayed home, she could also rely on people in the community to help. . . . People who did not have children often took responsibility for sharing in childrearing. (144)

"The centrality of women in African-American extended families," as Nina Jenkins concludes in "Black Women and the Meaning of Motherhood," "is well known" (Abbey and O'Reilly 1998: 206).

The practice of othermothering, as it developed from West African traditions, became in African American culture a strategy of survival in that it ensured that all children, regardless of whether the biological mother was present or available, would receive the mothering that delivers psychological and physical well-being and makes empowerment possible. Collins concludes:

> Biological mothers or bloodmothers are expected to care for their children. But African and African-American communities have also recognized that vesting one person with full responsibility for mothering a child may not be wise or possible. As a result, "othermothers," women who assist bloodmothers by sharing mothering responsibilities, traditionally have been central to the institution of Black motherhood. (1993: 47)

Community mothering and othermothering also emerged in response to black mothers' needs and served to empower black women and enrich their lives. "Historically and presently community mothering practices," Erica Lawson writes, "was and is a central experience in the lives of many Black women and participation in mothering is a form of emotional and spiritual expression in societies that marginalize Black women" (26). The self-defined and created role and identity of community mother also, as Lawson explains, "enabled African Black women to use African derived conceptions of self and community to resist negative evaluations of Black women" (26).

The practice of othermothering/community mothering as a cultural sustaining mechanism and as a mode of empowerment for black mothers has been documented in numerous studies. Carol Stack's early but important book *All Our Kin: Strategies for Survival in a Black Community* (1974) emphasizes how crucial and central extended kin and community are for poor urban blacks. "Black families in The Flats and the non-kin they regard as kin," Stack writes in her conclusion, "have evolved patterns of co-residence, kinship-based exchange networks linking multiple domestic units, elastic household boundaries, lifelong bonds to three-generation households, social controls against the formation of marriages that could endanger the network of kin, the domestic authority of women, and limitations on the role of the husband or male friend within a woman's kin network" (124).[2] Priscilla Gibson's recent article, "Developmental Mothering in an African American Community: From Grandmothers to New Mothers Again" (2000), provides a study of grandmothers and great-grandmothers who assumed the caregiving responsibilities of their (great) grandchildren as a result of the parent being unable or unwilling to provide that care. Gibson argues that "[in]creasingly grandmothers, especially African American grandmothers, are becoming kinship providers for grandchildren with absent parents. This absent middle generation occurs because of social problems such as drug abuse, incarceration, domestic violence, and divorce, just to name a few" (33). In "Reflections on the Mutuality of Mothering: Women, Children, and Othermothering," Njoki Nathani Wane explores in her research study of women in Kenya how precolonial African beliefs and customs gave rise to a communal practice of childrearing and an understanding that "parenting, especially mothering, was an integral component of African traditions and cultures" (111). "Most of pre-colonial Africa," explains Wane, "was founded upon and sustained by collectivism. . . . Labour was organized along parallel rather than hierarchical lines, thus giving equal value to male and female labour. Social organization was based on the principle of patrilineal or matrilineal descent, or a combination of both. Mothering practices were organized as a collective activity" (108). Today, the practice of othermothering, as Wane notes, "serves[s] to relieve some of the stresses that can develop between children and parents [and] provides multiple role models for children; [as well] it keeps the traditional African value systems of communal sharing and ownership alive" (113). Othermothering and community mothering, Wane concludes, "can be understood as a form of cultural work or as one way communities organize to nurture both themselves and future generations" (113).

Motherhood as Social Activism and as a Site of Power

The practices of othermothering and in particular community mothering serve, as Stanlie James argues, "as an important Black feminist link to the development of new models of social transformation" (45). Black women's role of community mothers, as Collins explains, redefines motherhood as social activism:

Black women's experiences as other mothers have provided a foundation for
Black women's social activism. Black women's feelings of responsibility for
nurturing the children in their extended family networks have stimulated a
more generalized ethic of care where Black women feel accountable to all
the Black community's children. (49)

In *Black Feminist Thought* Collins develops this idea further:

Such power is transformative in that Black women's relationships with children and other vulnerable community members is not intended to domi-
nate or control. Rather, its purpose is to bring people along, to—in the
words of late-nineteenth-century Black feminists—"uplift the race" so that
vulnerable members of the community will be able to attain the self-
reliance and independence essential for resistance. (132)

Various and diverse forms of social activism stem from and are sustained by the
African American custom of community mothering. Community mothering, as
Arlene Edwards explores it in her article "Community Mothering: The Relationship Between Mothering and the Community Work of Black Women," has been
expressed in activities and movements as varied as the Black Clubwomen and
Civil Rights movements and black women's work in the church. Drawing upon
the research of Gilkes, Edwards elaborates: "In reporting on Black community
workers, Gilkes found that these women often 'viewed the Black Community as
a group of relatives and other friends whose interest should be advanced, and pro-
moted at all times, under all conditions, and by almost any means'" (88). Bernard
and Bernard theorize black women's work as educators as a form of social
activism. "Education," they argue, "is considered a cornerstone of Black community development, and as such Black women, as community othermothers,
have placed a high value on education and have used it as a site for activism" (68).
Academic mothers, they continue, "also value education, and use their location
to facilitate the education of others. [As well] academic othermothers who operate within an Africentric framework, are change agents who promote student
empowerment and transformation" (68). They go on to elaborate:

Collins' definition of othermothers extends to the work we do in the academy. Othermothering in the community is the foundation of what Collins
calls the *"mothering the mind"* relationships that often developed between
African American women teachers and their Black female and male students. We refer to this as mothering in the academy, and see it as work that
extends beyond traditional definitions of mentorship. It is a sharing of self,
an interactive and collective process, a spiritual connectedness that epito-
mizes the Africentric values of sharing, caring and accountability. (68)

Collins argues that this construction of mothering as social activism
empowers black women because motherhood operates, in her words, as "a symbol of power." "A substantial portion of Black women's status in African-Amer-

ican communities," writes Collins, "stems not only from their roles as mothers in their own families but from their contributions as community othermothers to Black community development as well" (51). "More than a personal act," write Bernard and Bernard (1998), "Black motherhood is very political. Black mothers and grandmothers are considered the 'guardians of the generations.' Black mothers have historically been charged with the responsibility of providing education, social, and political awareness, in addition to unconditional love, nurturance, socialization, and values to their children, and the children in their communities" (47). Black motherhood, as Jenkins concluded, "is a site where [black women] can develop a belief in their own empowerment. Black women can see motherhood as providing a base for self-actualization, for acquiring status in the Black community and as a catalyst for social activism" (Abbey and O'Reilly 1998: 206).

MATRIFOCALITY

The African American model/practice of mothering, according to Patricia Hill Collins, differs from Eurocentric ideology in three important ways:

> First, the assumption that mothering occurs within the confines of a private, nuclear family household where the mother has almost total responsibility for child-rearing is less applicable to Black families. While the ideal of the cult of true womanhood has been held up to Black women for emulation, racial oppression has denied Black families sufficient resources to support private, nuclear family households. Second, strict sex-role segregation, with separate male and female spheres of influence within the family, has been less commonly found in African-American families than in White middle-class ones. Finally, the assumption that motherhood and economic dependency on men are linked and that to be a "good" mother one must stay at home, making motherhood a full-time "occupation," is similarly uncharacteristic of African-American families. (1993: 43–44)

Miriam Johnson in *Strong Mothers, Weak Wives* (1990) argues that the wife role and not the mother's role occasions women's secondary status in a patriarchal culture. In contrast, matrifocal cultures, such as African American culture, according to Johnson, emphasize women's mothering and are characterized by greater gender equality.[3] In matrifocal societies, Johnson writes, "women play roles of cultural and social significance and define themselves less as wives than as mothers" (226). "Matrifocality," Johnson continues,

> however, does not refer to domestic maternal dominance so much as it does to the relative cultural prestige of the image of mother, a role that is culturally elaborated and valued. Mothers are also structurally central in that mother as a status "has some degree of control over the kin unit's economic resources and is critically involved in kin-related decision making processes." . . . It is not the absence of males (males may be quite present)

but the centrality of women as mothers and sisters that makes a society matrifocal, and this matrifocal emphasis is accompanied by a minimum of differentiation between women and men. (226)

The wife identity, according to Collins, is less prevalent in African American culture because women assume an economic role and experience gender equality in the family unit. She writes:

African-American women have long integrated their activities as economic providers into their mothering relationships. In contrast to the cult of true womanhood, in which work is defined as being in opposition to and incompatible with motherhood, work for Black women has been an important and valued dimension of Afrocentric definitions of Black motherhood. (1993: 48)

"Whether they wanted to or not," Collins continues, "the majority of African-American women had to work and could not afford the luxury of motherhood as a noneconomically productive, female 'occupation'" (49). Thus, black women, at least among the urban poor, do not assume the wife role that Johnson identified as that which structures women's oppression. Moreover, in African American culture motherhood, not marriage, emerges as the rite of passage into womanhood. As Joyce Ladner emphasizes in *Tomorrow's Tomorrow* (1971): "If there was one common standard for becoming a woman that was accepted by the majority of the people in the community, it was the time when girls gave birth to their first child. This line of demarcation was extremely clear and separated the *girls* from the *women*" (215–16).[4] In African American culture, motherhood is the pinnacle of womanhood. The matrifocal structure of black families with its emphasis on motherhood over wifedom and black women's role as economic provider means that the wife role is less operative in the African American community and that motherhood is site of power for black women.

Nurturance as Resistance: Providing a Homeplace

The fourth way that African American mothering differs from the dominant model is the way in which nurturance of family is defined and experienced as a resistance. In African American culture, as theorist bell hooks has observed, the black family, or what she terms homeplace, operates as a site of resistance. She explains:

Historically, African-American people believed that the construction of a homeplace, however fragile and tenuous (the slave hut, the wooden shack), had a radical political dimension. Despite the brutal reality of racial apartheid, of domination, one's homeplace was one site where one could freely confront the issue of humanization, where one could resist. Black women resisted by making homes where all black people could strive to be subjects, not objects, where one could be affirmed in our minds and hearts despite poverty, hardship, and deprivation, where we could restore to ourselves the dignity denied to us on the outside in the public world. (1990: 42)

Hooks emphasizes that when she talks about homeplace she is not speaking merely of black women providing services for their families; rather, she refers to the creation of a safe place where, in her words, "black people could affirm one another and by so doing heal many of the wounds inflicted by racist domination . . . [a place where] [they] had the opportunity to grow an̄ develop, to nurture [their] spirits" (42).[5] In a racist culture that deems black children inferior, unworthy, and unlovable, maternal love of black children is an act of resistance; in loving her children the mother instills in them a loved sense of self and high self-esteem, enabling them to defy and subvert racist discourses that naturalize racial inferiority and commodify blacks as other and object. African Americans, hooks emphasizes, "have long recognized the subversive value of homeplace and homeplace has always been central to the liberation struggle" (42). Like hooks, Collins maintains that children learn at home how to identify and challenge racist practices and it is at home that children learn of their heritage and community. At home they are empowered to resist racism, particularly as it becomes internalized. Collins elaborates:

> Racial ethnic women's motherwork reflects the tensions inherent in trying to foster a meaningful racial identity in children within a society that denigrates people of color. . . . [Racial ethnic] children must first be taught to survive in systems that oppress them. Moreover, this survival must not come at the expense of self-esteem. Thus, a dialectal relationship exists between systems of racial oppression designed to strip a subordinated group of a sense of personal identity and a sense of collective peoplehood, and the cultures of resistance extant in various ethnic groups that resist the oppression. For women of color, motherwork for identity occurs at this critical juncture. (1994: 57)

The empowerment of minority children through resistance and knowledge occurs at home and in the larger cultural space through the communal mothering and social activism spoken of earlier. This view of mothering differs radically from the dominant discourse of motherhood that configures home as politically neutral space and views nurturance as no more than the natural calling of mothers.

The Motherline: Mothers as Cultural Bearers

The motherline, the fifth and final theme, considers the role black mothers play as cultural bearers and tradition keepers. Anglo-American feminist writer Naomi Lowinsky, author of *The Motherline: Every Woman's Journey to Find her Female Roots* (1992), defines the motherline:

> When a woman today comes to understand her life story as a story from the Motherline, she gains female authority in a number of ways. First, her Motherline grounds her in her feminine nature as she struggles with the many options now open to women. Second, she reclaims carnal knowledge of her own body, its blood mysteries and their power. Third, as she makes

the journey back to her female roots, she will encounter ancestors who struggled with similar difficulties in different historical times. This provides her
with a life-cycle perspective that softens her immediate situation. . . . Fourth,
she uncovers her connection to the archetypal mother and to the wisdom of
the ancient worldview, which holds that body and soul are one and all life is
interconnected. And, finally, she reclaims her female perspective, from
which to consider how men are similar and how they are different. (13)

Writing about Lowinsky's motherline in her book *Motherless Daughters: The
Legacy of Loss* (1994), Hope Edelman emphasizes that "Motherline stories ground
a . . . daughter in a gender, a family, and a feminine history. They transform the
experience of her female ancestors into maps she can refer to for warning or
encouragement" (201). Motherline stories, made available to daughters through
the female oral tradition, unite mothers and daughters and connect them to their
motherline. Naomi Lowinsky argues that many women today are disconnected
from their motherline and have lost, as a consequence, the authenticity and
authority of their womanhood. For Lowinsky, female empowerment becomes
possible only in and through reconnecting to the motherline.

In African American society the motherline represents the ancestral memory,
traditional values of African American culture. Black mothers pass on the teachings of the motherline to each successive generation through the maternal function of cultural bearing. Various African American writers argue that the very survival of African Americans depends upon the preservation of black culture and
history. If black children are to survive they must know the stories, legends, and
myths of their ancestors. In African American culture, women are the keepers of
the tradition: they are the culture bearers who mentor and model the African
American values essential the empowerment of black children and culture.
"Black women," Karla Holloway continues, "carry the voice of the mother—they
are the progenitors, the assurance of the line . . . as carriers of the *voice* [black
women] carry wisdom—mother wit. They teach the children to survive *and*
remember" (1987: 123). Black mothers, as Bernard and Bernard conclude, "pass
on the torch to their daughters, who are expected to become the next generation
of mothers, grandmothers, or othermothers, to guard future generations" (47).

The above five themes demonstrate that mothers and motherhood are valued by and regarded as central to African American culture; as well mothers and
mothering are recognized as that which makes possible the physical and psychological well-being and empowerment of African American people and the larger
African American culture. The following section will detail how the centrality
and significance of black motherhood gives rise to the empowerment of daughters. Black women, in connection with powerful mothers, become empowered as
daughters. "I come from / a long line of / Uppity Irate Black Women" begins
Kate Rushin's poem, "Family Tree." "And [when] you ask me how come / I think
I'm so cute," Kate Rushin replies, "I cultivate / Being uppity, / It's something /
My Gramon taught me" (Bell-Scott 1993: 176–77).

AFRICAN AMERICAN MOTHERS AND DAUGHTERS

Gloria Joseph and Jill Lewis, in their early but important work *Common Differences: Conflicts in Black and White Feminist Perspectives* (1981), contrast Anglo-American and African American women's experiences of motherhood and daughterhood. Joseph argues that respect for the mother was a central and organizing theme of the mother-daughter relationships examined. She also found that female socialization centered upon the teaching of survival skills and an insistence upon independence:

> What was startlingly evident, as revealed in the mother/daughter questionnaire, was the teaching of survival skills to females for their survival *in* and for the survival *of* the Black community. Intra-group survival skills were given more importance and credence than survival skills for dealing with the White society at large. There is a tremendous amount of teaching transmitted by Black mothers to their daughters that enables them to survive, exist, succeed, and be important to and for the Black communities. . . . Black daughters are actually "taught" to hold the Black community together. (106)[6]

The independence that mothers insist upon for their daughters is to be achieved through education and effort. This may be contrasted to the dominant narrative of Anglo-American feminine achievement that scripts marriage as the avenue through which women will "get ahead." The African American mothers' insistence upon independence for their daughters includes a critique of marriage, particularly the dependency inherent in the wife role. These mothers recognize with Miriam Johnson that it is the wife role and not the mother role that organizes women's secondary status. "Through Mom's guidance and direction," comments Candace Bernard in "Passing the Torch" (1998), "I learned the value of hard work, self-determination, goal-setting, and shared responsibility. . . . I experienced empowerment through Mom's ability to survive in a climate that was not conducive to survival." The daughter adds, "It is empowering to know that I have come from such a long line of strong Black women. . . . I feel honored that . . . I am able to carry on the struggle you began a generation ago" (48–49).

A black daughter also, as Barbara Turnage discusses in her article, "The Global Self-Esteem of an African-American Adolescent Female and Her Relationship with her Mother," develops high self-esteem through a secure and close attachment with her mother and knowledge of her African American heritage. Her study of 105 African American young women ranging in age from sixteen to eighteen, found that the most significant variable was "trust of the mother": "African American mothers play an important role in their daughters' self-esteem development. That is, the young women in this study who had high self-esteem also trusted their mothers to be there for them" (O'Reilly and Abbey 2000: 184). The second significant variable for self-esteem was "acknowledgment of an

African ancestry": "For an adolescent African-American female knowledge of her
African heritage helps her define her body image and structure her expectations"
(184). The message of this study, Turnage emphasizes, can not be "overstated":

> The relationship between these African-American young women and their
> mothers instilled in them the knowledge that they are competent and lov-
> able. Based on their trust in their mothers, these young women believed,
> when confronted with difficult situations, that they could rely on their
> mothers' assistance. Thus, as they grow into black womanhood, they grow
> with the knowledge that they can accomplish their goals and that they are
> worthy of love and respect. (184)

These daughters, connected with their mothers and motherline (awareness of
heritage), develop a strong and proud identity as black women and secure
empowerment.

Contemporary African American women's writing also celebrates mothers as
mentors and role models and illustrates the power daughters obtain in connection with their mothers and motherline. Readers of black women's literature have
long observed a deeply rooted matrilineal tradition in which daughters think
back through their mothers. In Marianne Hirsch's words, "[there is] in much of
contemporary black women's writing, a public celebration of maternal presence"
(177). In a 1980 article, appropriately entitled "I Sign My Mother's Name"
(Perry 1984), Mary Helen Washington speaks of a "generational continuity"
among African American women in which "a mother serves as the female pre-
cursor who passes on the authority of authorship to her daughter and provides a
model for the black woman's literary presence in this society" (147). "For black
women writers," as Dolana Mogadime observes in "A Daughter's Praise Poem for
her Mother," "the idea of thinking back through our mothers is rooted in the
notion of revisiting and learning about maternal knowledge and female-centred
networks as expressions of African continuities in contemporary society" (87).
Respect and gratitude for "women who made a way out of no way" is repeated
time and time again in the recent collection of writings on black mothers and
daughters, appropriately entitled *Double Stitch: Black Women Write About Mothers & Daughters* (Bell-Scott 1993).

In an introductory section to this collection, Beverly Guy-Sheftall writes: "In
selection after selection, daughters acknowledge how their mothers provided road
maps and patterns, a 'template,' which enabled them to create and define themselves. . . . Though daughters must forge an identity which is separate from the
mothers, they frequently acknowledge that a part of themselves is truly their
mothers' child" (61). Margaret Walker, in her poem appropriately entitled "Lineage," pays tribute to her grandmothers who "were strong / . . . full of sturdiness
and singing" (175). Sonia Sanchez writes: "My life flows from you Mama. My
style comes from a long line of Louises who picked me up in the night to keep
me from wetting the bed. . . . A long line of Lizzies who made me understand
love. . . . A Long line of Black people holding each other up against silence"

(25–26). Judy Scales-Trent writes: "my mother opened the door / . . . and set me free" (213). The first stanza of Irma McClaurin's poem, "The Power of Names," reads: "I slip my mother's name on like a glove / and wonder if I will become like her / absolutely. / Years number the times I have worn her pain / as a child, as a teenager, as a woman—my second skin— / as she sat, silver head bowed / silent / hedging the storm" (63).

In her moving autobiographical narrative, *Pushed Back to Strength: A Black Woman's Journey Home* (1993), some of which is excerpted in *Double Stitch,* Gloria Wade-Gayles argues that in the segregated South of the forties, "[s]urviving meant being black, and being black meant believing in our humanity, and retaining it, in a world that denied we had it in the first place" (6). The survival of black culture and black selfhood was sustained by the motherline. "The men in my family were buttresses and protectors," writes Wade-Gayles, "but it was the women who gave meaning to the expression 'pushed back to strength'" (13). Whether named mentor, role model, guide, advisor, wise woman, or advocate, the mother represents for the daughter a sturdy bridge on which to cross over. Even the author Renita Weems who was abandoned by her alcoholic mother writes: "Though not as sturdy as others, she is my bridge. When I needed to get across she steadied herself long enough for me to run across safely" (Bell-Scott 1993: 129).

Alice Walker's classic essay, "In Search of Our Mothers' Gardens" (1983), is a moving tribute to her African American foremothers who, in her words, "handed on the creative spark, the seed of the flower they themselves never hoped to see: or like a sealed letter they could not plainly read" (240). "[S]o many of the stories that I write," Walker emphasizes, "that we all write, are my mother's stories" (240). Walker delineates here a theory of creative identity that juxtaposes the male paradigm of literary achievement that demands separation and individuation. As Dannabang Kuwabong observes about Africaribbean women's writing, but germane, I argue, to all black female diaspora literature, "the mother-daughter relationship . . . is central to the development of identity and voice" (1998: 132). Cassie Premo Steele's observation about Audre Lorde is likewise applicable to many black women writers: "Grounding her narrative in matrilineal history and myth allows Lorde to find and take root: to form her identity" (8). Black female subjectivity generally, and creativity specifically, are formed, nurtured, and sustained through women's identification with, and connection to, their motherline. As Sylvia Hamilton, noted documentary writer and director, commented in the film *Black Mother, Black Daughter,* "[Our foremothers] created a path for us . . . we are bound to something larger than our selves. . . . I am moved by the example of their lives" (1989).

African American daughters seek and hold connection with mothers and the motherline; they achieve empowerment through this identification because motherhood is valued by and is central to African American culture and because the motherline bestows to the daughter affirming and empowering lessons and images of black womanhood. In *Not Our Kind of Girl: Unraveling the Myths of*

Black Teenage Motherhood (1997), Elaine Bell Kaplan, proposes a "poverty of relationship" thesis to account for the high incidence of black unwed teenage pregnancy. "[T]eenage mothers," she writes, "describe being disconnected from primary family relations, abandoned by their schools and by the men in their lives . . . at the time of adolescence, when it is most important that they experience positive relationships" (11). The absence of relationships in the adolescent girl's life, Kaplan argues, results from the loss of black neighborhood and community occasioned by the economic restructuring of the 1970s. In the 1950s and 1960s a strong sense of family and community prevailed in black neighborhoods; there was also a low incidence of unwed teenage pregnancy. Whether the two are causally related as Kaplan maintains, her argument explicates, albeit inadvertently, the connection-empowerment thesis advanced here. Disconnection, a word Kaplan herself uses, is at the core of the adolescent girl's aloneness and at the center of the community's despair. As African American women celebrate the power acquired through connection to a strong mother and a strong motherline, Kaplan's words remind us that the very survival of African American culture may depend on it.

AFRICAN AMERICAN MOTHERS AND SONS

Most of the writing by African American women has tended to focus on the mother-daughter relationship; little has been written on the mother-son relationship.[7] The notable exceptions are Joyce Elaine King and Carolyn Ann Mitchell's *Black Mothers to Sons: Juxtaposing African American Literature with Social Practice* (1995) and *Saving our Sons: Raising Black Children in a Turbulent World* (1995) by novelist Marita Golden.[8] In the introduction to their book, King and Mitchell, explaining their research interest in mothers and sons, write: "Considering the particular vulnerability of black males in this society and the role that mothers typically play as primary nurturers, this focus on black mother-to-son parenting is long overdue" (2). The initial question King and Mitchell explored in selected African-American fiction and asked of their research participants was: "What have you done to protect your son(s) from society's hostile forces?" (6). In their study of African American literature they found that protection was the primary aim of black mothering and manifested itself in two diametrically opposed modes of mothering: "mothers who whip their sons brutally 'for their own good' and mothers who love their sons to destruction through self-sacrifice and overindulgence" (9). The first strategy is sustained by the belief that, in their words, "a black man-child duly 'chastened' or broken at home will pose less of a threat to a society already primed to destroy him" (10); while the latter seeks to shield the child from all that is deemed harsh and upsetting. Each position, they argue, psychologically maims the son: the first by breaking the child's spirit, the latter by thwarting the child's maturation to true selfhood. The question black mothers ask in the raising of their sons is, in the authors' words, how can they "help sons develop the character, personality and integrity a black man-child needs to transcend these forces?" (1995, 19).

Golden's book also assumes as its central theme the survival of black men. Dedicated to the black men who have died violently in Washington, D.C., since 1988, Golden wrote this book, as she explains in her epilogue, "because at this moment there is no subject more necessary to confront, more imperative to imagine. Until I wrote about our sons, I could not speak or think or dream of anything else" (185). Homicide, Golden tells us, is the leading cause of death for young black men in America. The violence, drugs, crime, joblessness, and killing of black male youth mark, according to Golden, a new kind of Middle Passage. Her book narrates this crossing as it tells the story of her own son's journey into manhood; in this telling and testifying Golden lists possible causes, drafts solutions, and seeks to imagine what, in her words "we will look like, how will we sound, once we are spewed forth from the terrible hold of THIS ship" (9). "The major challenge . . . to a black mother raising sons today," as Claudette Lee and Ethel Wilson explain in "Masculinity, Matriarchy, and Myth: A Black Feminist Perspective," is "survival. . . . Racism, discrimination, and oppression define the childhood of an African-American male. Mothering for an African-American woman is defined by fear for her male child. Therefore her approach and relationship with her son must be different" (56–57).

Golden, as did King and Mitchell, recognizes that, for parents with the financial means, retreat has become the strategy of choice. Golden withdrew her son from public school in Washington, D. C., and enrolled him in a private boarding school, as she and her husband purchased a house in the suburbs. However, in saving your son this way, you remove him from the black community and its history, the "sites of resistance"—family, community, history—that have traditionally nurtured and empowered African Americans by creating black-defined narratives and identities. The women of King and Mitchell's study spoke of the "liberating, healing power of family lore, bloodlines and family secrets" (37). "[K]nowing about ancestors," King and Mitchell write, "strengthens identification with family values that can help a son overcome anger and hopelessness. Such family lore can also develop a son's confidence in himself. . . . [It] free[s] black males from the diminished definitions of their humanity and self-worth that society offers them" (38). Golden, too, recognizes that the double consciousness of which Dubois eloquently wrote more than a hundred years ago is, in her words, "draining and sometimes killing our spirits" (14). With integration came the loss of communities, traditions, beliefs, legends, narratives, and rituals, the "sites of resistance," that have long sustained and enriched black American culture.[9] While suburbs and boarding schools may save black sons from the killing fields of the so-called American inner cities, they also result in the further disintegration of black communities, the very thing that holds the promise of salvation for African Americans.

King, Mitchell, the women of their research group, and Golden agree that sons must be taught, in Golden's words, "that the first line of defense against racism is to mold themselves into disciplined, self-respecting refutations of its ability to destroy our souls or ourselves" (186). Or as James Baldwin wrote in

1971: "[I]t evolves upon the mother to invest the child, her man child, with some kind of interior dignity which will protect him against something he really can't be protected against, unless he has some kind of interior thing within him to meet it" (quoted in King 1995: 39). Audre Lorde wrote in "Manchild: A Black Lesbian Feminist Response" (1984) that "[f]or survival, Black children in America must be raised to be warriors. For survival they must also be raised to recognize the enemy's many faces" (75). She goes on to say:

> The strongest lesson I can teach my son is the same lesson I teach my daughter: how to be who he wishes to be for himself. And the best way I can do this is to be who I am and hope that he will learn from this not how to be me, which is not possible, but how to be himself. And this means how to move to that voice from within himself, rather than to those raucous, persuasive, or threatening voices from outside, pressuring him to be what the world wants him to be. (77)

The aim of the black mothering is thus to nurture and sustain the "soul," "voice within," and "the interior thing" of black sons so that they are able to transcend the maiming of racism and grow into manhood whole and complete. Mothers of black sons, according to these writers, while they must negotiate between the need to keep their sons physically safe while simultaneously promoting their psychological maturation, must primarily aim to nurture and sustain that "soul," "voice within," and "interior thing."[10] For mothers of black sons this is achieved by grounding sons in their culture of origin, the black community, and connecting them to their African American motherline[10].

The presence and involvement of the mother are recognized as crucial and essential to the son's maturation. African American mothering foregrounds the importance and centrality of the mother in the son's life for it is she who both provides protection and teaches her son how to protect himself, physically and otherwise, and passes on the important teachings of the African American motherline. Presence and participation in the sons' lives are emphasized in African American culture because black boys' lives are at risk. Black mothers must protect their sons to ensure their survival, both physically and psychologically, and teach them how to do the same for themselves. The son's well-being thus depends upon, as it does with his sister, the presence and involvement of his mother in his life. The emphasis upon maternal involvement with sons and maternal connection for daughters underscores the importance of mothers and motherline in African American culture. The African American tradition of motherhood—othermothering, matrifocality, social activism, providing a homeplace, and cultural bearing—gives mothers, motherhood, and the motherline power and prominence in African American culture. Mothers from this site of authority empower their children through the above five themes or tasks of African American mothering; children, in turn, secure this empowerment through connection with their mothers and motherline.

Reflecting upon these five themes of black motherhood I am reminded of the chorus from Canadian singer-songwriter Jann Arden's song "Good Mother":

> I've got a good mother
> and her voice is what keeps me here
> Feet on ground
> Heart in hand
> Facing forward
> Be yourself.

African American motherhood, in the five themes detailed above, bestows upon black children a loved, strong, and proud selfhood. The mother, in fulfilling these tasks of black motherhood, becomes, to borrow the metaphor from the song, "the voice that keeps [the children] here." She is the "heart in the hand" that enables the children to "face forward with feet on the ground and be themselves." Whether it be connection that it is emphasized, as in the mother-daughter relationship, or involvement, as with mothers and sons, mothering in black culture is what ensures physical and psychological survival and well-being and is what makes resistance possible.

MOTHERHOOD AS A SITE OF POWER IN MORRISON: THE "ANCIENT PROPERTIES" AND THE "FUNK"

The above five themes provide the foundation for Morrison's theory of motherhood as a site of power for black women and motherwork as concerned with the empowerment of children. Building upon the traditions of matrifocality, cultural bearing, social activism, providing a home place, and othermothering discussed above, Morrison defines motherhood, and in particular maternal identity, as a site of agency and authority for black women. More specifically these practices and beliefs in Morrison become elaborated and refined as particular characteristics, which she calls the ancient properties and the funk, that together make motherhood a site of power for black women.

In an interview with Bill Moyers (1989), Morrison describes motherhood as

> the most liberating thing that ever happened to me. . . . Liberating because the demands that children make are not the demands of a normal "other." The children's demands on me were things that nobody ever asked me to do. To be a good manager. To have a sense of humor. To deliver something that somebody could use. And they were not interested in all the things that other people were interested in, like what I was wearing or if I were sensual. All that went by. You've seen the eyes of your children. They don't want to hear it. They want to know what you are going to do now—today. Somehow all of the baggage that I had accumulated as a person about what was valuable just fell away. I could not only be me—whatever that was—but somebody actually needed me to be that. It's different from being a daughter. It's different from being a sister. If you listen to your children and look at them, they make demands that you can live up to. They don't need all that overwhelming love either. I mean, that's just you being vain about it. If you listen to them, somehow you are able to free yourself from baggage

and vanity and all sorts of things, and deliver a better self, one that you like. The person that was in me that I liked best was the one my children seemed to want. Not the one that frowned when they walked in the room and said "Pull your socks up." Also, you could begin to see the world through their eyes again—which are your eyes. I found that extraordinary. (Taylor-Guthrie 1994: 270–71)

In this statement Morrison defines mothering, in the words of Donna Bassin, Margaret Honey, and Meryle Mahrer Kaplan, "as a freeing, generative experience" (2). Such a view, they emphasize, contrasts sharply with "the predominant image of the mother in white Western society [which assumes mothers are] ever-bountiful, ever-giving, self-sacrificing . . . not destroyed or overwhelmed by the demands of [their] child[ren]" (2–3).[11] Motherhood in a Western context, as numerous Anglo-American feminist theorists on motherhood have pointed out, is organized as a patriarchal institution that is deeply oppressive to women. When white middle-class mothers write about motherhood, as Elizabeth Johnson explains, "they write about their own struggles for identity in the institution of motherhood" (33). Morrison, in contrast, states that motherhood *liberated* her and gave her a "better self." Motherhood, for Morrison, is a site of liberation and self-realization, because her standpoint on motherhood is developed from black women's everyday practices and meaning of motherhood wherein motherhood is a site of power for black women. More specifically, Morrison takes traditional conceptions of black womanhood—what Morrison terms "the ancient properties"—and traditional black values—what she calls the funk—and makes them central to her definition of motherhood as a site of power for black women.

Black women, Toni Morrison commented in an *Essence* interview with Judith Wilson (1981),

[need to] pay . . . attention to the ancient properties—which for me means the ability to be "the ship" *and* the "safe harbor." Our history as Black women is the history of women who could build a house *and* have some children and there was no problem. . . . What we have known is how to be complete human beings, so that we did not let education keep us from our nurturing abilities . . . [t]o lose that is to diminish ourselves unnecessarily. It is not a question, it's not a conflict. You don't have to give up anything. You *choose* your responsibilities. (Taylor-Guthrie 1994: 135)

In a conversation with Gloria Naylor, Morrison elaborates further:

[T]he point is that freedom is choosing your responsibility. . . . [It]'s choosing the ones you want. . . . A lady doctor has to be able to say, "I want to go home." And the one at home has the right to say, "I want to go to medical school." That's all there is to that, but then the choices cause problems where there are no problems because "either/or" seems to set up the conflict, first in the language and then in life. . . . I tried hard to be both the ship and the safe harbor at the same time, to be able to make a house and be on the job market and still nurture the children. . . . No one should be asked to make a choice between a home or a career. Why not have both? It's all possible. (Taylor-Guthrie 1994: 195, 197)[12]

Speaking of her own family to Anne Koenen (1980), Morrison elaborates:

> One of the characteristics of Black women's experiences was that they did not have to choose between a career and a home. They did both. . . . I know my mother and father, my grandmother and grandfather, and the people that lived around me, they thought they were doing something important. And I don't know if they "loved" each other or not, but they took careful care of one another and there was something clear and common about what they were doing. They worked with each other. Sometimes they complained about things, but you always knew that there was some central thing that was bigger than they were, that they were doing. It had to do with raising children, with being morally coherent people. Maybe that's a boring little life, but it seemed to me that was what was strong about it. Because of the dual responsibility that Black women had—when they were left, they didn't collapse. They didn't have crutches in the first place, so with nothing but themselves to rely on they just had to carry on. And that, I think, is absolutely extraordinary and marvelous. (Taylor-Guthrie 1994: 72–73)

Morrison's concept of black woman as ship and safe harbor is developed from what she has termed the ancient properties of traditional black womanhood. Models, manifestations, and metaphors of these ancient properties may be found in the "herstories" of black women. Morrison continues:

> [I]f women are to become full, complete, the answer may not be in the future, but the answer may be back there. And that does interest me more than the fully liberated woman, the woman who understands her past, not the woman who merely has her way. Because that woman did know how to nurture, *and* survive. . . . It seems to me that the most respectable person is that woman who is a healer and understands plants and stones and yet they live in the world. Those people are always strange, when they get to the city. These women know what time it is by looking at the sky. I don't want to reduce it to some sort of heavy know-how, but it's paying attention to different sets of information, and that information certainly isn't useful in terms of a career. . . . It's a quality that normally one associates with a mammy, a black mammy. She could nurse, she could heal, she could chop wood, she could do all those things. And that's always been a pejorative word, a bad thing, but it isn't. That stereotype is bad only when people think it's less. . . . Those women were terrific, but they were perceived of as beastly in the very things that were wonderful about them. (Taylor-Guthrie 1994: 81–82)

The black mammy figure represents for Morrison, the "full and complete" manifestations of the ancient properties and thus may be viewed as an archetypical representation of Morrison's standpoint on black maternal identity. However, as this model of traditional womanhood is drawn from the past, it represents for Morrison her vision of the future. Speaking to a group of young women at a 1979 commencement address at Barnard College, Morrison insists upon the contemporary value and relevance of the ancient properties of the black mammy figure:

> I am suggesting that we pay as much attention to our nurturing sensibilities as to our ambition. You are moving in the direction of freedom and the function of self-fulfillment and the consequences of that fulfillment should be to discover that there is something just as important as you are. In your rainbow journey toward the realization of personal goals, don't make choices based only on your security and your safety. . . . Let your might and power emanate from the place in you that is nurturing and caring.[13]

Though these young women are living a life radically different from their ancestors, Morrison calls upon them to live their modern lives according to the ancient properties of traditional black womanhood.

These quotes by Morrison, drawn from interviews that span a twenty-five-year period, illustrate Morrison's particular standpoint of maternal identity, namely the traditional view of black women as both ship and safe harbor, inn and trail. Significantly and appropriately, Morrison illustrates her standpoint by way of personal example. Morrison, speaking about her writing practices to Jane Bakerman (1977), commented:

> I used to go to the back room to write, and they [her two sons] would come in there frequently, asking for things or fighting each other. And then it occurred to me that they *didn't* want me to separate myself from them, so now I write in the big room where we all generally stay. They didn't *want* me and they didn't have anything to say to me particularly; they just wanted the presence. (Taylor-Guthrie 1994: 32)

"When I'm writing a book," Morrison explains further, "there's almost no time when it's not on my mind—when I'm driving, doing dishes, or what have you" (Taylor-Guthrie 1994: 31–32). Morrison's view of mothering and writing stands in sharp contrast to the received feminist view of women and creativity, which asserts, following the advice of Virginia Woolf, that "a woman must have money and a room of her own if she is to write fiction" (6). Adrienne Rich wrote, in "When We Dead Awaken: Writing as Re-Vision":

> [T]o be maternally with small children all day . . . requires a holding back, a putting-aside of that imaginative activity, and demands instead a kind of conservatism. . . . [T]o be a female human being trying to fulfil traditional female functions in a traditional way *is* in direct conflict with the subversive function of the imagination. (43)[14]

In *Of Woman Born* Rich wrote:

> Once in a while someone used to ask me, "Don't you ever write poems
> about your children?" The male poets of my generation did write poems
> about their children—especially their daughters. For me, poetry was where
> I lived as no-one's mother, where I existed as myself. (31)

Women in the dominant Anglo-American culture often experience the demands
of work, in this instance writing, in conflict with those of mothering because of
the way this culture defines and positions the public sphere of work in opposition to the private/reproductive sphere of the home/family. Women, according to
this maternal ideology, are categorized and regulated by what has been termed
the "either-or dichotomy": women must choose between work and motherhood.
In contrast, African American thought on mothering, as noted earlier, recognizes
that black women have always worked in and outside the home and mothering
itself is understood to be a public and political enterprise. Morrison, drawing
upon this important theme of black maternal practice and thought, develops a
specific standpoint of black maternal identity; namely that black women, as
defined by the ancient properties, regard nurturance and work as integrated—
not oppositional—dimensions of their selves and lives. "It is not a question, it's
not a conflict," as Morrison explains, "You don't have to give up anything. You
choose your responsibilities" (Taylor-Guthrie 1994: 135).

In her article, "The Convergence of Feminism and Ethnicity in the Fiction
of Toni Morrison," (McKay 1988), Denard argues that "[black women] always
maintain, whether they desire it or not, a connection to their ethnic community."
They are the "cultural bearers, they function as a parent . . . as a sort of umbrella
figure in the community not just with [their] children but with all children"
(174). Morrison in her maternal standpoint uses the term *ancient properties* to
signify those black woman who are these cultural bearers and define themselves
in connection with African American culture and history, and who serve as
ambassadors for their people, bringing the past to the present and keeping
African American culture in the community of black people. To have the ancient
properties is to live life according to the ways of the foremothers; it is to define
oneself according to the script of traditional black womanhood of being both
ship and harbor.

Morrison, thus, does not endorse the existentialist or power feminism championed by much of Anglo-American feminism. As she said in her interview with
Koenen: "[I]f women are to become full, complete, the answer may not be in the
future, but the answer may be back there. And that does interest me more than
the fully liberated woman, the woman who understands her past, not the woman
who merely has her way" (Taylor-Guthrie 1994: 81). The feminist stance that
Morrison advocates is thus an ethnic and cultural one. Carolyn Denard explains:

> Among black women, who have historically suffered oppression because of
> both race and gender, there is usually a simultaneous concern for both these

issues. They abhor both sexist and racist oppression. But because of their minority ethnic status, which keeps their allegiance to ancestral group foremost, most shun an advocacy of the kind of political, existential feminism embraced by many women of the majority culture. For black women, their concern with feminism is usually more group-centred than self-centred, more cultural than political. As a result, they tend to be concerned more with the particular female cultural values of their own ethnic group rather than with those of women in general. They advocate what may be termed ethnic cultural feminism. (171–72)

In Morrison's fiction women who shun the ancient properties of ethnic cultural feminism and embrace Anglo-American definitions of feminism do not achieve what Morrison calls, "complete[ness]" and "full[ness]" of self. These qualities are obtained only by those women who live their lives according to the ancient properties of their foremothers.

THE FUNK

As the term *ancient properties* in Morrison signifies the ways of traditional black womanhood, the term *funk* signals traditional black values. Morrison's first novel *The Bluest Eye* defines funkiness as "the funkiness of passion, the funkiness of nature, the funkiness of a wide range of emotions" (68). "Funky" people, as Elizabeth House observes, "remain true to their heritage" (1984: 181). Morrison, however, does not define or detail the funk as she did with her concept of the ancient properties. Rather, the funk is explicated indirectly through literary devices such as metaphor, personification, and juxtaposition. Images of the funk explode with color, aroma, and flavor. Pauline's description of her childhood in the folk rural South functions as a metaphor for the funk: "[M]y whole dress was messed with purple, it never did wash out. Not the dress nor me. I could feel that purple deep inside me. And that lemonade Mama used to make when Pa came in out of the fields. It be cool and yellowish" (92). Food imagery also, as in *Song of Solomon,* is used to suggest funkiness. Raw foods such as fruits or eggs represent the funk while commercially prepared foods, like candies and jams, signify the capitalistic values of the dominant culture, in particular the competitive acquisition of money and power. The funk is also developed through personification. Pilate in *Song,* for example, as many critics have observed is, in the words of Patrick Bjork, "the embodiment of black heritage" (91). Pilate, as Joseph T. Skerrett writes, "is Morrison's most complete and concentrated image of an Afro-American in touch with the spiritual resources of Afro-American folk traditions" (195). The funk is also frequently conveyed by means of juxtaposition. The oppositional structuring of Pilate's and Macon's households in *Song of Solomon* and the convent and the town in *Paradise,* for example, details the life-affirming funk values of the women's households by contrasting them to the life-denying ambitions of Macon and the men of Ruby.

Morrison is often read as a critic of the traditional nuclear family: namely, a familial structure composed of a mother and a father and their biological children in which the husband's role is to be the provider while the wife is to be the "at home" nurturer. The majority of families in Morrison's fiction are female-headed households in which three generations of women reside together, or, as with the three whores in *The Bluest Eye* and the convent women in *Paradise,* are families made up of a community of non–biologically related women. Readers are quick to point out that we can find only one "successful" nuclear family in all of Morrison's fiction, they being the MacTeers who appear in Morrison's first novel. What has not been considered, however, is why Morrison is so critical of the nuclear family arrangement.

The traditional nuclear family, in Morrison's view, is structured both by male dominance and the privileging of "white" hegemonic values—money, ownership, individualism—over the traditional black values of the funk and the ancient properties of traditional black womanhood discussed above. Writers on the black family have long observed a tradition of egalitarian marriages in African American culture. About her parents' and grandparents' marriages, Morrison observes:

> There was a comradeship between men and women in the marriages of my grandparents, and of my mother and my father. . . . There was not conflicts of gender in that area, at the level at which such are in vogue these days. My mother and my father did not fight about who was supposed to do what. Each confronted whatever crisis there was. . . . I didn't find imbalance or unevenness in these relationships. I don't think that my mother's talents were hidden from males or white society, actually they were very much on display. So I don't find a tension there, or the struggle for dominance. . . . The women in my family were very articulate. . . . I feel the authority of those women more than I do my own. (140–41)

When African American men and women emulate the white nuclear family structure, the hitherto assumed equality is jeopardized because the patriarchal nuclear family is structured on male dominance, or what may be termed "husband-on-top heterosexuality." To be a wife in a male-dominated marriage is to fulfill the ideological role of patriarchal wifedom, specifically to live in subservience to men and masculine values. When African American women, such as Geraldine in *The Bluest Eye* and Ruth in *Song,* take on the traditional role of wife they, by necessity, forsake the funk and in particular the ancient properties of traditional black womanhood, because woman cannot be ship and safe harbor in a patriarchal marriage that assumes women are inferior and assigns them exclusively to the reproductive realm of the home.

Adrienne Rich has argued that for women who mother in the patriarchal institution of motherhood, raising daughters has meant turning them over to the patriarchy, or, more specifically, socializing daughters so that they conform to the passive, dependent, subordinate identity expected of them as wives. This is particularly problematic for Morrison in two ways. First, as a "wife," African

American women, as noted above, cannot assume the maternal identity or motherself of the funk and the ancient properties that Morrison champions and considers essential for women's "fullness and completeness of being." Secondly, in the wife role, mothers are prevented from assuming their central and crucial cultural role of, in Trudier Harris's (1991) words, "keepers of the tradition." As will be examined later in the following section, Morrison's fiction details a particular mode of mothering that empowers children by connecting them to their African American motherline. However, this mode of mothering, according to Morrison's maternal standpoint, is possible only by way of mothers modeling and mentoring the funk of traditional black culture and for daughters, the ancient properties of traditional black womanhood. This is not possible in the patriarchal role of wife. In her rearticulation of commonplace black values—the funk—and everyday maternal practices and beliefs—the ancient properties—Morrison formulates a maternal standpoint that views motherhood as a site of power for black women. From this perspective she develops a model of maternal practice that assumes as its explicit aim the empowerment of black children. To this discussion I now turn.

MORRISON'S THEORY OF MATERNAL PRACTICE: MOTHERWORK AS CONCERNED WITH THE EMPOWERMENT OF CHILDREN

Morrison's maternal standpoint on black motherhood as a site of power gives rise to a particular model of maternal practice that I will be calling motherwork. This section of the chapter will explore how and in which ways motherwork in Morrison centers upon the empowerment of children. In particular, I will examine how Morrison defines the responsibilities of motherwork in terms of four distinct yet interrelated tasks; namely, preservation, nurturance, cultural bearing, and healing. Together these four tasks enable mothers to (1) protect their children, physically and psychologically, (2) teach children how to protect themselves, and (3) heal adults who were unprotected as children and hence harmed. This discussion will be built from Sara Ruddick's theory of maternal practice and maternal thinking.

SARA RUDDICK'S THEORY OF MATERNAL PRACTICE AND MATERNAL THINKING

In *Maternal Thinking: Toward a Politics of Peace,* Sara Ruddick argues that the work of mothering "demands that mothers think; out of this need for thoughtfulness, a distinctive discipline emerges" (24). Ruddick elaborates:

> I speak about a mother's thought—the intellectual capacities she develops, the judgements she makes, the metaphysical attitudes she assumes, the values she affirms. Like a scientist writing up her experiment, a critic poring over a text, or a historian assessing documents, a mother caring for her children engages in a discipline. She asks certain questions—those relevant to

her aims—rather than others; she accepts certain criteria for the truth, adequacy, and relevance of proposed answers; and she cares about the findings she makes and can act on. The discipline of maternal thought, like other disciplines, establishes criteria for determining failure and success, sets priorities, and identifies virtues that the discipline requires. Like any other work, mothering is prey to characteristic temptations that it must identify. To describe the capacities, judgements, metaphysical attitudes, and values of maternal thought presumes not maternal achievement, but a *conception* of achievement. (24)

Ruddick argues that motherwork is characterized by three demands: preservation, growth, and social acceptance. "To be a mother," continues Ruddick, "is to be committed to meeting these demands by works of preservative love, nurturance, and training" (17).

The first duty of mothers is to protect and preserve their children: "to keep safe whatever is vulnerable and valuable in a child" (80). "Preserving the lives of children," Ruddick writes, "is the central constitutive, invariant aim of maternal practice: the commitment to achieving that aim is the constitutive maternal act" (19). "To be committed to meeting children's demand for preservation," Ruddick continues, "does not require enthusiasm or even love; it simply means to see vulnerability and to respond to it with care rather than abuse, indifference, or flight" (19). "The demand to preserve a child's life is quickly supplemented," Ruddick continues, "by the second demand, to nurture its emotional and intellectual growth" (19). Ruddick explains:

> To foster growth . . . is to sponsor or nurture a child's unfolding, expanding material spirit. Children demand this nurturance because their development is complex, gradual, and subject to distinctive kinds of distortion or inhibition. . . . Children's emotional, cognitive, sexual, and social development is sufficiently complex to demand nurturance; this demand is an aspect of maternal work . . . and it structures maternal thinking. (83)

The third demand of maternal practice is training and social acceptability of children. This third demand, Ruddick writes,

> is made not by children's needs but by the social groups of which a mother is a member. Social groups require that mothers shape their children's growth in "acceptable" ways. What counts as acceptable varies enormously within and among groups and cultures. The demand for acceptability, however, does not vary, nor does there seem to be much dissent from the belief that children cannot "naturally" develop in socially correct ways but must be "trained." I use the neutral, though somewhat harsh, term "training" to underline a mother's active aims to make her children "acceptable." Her training strategies may be persuasive, manipulative, educative, abusive, seductive, or respectful and are typically a mix of most of these. (21)

"In any mother's day," Ruddick concludes, "the demands of preservation, growth and acceptability are intertwined. Yet a reflective mother can separately identify each demand, partly because they are often in conflict" (23).[15]

The many and various children's needs that arise from each demand of motherwork and the various and many responses of the mother coalesce to form the discipline of maternal thought. Specifically, motherwork gives rise to particular cognitive styles, particular ways of seeing and dealing with the world. For example, because the job of raising children is complex and often contradictory, where there is seldom a right or wrong, and because the mother's own feelings about her children are so ambivalent—as one mother put it "I love them [my children] more than life itself and I wish they would go away forever"[16]—mothers become accepting of ambiguity. Moreover, because so much of motherwork is beyond the control of the mother, mothers develop what Ruddick calls humility: "In a world beyond one's control, to be humble is to have a profound sense of the limits of one's actions and of the unpredictability of the consequences of one's work" (72). Motherwork also gives rise to what Ruddick calls "cheerfulness": "To be cheerful means to respect chance, limit, and imperfection and still act as if it is possible to keep children safe" (74). Humility, cheerfulness, and acceptance of ambiguity are only a few of the many attitudes that mothers learn and develop as they respond to the demands of motherwork. "Mothers, like gardeners or historians," writes Ruddick, "identify virtues appropriate to their work. But to identify a virtue is not to possess it" (25). Ruddick explains further:

> Mothers meeting together at their jobs, in playgrounds, or over coffee can be heard thinking. This does not necessarily mean that they can be heard being good. Mothers are not any more or less wonderful than other people—they are not especially sensible or foolish, noble or ignoble, courageous or cowardly. . . . When mothers speak of virtues they speak as often of failure as of success. Almost always they reflect on the *struggles* that revolve around the temptations to which they are prey in their work. What they share is not virtuous characteristics but rather an identification and a discourse about the strengths required by their ongoing commitments to protect, nurture, and train. (25)

When mothers set out to fulfill the demands of motherwork—to protect, nurture, train—they are engaged in maternal practice; and this engagement, in turn, gives rise to a specific discipline of thought—a cluster of attitudes, beliefs, values—which Ruddick calls maternal thinking.

MORRISON'S THEORY OF MOTHERWORK

Toni Morrison, in a manner similar to the model developed by Sara Ruddick, positions motherwork as a practice committed to meeting specific tasks. Like Ruddick, Morrison foregrounds the aims of preservation and nurturance in her theory of motherwork. As well, Morrison is attentive to the task of "training" children so that they are acceptable to their social group. However, with Morrison the aim of training is amplified to include the African American maternal custom of cultural bearing discussed above: raising children in accordance with the values, beliefs, and customs of traditional African American culture and in particular the values of the funk and ancient proprieties. In each of these tasks—preservation, nurturance, cultural bearing—Morrison is concerned with protecting children from the hurts of a racist and, for daughters, sexist culture, and with teaching children how to protect themselves so they may be empowered to survive and resist the racist and patriarchal culture in which they live and to develop a strong and authentic identity as a black person. Finally, Morrison advances a fourth aim, healing, which is developed from the African American maternal practice of nurturance as resistance discussed earlier. With this aim, Morrison's focus is upon those adults who never received protection, nurturance, and cultural bearing as children and thus grew to be adults psychologically wounded by the hurts of racism and/or sexism. In Morrison's reformulation of these tasks, maternal practice is defined and represented specifically as a political undertaking with the explicit objective of empowering children and/or healing adults so that they may survive and resist racism and sexism through the creation of a strong self-defined identity. In other words, Morrison, building upon the African American maternal practices of nurturance as resistance and cultural bearing discussed above, argues that motherwork, through the tasks of preservation, nurturance, cultural bearing, and healing, is what makes survival and resistance possible for African American people.

In her reformulation of motherwork as a political enterprise Morrison challenges the received view or, what she calls in another context the master narrative of motherhood. Motherhood is a cultural construction that varies with time and place; there is no one essential or universal experience of motherhood. However, these many and diverse meanings and experiences of mothering become marginalized and erased through the construction of an official definition of motherhood. Through a complex process of intersecting forces—economics, politics, cultural institutions—the dominant definition of motherhood is codified as the official and only meaning of motherhood. Alternative meanings of mothering are marginalized and rendered illegitimate. The dominant definition of motherhood is able to suppress its own construction as an ideology and thus can naturalize its specific construction of motherhood as the universal, real, natural maternal experience.

The dominant discourse of motherhood is, however, historically determined and thus variable. In the Victorian era, the ideology of moral motherhood that saw mothers as naturally pure, pious, and chaste emerged as the dominant discourse of motherhood. This ideology of moral motherhood, however, was race and class specific. Only white and middle-class women could wear the halo of the Madonna and transform the world through their moral influence and social housekeeping. Slave mothers, in contrast, were defined as breeders; placed not on a pedestal, as white women were, but on the auction block. After World War II the discourse of the happy homemaker made the "stay-at-home-mom and apple pie" mode of mothering the normal and natural motherhood experience. Again, only white and middle-class women could, in fact, experience what discursively was inscribed as natural and universal. With the sixties a new discourse of motherhood emerged, that of "sensitive" mothering that positioned middle-class mothering as the normative maternal practice. However, while each new discourse differs in its definition of ideal motherhood, each views mothering as an individual act undertaken in the privacy of one's home, separate and isolated from the public, political, and social realm. Additionally, normative discourses of motherhood, in particular the contemporary one of "sensitive" mothering, focus exclusively upon the tasks of nurturance and training; consequently, they disregard the task of preservation and view maternal practices that focus on this task as inadequate and inferior.

Morrison's maternal standpoint of mothering as a site of power and her model of motherwork as concerned with the empowerment of children means that mothering, in Morrison's view, is profoundly a political act with social and public connections and consequences. Moreover, Morrison foregrounds the importance of preservation in her theory of mothering as empowerment. In this, Morrison's theory counters and challenges the dominant view that mothering is an individualized and private act, focused upon the nurturance of children, and having no or little political import, social significance, or cultural value. The aim of this section is to explore how Morrison positions motherwork, in the functions of preservation, nurturance, cultural bearing, and healing, as committed to the empowerment of children, and how Morrison in doing so deconstructs the "master narrative" of motherhood. However, because Morrison's view of mothering differs so radically from the received view of motherhood, and since most readers of Morrison come to her texts from the perspective of the dominant discourse of motherhood, her theory of motherhood as power and motherwork as empowerment may be misunderstood or missed by critics and readers alike. In order to best demonstrate how Morrison's view of mothering both differs from and becomes a challenge to the dominant discourse of motherhood, I will briefly sketch the tenets of the "sensitive" mothering discourse that stands in opposition to Morrison's model and is critiqued by it. While this narrative of motherhood is anachronistic to Morrison's renditions of motherhood, given that it emerged in the 1960s and most of Morrison's portrayals take place before this date, it nonetheless is the ideological viewpoint from which readers will assess Morrison's representations of motherhood and is the one, I believe, of which Morrison is most critical. To this discussion I now turn.

In their landmark book, *Democracy in the Kitchen: Regulating Mothers and Socializing Daughters* (1989), Valerie Walkerdine and Helen Lucey examine how the maternal behavior of the middle class becomes culturally constructed and codified as the real, normal, and natural way to mother. Natural mothering begins with the ideological presupposition that children have needs that are met by the mother. To mother, therefore, is to be sensitive to the needs of children; to engage in sensitive mothering. The first characteristic of the sensitive mother, Walkerdine and Lucey explain, is that her domestic life is centred around her children and not around her housework. The boundaries between this work and children's play have to be blurred. . . . While the mother is being sensitive to the child's needs, she is not doing any housework. She has to be available and ready to meet demands, and those household tasks which she undertakes have to become pedagogic tasks. . . . The second feature of the sensitive mother is the way she regulates her children. Essentially there should be no overt regulation; regulation should go underground; no power battles, no insensitive sanctions as these would interfere with the child's illusion that she is the source of her wishes, that she has "free will." (20, 23–24)

This mode of mothering is drawn from the parenting styles of the so-called Baby Boom generation. Today good mothering is defined as child-centered and is characterized by flexibility, spontaneity, democracy, affection, nurturance, and playfulness. This mode of mothering is contrasted to the earlier stern, rigid, authoritative, "child should be seen and not heard" variety of parenting. Today's ideal mother is not only expected to be "at home" with her children, as her mother was with her in the fifties; she is also required to spend, in the language of eighties parenting books, "quality time" with her children. While the fifties mom would put her children in the pram or playpen to tend to her household chores, today's mom is to "be with" her child at all times psychically and, most importantly, psychologically. Whether the activity be one of the numerous structured moms and tots programs—swimming, kindergym, dance—or whether it be an at home activity—reading, gardening, cooking, playing—the mother's day is to revolve around the child, not her housework as it was in the fifties, and is to be centered upon the child's educational development. The child is to be involved in any domestic labor performed and the chore at hand is be transformed into a learning experience for the child.

Working-class mothers, Walkerdine and Lucey emphasize, do not practice so-called sensitive mothering; work does not become play nor do power and conflict go underground. Working-class mothers, in their study, do play with their children but only after domestic chores have been tended to. In working-class households the boundaries between mothering and domestic labor are maintained and the very real work of domestic labor is not transformed—or trivialized—into a game for the child's benefit. This type of mothering, however, becomes pathologized as deficiency and deviance because the middle-class style of sensitive mothering has been codified, both socially and discursively, as natural. Working-class mothering is, thus, not simply different, it is deemed unnatural. Working-class mothers are unfit mothers in need of regulation. In other words, "there is something wrong with working-class mothering which should be put right by making it more middle-class" (Walkerdine 1989: back cover).

Morrison, in her writings, deconstructs the normative discourse of sensitive mothering and inscribes mothering as a culturally determined experience. Morrison, building upon the traditions of black motherhood, positions motherwork in African American culture as a political undertaking in its commitment to empowerment and thus can not be understood or appreciated from the ideological lens of sensitive mothering. With the dominant discourse of motherhood introduced, I will, in the pages that remain, detail how and in which ways Morrison positions motherwork, through the tasks of preservation, nurturance, cultural bearing, and healing, as committed to the empowerment of children.

Preservation

Central to Morrison's counternarrative of motherhood and her critique of the dominant discourse is a challenge to the received view that links "good" mothering solely with nurturance. Morrison, in her model of motherwork as empowerment, foregrounds the importance of preservation, a dimension of motherhood minimized and trivialized in the dominant discourses of motherhood, most notably with sensitive mothering discussed above. Sara Ruddick argued, as noted above, that the first duty of mothers is to protect and preserve their children: "to keep safe whatever is vulnerable and valuable in a child" (80). "Preserving the lives of children," Ruddick writes, "is the central constitutive, invariant aim of maternal practice" (19). Though maternal practice is composed of two other demands—nurturance and training—this first demand, which Ruddick calls preservative love, is what describes much of African American women's motherwork. In a world in which, to use Patricia Hill Collins's words, "racial ethnic children's lives have long been held in low regard" (Forcey 1987: 49), mothering for many black women, particularly among the poor, is about ensuring the physical survival of their children and those of the larger black community. Securing food and shelter, struggling to build and sustain safe neighborhoods is what defines both the meaning and experience of black women's motherwork. Preservation, as Collins explains further, is, "a fundamental dimension of racial ethnic women's motherwork" (Forcey 1987: 48–49). However, normative discourses of motherhood, particularly in their current configuration as sensitive mothering, define motherwork solely as nurturance. "Physical survival," writes Collins, "is assumed for children who are white and middle class. The choice to thus examine their psychic and emotional well-being . . . appears rational. The children of women of color, many of whom are 'physically starving' have no such choices however " (Forcey 1987: 49). While exclusive to middle-class white women's experiences of mothering, the normative discourse of mothering as nurturance has been naturalized as the universal normal experience of motherhood. Consequently, preservative love, such that practised by Eva in *Sula* and Mrs. MacTeer in *The Bluest Eye,* is often not regarded as real, legitimate, or "good enough" mothering. However, for Morrison, keeping children alive through preservative love is an essential and integral dimension of motherwork.

Nurturance

The aim of black mothering, once preservation has been ensured, is to nurture children so that they may survive and resist the maiming of racism and, for daughters, sexism and grow into adulthood whole and complete. Nurturance requires that black mothers immunize their children from racist ideologies by loving them so that they may love themselves in a culture that defines them as not deserving or worthy of love. In loving her children the mother instils in them a loved sense of self and self-esteem, enabling them to defy and subvert racist discourses that naturalize racial inferiority and commodify blacks as object and other. This maternal nurturance is described in *Paradise*: "Parents who wiped the spit and tears from their children's faces and said 'Never mind, honey. Never you mind. You are not and never will be a nigger, a coon, a jig, a jungle bunny nor any other thing white folks teach their children to say. What you are is God's'" (212). Morrison's thinking on nurturance as an act of resistance builds upon the African American view of homeplace as a site of resistance. Homeplace, as discussed ealier, refers to a haven or refuge, where "black people could affirm one another and by so doing, heal many of the wounds inflicted by racist domination . . . [a place where they] had the opportunity to grow and develop, to nurture their spirits" (42).

Time and time again in her writing Morrison emphasizes the need for the parent to have a strong sense of self so that he or she may nurture the same in the growing child. The nurture of self-love in children, Morrison believes, depends on self-love in parents. Morrison argues that self-love depends on the self first being loved by another self. Before the child can love herself, she must experience herself being loved and learn that she is indeed valuable and deserving of affection. Informing Morrison's writing is her belief that mothering is essential for the emotional well-being of children because it is the mother who first loves the child and gives to that child a loved sense of self. Rich writes in *Of Woman Born*: "The nurture of the daughters in a patriarchy calls for strong sense of self-nurture in the mother" (247). The self-love that Morrison deems as essential for the motherlove is derived from the ancestral memory and ancient properties discussed in the following section on cultural bearing. Parents, and in particular mothers, Morrison argues, must identify with the ancestral memory and ancient properties of the African American motherline in order to love themselves as black people and to teach the same to their children so that they can develop a strong and proud black identity. This is particularly true for girl children. Daughters need strength and confidence from their mothers because, in patriarchy, female selves are susceptible to erasure and displacement. In an interview (Ross 1992), Morrison commented: "Women sabotage themselves. . . . They locate the true beloved out of themselves." These women, Morrison goes on to say, "have girl children . . . [they] bring them up to be broken in half . . . to loath themselves." Mothers must, Morrison emphasizes, "take their daughters in their arms and hold them and say, you are just fine the way you are" (C1). Rich writes in *Of Woman Born* that "[what] women [need] growing into a world so hostile to us . . . [is] a very profound kind of loving in order to love ourselves" (246). Morrison's children thus move from motherlove to self-love to selfhood. This is why the comment about Gideon in *Tar Baby* upsets

Son: "[It] bothered him that everybody called Gideon Yardman, as though he had not been mothered" (161). Son's statement makes clear the connection between mothering and selfhood.

Frequently in Morrison, a woman other than the child's biological mother is the one who provides this nurturance. Building upon the African American tradition of othermothers and woman-centered networks discussed above, Morrison defines mothering to include, as Patricia Hill Collins has observed, a "generalized ethic of caring and personal accountability among African American women who often feel accountable to all the Black community's children" (1991: 129). Speaking of the character Hagar in *The Song of Solomon,* Morrison writes: "She needed what most colored girls needed: a chorus of mamas, grandmamas, aunts, cousins, sisters, neighbors, Sunday school teachers, best girl friends, and what all to give her the strength life demanded of her and the humor with which to live it" (311). In Morrison, surrogate mothers or a community of women mother the child in the event of the mother's death or abandonment, psychological or otherwise. These mothers are also, as with Pilate in *Song,* the singing teachers or story tellers who tell the orphaned or neglected child the stories and provide them with nurturance not made available by the biological mother. The act of nurturance, whether it be conveyed by the biological mother or an othermother, bestows upon the child a loved sense of self that both shields him/her from the hurts of a racist and sexist culture and fortifies that child to survive and resist racism and sexism.

Nurturance, or more specifically failed maternal nurturance, in Morrison is also positioned as a subversion of patriarchal culture and, in particular, an act of resistance against the institution of motherhood. Black women, in loving their children, seek to subvert racist ideologies and to protect their children from these same ideologies. They also recognize that the institution of motherhood, as it is organized in patriarchal culture, prevents them from loving their children well, particularly because, as noted earlier, patriarchal motherhood prohibits black women's cultural bearing function. In Morrison, resistance against patriarchal motherhood is conveyed either as "deviant" maternal nurturance, as with Ruth's late nursing of her son Milkman, or as failed maternal nurturance, as with Margaret's child abuse. Whether it is expressed as resistance against racism's dehumanization of her children or resistance against the mother's own oppression in the patriarchal institution of motherhood, nurturance is viewed as essential for the empowerment of children.

CULTURAL BEARING

The third aim, cultural bearing, is the central and most significant task in Morrison's theory of motherwork. Cultural bearing refers to the task of raising children in accordance with the values and beliefs of traditional African American culture. The aim of nurturance is to develop in the child a loved sense of self so that he/she will see themselves as worthy and deserving of love in a culture that largely deems them otherwise. In this way nurturance could be seen as an act of immunization in that it shields children from the disease of racism and sexism and then fortifies them so that children are able to protect themselves from this same disease to survive and resist racism/sexism. The task of cultural bearing functions in a similar manner: by way of cultural bearing, mothers pass on to each successive generation of children African American culture and instill in their children knowledge about and pride in their African American heritage. More specifically, mothers pass on what I will be calling the motherline: the ancestral memory and the ancient proprieties of traditional black culture. By way of cultural bearing or what may be termed mothering from the motherline, mothers transmit ancestral memory and the ancient proprieties to their children. In so doing, cultural bearing or motherline mothering confers affirming images of black people and their history that, in turn, impedes the internalization of the controlling images of blackness put forward by the dominant culture and allows the child to develop a strong and authentic selfhood as a black person. Therefore, as with nurturance, cultural bearing both protects black children from racism and sexism and enables children to protect themselves.

THE MOTHERLINE: THE ANCIENT PROPERTIES AND ANCESTRAL MEMORY

There is "a worldview," writes Naomi Lowinsky, "that is as old as humankind, a wisdom we have forgotten that we know: the ancient lore of women—The Motherline" (1). The motherline, as noted above, enables daughters to derive strength from their identities as women. In Morrison, the motherline signifies the ancient properties of traditional black womanhood and ancestral memory more generally of black culture. Mothers pass on the ancient properties of black womanhood and ancestral memory through the maternal task of cultural bearing. Women, however, are often, as Naomi Lowinsky has observed "cut off from their motherline, and [have] paid a terrible price for cutting [themselves off from] [their] feminine roots" (26). What is lost, she emphasizes, is female authenticity and authority. Morrison, likewise, argues that fullness and completeness of being are assured only in connection with the motherline and by living life in accordance with the ancient properties ancestral memory. According to Morrison, daughters need mothers to become women and mothers need women to stay daughters. "A woman," Morrison argues, "has to be a daughter before she can be any kind of woman. If she doesn't know how to relate to her ancestors, to her tribe, so to speak, she is not good for much" (Taylor-Guthrie 184). "When I talked to a very young black girl recently," Morrison continues, "it seemed to me that she had never heard of anything. They've grown up like they never had grandmothers. Or if they had them, they never paid them any attention. Kill your ancestors, you kill all" (Taylor-Guthrie 73).

One could argue that the main theme of Morrison's fiction is summed up in her oft-cited quotation: "When you kill the ancestor you kill yourself. I want to point out the dangers, to show that nice things don't always happen to the totally self-reliant if there is no conscious historical connection" (1984: 344). "From the outset of her literary career," critic Angelita Reyes emphasizes, "Toni Morrison . . . has been deeply concerned with the preservation of black folklore, and with sustaining positive black cultural values" (19). Speaking specifically of Morrison's fourth novel *Tar Baby,* but applicable to all of her writings, Reyes maintains that what Morrison asks is that "Black people of the New World diaspora must not lose sight of their African consciousness" (19). In a conversation with Elsie B. Washington (1987), Toni Morrison comments:

> [Grandparents and ancestors are] DNA, it's where you get your information, your cultural information. Also it's your protection, it's your education. They were responsible *for* us, and we have to be responsible *to* them. . . . You can't just *take.* Our ancestors are part of that circle, an ever widening circle, one hopes. And if you ignore that, you put yourself in a spiritually dangerous position of being self-sufficient, having no group that you're dependent on. (Taylor-Guthrie 1994: 238)

Toni Morrison describes the memory of black people as a "spoken library":

> The spoken library was . . . children's stories my family told, spirituals, the ghost stories, the blues, and folk tales and myths, and the everyday . . . instruction and advice of my own people. . . . I wanted to write out of the matrix of memory, of recollection, and to approximate the sensual and visceral response I had to the world I lived in . . . to recreate the civilization of Black people . . . the manners, judgements, values, morals. . . . (Holloway 1987: 104–105)

Morrison, thus, as critic Theodore Mason has observed,

> is an example of the novelist as *conservator.* She is a writer particularly interested in depicting, and thereby preserving and perpetuating, the cultural practices of black communities. Her work displays a commitment to the capacity of fiction to provide ways of maintaining and communicating important cultural values which otherwise might be lost. The novelist, then, is not a figure isolated from history and culture but rather is someone who conserves cultural forms and practices by depicting them in the public act of fiction. (172, emphasis in original)

The motherline in Morrison signifies ancestral memory; therefore men, as well as women, must live their lives in accordance with the values of the motherline, or more specifically the ancestral memory of black culture. In this, Morrison differs radically from conventional thinking on the mother-son relationship. Psychoanalytic discourse, childrearing manuals, literature from the men's movement, and popular wisdom argue that sons must separate from their mothers in order to assume a "normal" masculine identity. A close and caring relationship between a mother and her adolescent son is pathologized as somehow aberrant—she's making a mama's boy out of him—while a relationship structured upon separation is naturalized as the real, normal, and hence natural way to experience mother-son attachment.[17] In contrast to this, Morrison argues that men are made complete and whole through connection to the mother and identification with the motherline and the ancestral memory it conveys and embodies. In Morrison, to use the words of Baby Suggs from *Beloved:* "A man ain't nothing but a man. . . . But a son well now, that's *somebody*" (23). Therefore, sons as well as daughters must live their lives in accordance with the values of the motherline to develop a healthy sense of self. And it is the mother who, in the task of cultural bearing, models and mentors the teachings of the African American motherline. To this task I now turn.

Cultural Bearing: Mothering from Motherline

In *Maternal Thinking,* Sara Ruddick writes: "Many mothers find that the central challenge of mothering lies in training a child to be the kind of person whom others accept and whom the mothers can actively appreciate" (104). With Morrison, training or more specifically cultural bearing means socializing children in the values of the African American motherline so that a child will not only be accepted by African American values but more significantly develop self-esteem as a black person that will enable him/her to survive and challenge the racism of the dominant culture.

Karla Holloway observes that there are "archetypal children's needs, and these show in Black children's special need for memory" (1987: 104). If black children are going to survive they must know the stories, legends, and myths of their ancestors. Black women, writes Barbara Hill Rigney, "are the primary tale-tellers and the transmitters of history, as well as the singing teachers" (10). Trudier Harris describes these women as "keepers of the tradition" and "culture bearers . . . they are women who have kept their funkiness intact" (1991: 41). "These women are free," Harris continues, "but the freedom they experience is one wrought in nurturing their children and grandchildren, not in defiance and destruction of them" (40). Speaking to Nellie McKay (1983) about her ancestors, Morrison commented: "What is uppermost in my mind . . . is that my life seems to be dominated by information about black women. They were the culture bearers, and they told us [children] what to do . . ." (Taylor-Guthrie 1994: 140). "Black women," critic Karla Holloway writes, "carry the voice of the mother— they are the progenitors, the assurance of the line. . . . Women as carriers of the voice," Holloway continues, "carry wisdom—mother wit" (1987: 123). In an interview with Bessie Jones and Audrey Vinson (1985), Morrison talks about her own mother's soliloquies: "[She had the] habit of getting stuck like a record on some problem, going on for days and days and then singing in between . . . just like a saga" (Taylor-Guthrie 1994: 172). Stories also bestow, in Holloway's words, "endurance, staying power, and spiritual dominion" (114).[18] In this cultural bearing function, mothers, by way of storytelling, song, or soliloquies, impart important life lessons about black strength and courage as well as instill knowledge about, and pride in African American heritage that enable children to refuse the controlling images of blackness put forward by the dominant culture.

HEALING

In meeting the three tasks of motherwork, whether it be in the form of nurturance, preservation, or cultural bearing, mothers seek to protect children and teach them how to protect themselves from the hurts of the racist and, for daughters, sexist culture in which they live by enabling the child to develop a loved and proud sense of self as a black person. In this, these three functions of motherwork may be viewed as preventive or pro-active acts in so far as mothers through preservation, nurturance, and cultural bearing empower children to survive and resist. Alive and armed with the self-esteem of a beloved child who is proud of his/her black identity, this son or daughter is physically and psychologically readied and prepared to keep his selfhood intact and withstand the many and varied racist and sexist assaults that threaten to harm him or her physically and psychologically. Morrison's final task of motherwork, what I have termed healing, may be read as a re-active or restorative practice insofar as it seeks to repair those people, in particular women, whose selfhood has been displaced or damaged by the hurts of a racist and a patriarchal culture.

In her interviews Morrison has spoken about the tendency in women to place what she calls the beloved outside of themselves. In her interview with Gloria Naylor (1985), Morrison tells of how she became, in her words, "obsessed . . . with fragments of stories" she had heard of women who displaced their selves. The first was the story of Margaret Garner, the fugitive slave mother who chose to kill her children rather than see them returned to slavery. The second was the photo of a young dead girl from Van der Zee's *The Harlem Book of the Dead* (Taylor-Guthrie 1994: 207). This young girl was shot and, as she lay dying, she was asked, "What happened to you?" To which she responded, "I'll tell you tomorrow," giving the man responsible time to get away. "[I]n both instances" Morrison explains,

> something seemed clear to me. A woman loved something other than herself so much. She had placed all the value of her life in something outside herself. That woman who killed her children loved her children so much; they were the best part of her and she would not see them sullied. She would not see them hurt. . . . And . . . this woman had loved a man or had such affection for a man that she would postpone her own medical care or go ahead and die to give him time to get away so that, more valuable than her life, was not just his life but something else connected with his life. (Taylor-Guthrie 1994: 206–208)

Morrison goes on to say:

> Now both of those incidents seem to me . . . very noble, you know, in that old-fashioned sense, noble things, generous, wide-spirited, love beyond the call of. . . . It's peculiar to women. And I thought, it's interesting because the best thing that is in us is also the thing that makes us sabotage ourselves, sabotage in the sense that our life is not as worthy. [W]hat is it that really

compels a good woman to displace the self, her self. . . . [W]hat I started . . . thinking about . . . was to project the self not into the way we say "yourself," but to put a space between those words, as though the self were really a *twin* or a thirst or a friend or something that sits right next to you and watches you. (208)

In this conversation with Gloria Naylor, Toni Morrison described her writing as a "process of reclamation"—a journey of remembering which brings into being the life of the dead girl:

[B]it by bit I had been rescuing her [the dead girl] from the grave of time and inattention. Her fingernails may be in the first book; face and legs, perhaps, the second time. Little by little bringing her back into living life. So that now she comes running when called—walks freely around the house, sits down in a chair; looks at me, listens. . . . She cannot lie. Doesn't know greed or vengeance. Will not fawn or pontificate. . . . She is here now, alive. I have seen, named and claimed her—and oh what company she keeps. (217)

Eight years later during a radio interview with Eleanor Wachtel on *Jazz* (1993), Morrison was asked about the relationship between the dead girl inside who is brought back to life through writing and the dead girl that is killed by Violet and yet lives with her. Morrison responded:

[Violet's] dead in the sense of being asleep. No one can bring that person back to life except the person who has enfolded it. The soul or spirit . . . what…we mean when we say me. [It] is so ignored, so silent, so unappreciated by forces that are in the world. . . . That is where self esteem is born or destroyed . . . need to release . . . honor that part of our selves. . . . That seems to be critical and very important for human beings to be able to do that. [The] search for that person, concept or idea informs a great deal of my work. (Wachtel 1993)

Morrison's writings call upon her readership to recognize, affirm, and celebrate the "me"; and to love, as Baby Suggs preaches in *Beloved,* the person we are. The self must be known and loved, in Morrison's terms, "honored and released." When we do not name or nurture our own authentic self, we lose, forget about, or put to sleep the person we are. Morrison comments further: "[What concerns me] is when you displace the self, so completely that you do not have value if you are not worried about someone else. When are you going to worry about your self?" She goes on to ask:

Who is Beloved? . . . Where is that part of you that you know loves you and will never let you down. . . . Why are we ignoring that part of ourselves—we keep strangling it every minute and we know that one will always be there, will always love and give no judgement. That is the one we put to sleep all the time and transfer energy of that into the thing outside. (Wachtel, 1993)

Morrison asks us to recognize, as Sethe eventually does in *Beloved,* that our "me" is indeed our "best thing" (1987: 273).

In her 1993 radio interview, Morrison spoke about the need to "honor and release the soul or spirit . . . what we mean when we say me, the part of you that you know loves you and will never let you down" (Wachtel 1993). In a 1990 interview with Bill Moyers, Morrison commented: "We have to embrace our-selves [and have] Self regard" (57). In her 1983 interview with Nellie McKay, Morrison described the woman in yellow from *Tar Baby* as

> a real, a complete individual who owns herself—another kind of Pilate. There is always someone who has no peer, who does not have to become anybody. Someone who already "is." . . . She is the original self—the self that we betray when we lie, the one that is always there. And whatever that self looks like—if one ever sees that thing, or that image—one measures one's other self against it. (Taylor-Guthrie 1994: 147–48)

In her 1985 conversation with Gloria Naylor, Morrison discusses again the woman in yellow and says:

> [She] is somehow transcendent and whatever she really was, what she was perceived as by Jadine, is the real chic. The one that authenticates every-thing. The one that is very clear in some way about what her womanhood is. . . . [T]he memory of that one is somehow a basis for either total repres-sion or a willingness to let one's true self surface. (Taylor-Guthrie 1994: 194)

The interviews cover a ten-year period, and yet in each the idea of an authentic or true self is emphasized. This authenticity of self is specifically the selfhood made possible through the preservation, nurturance, and cultural bearing of motherwork. Morrison's emphasis on an authentic or true self informs all of her writings and has particular relevance for her women characters.

In Morrison's work, children who do not receive the preservation, nurtu-rance, and cultural bearing of motherwork never develop the authentic selfhood Morrison champions and thus grow to be psychologically wounded as adults. Never having been loved—protected, nurtured, and sustained through cultural bearing—by their mothers, unmothered children never learn how to love them-selves. Without this self-love, the "me" of which Morrison speaks is lost, forgot-ten, or "put to sleep." The aim of healing, the fourth task of motherwork, is to mend the unmothered and wounded children. Normally, this healing takes place when these children have become adults and centers upon the recovery of dis-placed selfhood for those individuals who were denied nurturance and cultural bearing in childhood. Specifically, these adults finally acquire self-love and achieve selfhood by being remothered as adults. This remothering is achieved by way of a spiritual or physic reconnection with a lost mother and by way of a recla-mation of a lost or displaced mother/daughter selfhood. This reconnection and reclamation is achieved through what Morrison has termed rememory. Healing occurs when the son or daughter is able to remember the mother, mourn her loss, reconnect with her and recreate for themselves an identity as a mothered child. This connection, however, is not with an actual flesh and blood mother but with the spirit or memory of the lost mother. This psychic journey of return, reconnection, and reclamation while directed to a spirit of a lost mother, is often initiated and overseen by an actual mother figure, a close female friend of the troubled woman who serves as an othermother for her. "Black women," as Carole Boyce Davies has observed, "at certain junctures in their lives, require healing and renewal and . . . Black women themselves have to become the healers/mothers for each other when there is such a need" (1991: 41). The othermother heals the woman by prompting her to take this journey of rememory and reconnection and assisting, comforting, and sustaining her as she does so. The me-ness that Morrison argues is central to well-being therefore is either imparted to us as children through cultural bearing and nurturance or restored to us as adults through healing. And it is this me-ness that empowers the child to survive and resist. In both instances it is women, though not necessarily or exclusively a biological mother or even a real flesh-and-blood mother, who provide this healing that makes possible the achievement of this sustaining selfhood.

MORRISON'S THEORY OF MOTHERHOOD AS A SITE OF POWER AND MOTHERWORK AS CONCERNED WITH THE EMPOWERMENT OF CHILDREN AS DEVELOPED IN HER NOVELS

The traditions and practices of black motherhood discussed above give rise to a distinct black experience of, and perspective on mothering. Building upon this, Morrison argues that the ancient properties make motherhood a site of power. In each of her seven novels we find representations of women who embody the ancient proprieties of traditional black womanhood. Mrs. MacTeer in *The Bluest Eye,* Eva in *Sula,* Pilate in *Song of Solomon,* and Sethe in *Beloved* are women who, to use Morrison's words, "could build a house and have some children . . . they are both ship and safe harbor at the same time." Other women, while not mothers themselves, are ship and safe harbor to children through the practice of othermothering: Ondine in *Tar Baby,* Violet and Alice in *Jazz,* and Connie in *Paradise* provide care, both economic and emotional, for children and adults. Likewise, women such as the "woman in the yellow," the Tar Women, and Therese from *Tar Baby,* while not central to the novel's plot, signify the "black mammy" characteristics Morrison seeks to reclaim as essential for the empowerment of black women. They are women, again to use Morrison's words, "who understand [their] past, not women who merely [have] [their] way. . . . [These] women did know how to nurture and survive." While their jobs are varied—hairdresser (Violet), cook (Sethe), bootlegger (Pilate), domestic service (Ondine, Mrs. MacTeer), landlady (Eva)—none of these women experiences her work as being in conflict with the duties of home and nurturance. Rather, paid work is regarded simply as a dimension or extension of motherwork. Noticeably absent in Morrison's fiction, and found in much of white middle-class women's writing on motherhood, is a narrative or thematic conflict between the duties of home and the demands of work. While motherhood and work in white women's writing are usually conveyed in terms of "a struggle to juggle the load" theme, in Morrison, motherhood and work are understood to be essential and integrated dimensions of black women's role and identity. Again, to quote from one of Morrison's interviews on this topic: "[Black women] have known . . . how to be complete human beings . . . it's not a question, it's not a conflict. You don't have to give up anything. You choose your responsibilities." The challenge for Morrison's mothers therefore, is not how to combine motherhood and work, but rather how, in the face of racism and sexism, to best provide the motherwork—both in and outside the home—necessary for the empowerment of children. The struggle for Morrison's mothers is not how to balance work and family but rather how to fulfill the important tasks of motherwork in the face of racism and poverty. In Morrison's fiction, black mothers, despite the power of their maternal standpoint, must mother their children in a world hostile to them and often must battle to provide the preservation, nurturance, and cultural bearing necessary for the empowerment of their children.

THE MOTHERLINE: DISCONNECTIONS, FRACTURES, AND RECONNECTIONS: CHAPTERS 2, 3, AND 4

The ancient properties of traditional black womanhood accord black women power and from this position black mothers engage in a maternal practice that has as its explicit goal the empowerment of children. Motherwork, in its tasks of preservation, nurturance, cultural bearing, and healing seeks to empower children by protecting them and teaching children how to protect themselves. This protection centers upon the formation of a loved and proud black selfhood that makes survival and resistance possible. However, mothers must, to fulfill these tasks, be the women of the ancient properties. Motherwork—in particular the essential aim of cultural bearing—requires that mothers be the women of the ancient properties because only these women can pass on the teachings of African American motherline that make possible a loved and proud black selfhood. While the four tasks are represented in each of Morrison's novels, generally her fiction tends to move from a preoccupation with the loss of the ancient properties though disconnections and fractures to the motherline to a concern with the healing of those adults who never received cultural bearing and nurturance from mothers of the ancient properties. Morrison, in her early and middle books, is concerned with how people become disconnected from the motherline, how the motherline itself becomes severed, and how people may be reconnected to their motherline. Of particular concern to Morrison, and the subject of chapter 2, is how women become disconnected from their motherline, lose the ancient properties through identification with normative gender ideologies, specifically those of family, beauty, motherlove, and female success. These gender hegemonies trouble Morrison because they cause black women to shun the very values that would empower them, namely, the funk and ancient proprieties of the African American motherline. Morrison's fiction, in particular *The Bluest Eye, Sula,* and *Tar Baby,* seeks to dismantle, destabilize, and deconstruct these master narratives so as to enable black women to write their own scripts of family, beauty, motherlove, and female fulfilment in accordance with ancient properties of the motherline.

Disconnection from the motherline is central to Morrison's first, second, and fourth novel and is the topic of the second chapter of this book. The third chapter looks at how the African American motherline itself is fractured by historical trauma, in particular slavery, migration, and assimilation, a theme most fully developed in *Song of Solomon* and *Beloved.* Migration and assimilation seriously impair black women's maternal function as cultural bearer and hence weakens their ability to pass on the teachings of the motherline. Migration does this by geographically separating women from the rural South—the place wherein the funk and ancient properties originated and are most fully sustained. Assimilation achieves this by socializing girls into the patriarchal role of wife—as opposed to the black motherself role of ship and harbor. Slavery ruptured the motherline by separating families through sale and by denying African people their humanity and history. As chapters 2 and 3 examine disconnections from and disruptions of the motherline, chapter 4 explores the theme of reconnection to the motherline in Morrison's middle books*, Song of Solomon* and *Tar Baby,* under the interrelated questions: How is reconnection made possible, and by whom? In particular, these novels map the way back to the motherline and describe the person best suited to guide and mentor us on this journey.

Cultural bearing, as noted above, is the way by which mothers pass on the motherline to each successive generation of children. Cultural bearing, in other words, delivers children to, and keeps them connected with the motherline and thereby works to prevent the motherline disconnections and fractures described above and explored in chapters 2, 3, and 4 of this book. However, in Morrison, there are no representations of cultural bearing with the notable exception of Mrs. MacTeer in *The Bluest Eye.* There are some examples of cultural bearing for adults, as with Pilate and Milkman in *Song* and arguably Son with Jadine, but in these two instances cultural bearing is concerned with reconnecting an adult to a motherline rather than with raising a child by way of the teachings of the African American motherline. The question to be asked, then, is, "If cultural bearing, the passing on of the ancient properties and ancestral memory, is so central and integral to Morrison's model of motherwork as the empowerment of children, why then is it not represented in her fiction?" I suggest that the significance of cultural bearing for the well-being of children is conveyed by showing the suffering that occurs when cultural bearing *does not* take place and mothers lose and children do not acquire the ancient proprieties that would empower them. In other words, the need for cultural bearing is affirmed and confirmed in and through its absence, in particular through detailing the costs and consequences of motherline disconnections and fractures.

PRESERVATION, NURTURANCE, CULTURAL BEARING;
MATERNAL POWER AND RESISTANCE: CHAPTER 5

The significance of the tasks of preservation and nurturance for the well-being of children is, similarly, emphasized not through the achievement of these aims but through detailing the difficulty of fulfilling these tasks in a racist world hostile to black children and a mother's struggle to protect and love them. Morrison's fiction affirms and confirms the importance of motherwork by detailing the personal and cultural suffering that occurs when it is absent. Likewise, Morrison's fiction bespeaks the despair and rage of mothers who, in the face of racism and poverty, are not able to fulfill these essential tasks of motherwork. What is described in Morrison is not the successful completion of this work but a mother's arduous, usually desperate, struggle to protect and nurture her children. Consequently, novels such as *The Bluest Eye* and *Sula* describe a mother's struggle to preserve and nurture; they also convey the mother's grief and rage at not being able to do so effectively, because of both racism and the patriarchal institution of motherhood. The mothers' rage and grief emerge as the central and organizing theme and perspective of the narrative. Specifically, Morrison is concerned with how and in which ways mothers resist racist and patriarchal practices that prevent them from being the protective and nurturing mothers they wish to be. From this consideration, Morrison explores how mothers, such as Eva in *Sula* and Sethe in *Beloved,* in their struggle to provide care and love in resistance against a culture that denies them, claim a maternal power that upsets comfortable notions of maternal powerlessness, particularly as such pertains to black women who are expected to be powerless in a racist and sexist culture. While such expressions of maternal power may disturb readers, maternal power is, according to Morrison, essential for black mothers to perform the necessary tasks of motherwork.

Chapter 5 will explore the above issues through an examination of the preservative love of Mrs. MacTeer and Eva, in *The Bluest Eye* and *Sula* respectively, as well as the nurturance of Sethe in *Beloved* and the cultural bearing of Mrs. MacTeer. At issue will be how the mothers' struggles to do this motherwork are represented as acts of resistance against a racist and patriarchal culture that renders a black mother powerless to preserve and nurture her own. The chapter will also explore how the failed mothering of Ruth in *Song* and Margaret in *Tar Baby* can be read as acts of resistance against patriarchy, and in particular the patriarchal institution of motherhood. Informing the above discussions will be a larger question of how these mothers, in seeking to claim power as mothers, disturb the cultural view that all mothers, and in particular oppressed mothers, are and should be powerless. Finally, the chapter will consider how these representations of motherhood as resistance and a mother's assertion of power both disturb readers and challenge normative discourses of motherhood.

Morrison's fiction attests to the importance of preservation, nurturance, and cultural bearing by detailing the suffering for children and the rage of mothers that occurs when such are absent. This strategy is underscored by the frequency of maternal deaths in Morrison's fiction. In each of her seven novels, a mother or her surrogate dies or leaves before the child reaches adulthood. Cholly as an infant is abandoned on a trash pile by his mother; while his aunt, his surrogate mother, dies before his thirteenth year. Hannah, Ruth, Jadine, and Violet, die just as their daughters are becoming women; while the women who inhabit or visit the convent in *Paradise* are either orphaned or estranged from their mothers. When a mother dies the essential tasks of preservation, nurturance, and cultural bearing remain unfulfilled or, at best, only partially fulfilled unless an othermother performs this role. These maternal deaths also function metaphorically in that they signify the cultural and personal loss that occurs when preservation, nurturance, and cultural bearing are not provided. Morrison is often remembered and known for her disturbing renditions of motherhood: an adult son burnt to death; a baby whose throat is slit; a toddler whose bottom is pricked by pins; and newborn twins smothered in the back seat of a car. These harrowing and horrifying events that permeate her narrative have indeed come to characterize the work of Toni Morrison. Symbolically they represent the suffering of unmothered children and the despair of mothers not able to mother these children. However, as Morrison's fiction portrays the suffering and despair in the absence of mothering, her texts also offer hope in mothers' resistance against denied mothering, the topic of chapter 5, and in maternal redemption, healing the unmothered adult children, the concern of the final chapter of this book.

MATERNAL HEALING: CHAPTER 6

The fourth task of motherwork, the healing of the unmothered and wounded children, is the concern of Morrison's last two novels, *Jazz* and *Paradise*. These two novels center upon the recovery of displaced selfhood for those individuals who were denied nurturance and cultural bearing in childhood. Joe and Violet in *Jazz* are healed when they remember the mother, mourn her loss, reconnect with her, and recreate for themselves an identity as a mothered child. In *Paradise*, the convent women, under the care of Consolata, are able to confront "the monsters that slavered them" (303) and "rememory" the reproductive traumas that haunt them. Healed, they may reclaim their identities of mothers and/or daughters that their maternal failures caused them to deny. As Joe and Violet must go in search of their lost mother to find their lost selves, the convent women must remember the daughters and mothers they once were to become the women they wish to be. Remothering is performed not by the actual flesh-and-blood mothers of Joe, Violet, and the convent women; rather, it is achieved by the children reconnecting with the memory of their lost mother and reclaiming an identify as a loved child.

CONCLUSION

Morrison's maternal standpoint defines motherhood as a site of power and her model of motherwork is concerned with the empowerment of children. By way of motherwork, children develop a loved and proud African American identity that makes survival and resistance possible. However, this theoretical trajectory of Morrison's is not, as noted above, delineated in the fiction itself. Only with the task of healing is the redemptive power of mothering conveyed and in this instance such is achieved by a child's psychic return to his lost mother rather than by an actual woman mothering her children (though an othermother does oversee this adult child's journey of remembering, return, and reconnection). From this perspective, it would seem that there is a disparity or divergence between the idealized view of motherhood put forward in Morrison's theory and the "ineffectual" mothering portrayed in her fiction, that the promise of the power of mothers and motherhood celebrated in her theory is not delivered in her fiction. However, this book will argue that the reverse is, in fact, the case. Morrison affirms and confirms the importance of mothers and motherwork by describing in poignant and often agonizing detail the personal and cultural suffering and loss that occur when children are not mothered and do not receive the preservation, nurturance, and cultural bearing needed for personal resistance and cultural renewal. Morrison, in her many interviews, explains why and how motherwork empowers children. In contrast, Morrison's novels, as fiction, do not describe or prescribe how such motherwork is to be performed; rather, they portray mothers' despair at not being able to fulfill the essential tasks of motherwork and the inevitable suffering of children and the larger African American culture in the absence of maternal preservation, nurturance, and cultural bearing. Frequently, we understand or appreciate the importance of something or someone only when that something or someone is lost or absent. Morrison's dedication in *Sula* bespeaks this theme: "It is sheer good fortune to miss somebody long before they leave you. This book is for Ford and Slade, whom I miss although they have not left me." This, as the following chapters will show, is the strategy of Morrison's fiction.

chapter two

Disconnections from the Motherline

Gender Hegemonies and the Loss of the Ancient
Properties: *The Bluest Eye, Sula, Tar Baby*

MOTHERS, THROUGH THE TASK of cultural bearing, pass on to each successive generation of children African American culture and instill in their children knowledge about and pride in their African American heritage. More specifically, mothers pass on what I have called the motherline: the ancestral memory and ancient properties of traditional black culture. In so doing, cultural bearing or motherline mothering confers affirming images of black people and their history that, in turn, impedes the internalization of the controlling images of blackness put forward by the dominant culture and allows the child to develop a strong and authentic selfhood as a black person. Morrison, as noted in the previous chapter, affirms and confirms the importance of this task of cultural bearing by showing the suffering that occurs when cultural bearing *does not* take place and mothers lose and children do not acquire the ancestral memory and ancient properties that would empower them. In particular, Morrison is concerned with examining how and why women become disconnected from the motherline as well as detailing the costs and consequences of motherline disconnections for mothers as well as their daughters. This chapter will explore this theme of disconnection from and loss of the motherline in *The Bluest Eye, Sula,* and *Tar Baby*. In particular, it will examine how women become disconnected from their motherline through identification with normative gender ideologies. Pauline, Sula, and Jadine, the women examined in this chapter, each become disconnected from their motherline and disregard, as a consequence, their ancient properties as a result of their internalization of a particular normative gender belief or behavior.

In the instance of Pauline, the normative gender ideology internalized is that of the family and female beauty, while for Sula it is that of motherlove and for Jadine it is that of female fulfillment. Morrison's first novel, *The Bluest Eye* describes a mother's, Pauline's, loss of the funk and the ancient properties through her internalization of the hegemonic view of the model family and ideal female beauty, and details the devastating impact of this on her ability to mother. In *Sula,* disconnection occurs as a result of a daughter's, Sula's, adherence to normative definitions of motherlove, in particular the ideology of unconditional love, which causes her to reject her mother Hannah and her motherline. In Morrison's fourth novel, *Tar Baby,* Jadine's belief in modern gender ideologies of female fulfillment—autonomy, self-sufficiency, independence—results in her rejection of the ancient properties and the funk of traditional black womanhood. With Pauline, a mother does not engage in cultural bearing to pass on the teachings, in particular the ancient properties, of the motherline, while in the instance of Jadine and Sula, a daughter shuns the teachings of the motherline and separates herself from it. Morrison, as critical commentary on her fiction has long observed, is particularly and deeply troubled by normative gender ideologies, in particular those of female beauty, the family, motherlove, and female fulfillment. Less acknowledged is the question of why Morrison is so preoccupied with these issues. These gender ideologies worry Morrison precisely because they cause black women to shun the very values that would empower them, namely, the funk and ancient properties of the African American motherline. Morrison's fiction seeks to dismantle, destabilize, and deconstruct these master narratives so as to enable black women to write scripts of family, beauty, motherlove, and fulfillment in accordance with the teachings of the African American motherline.

THE BLUEST EYE

Much critical commentary on *The Bluest Eye* has centered on the primer that opens the text and introduces each chapter. The primer presents the ideal family: in "the very pretty house" live Dick and Jane with their "nice" mother and "big and strong" father. The white middle-class nuclear family of the primer is scripted as the normal family arrangement. Families are measured by this ideal and are encouraged to emulate it. The "Dick and Jane" family however is available only to a select few. Families like the Breedloves in *The Bluest Eye* can never be a Dick and Jane family though they will continually aspire to achieve the ideal and forever measure their own selves against it. The primer in *The Bluest Eye* serves to emphasize the inappropriateness of this ideal for black families and reminds us of the inevitable feelings of inferiority that come with not achieving what is presented as the ideal and normal way of being. In a 1981 interview Morrison discusses how she used "the primer story, with its picture of a happy family, as a frame acknowledging the outer civilization. The primer with white children," Morrison continues, "was the way life was presented to the black people" (Taylor-Guthrie 1994: 127).

In this interview Morrison goes on to discuss how she "wanted that primer version broken up and confused" (Taylor-Guthrie 1994: 127). The initial primer paragraph conforms to conventional grammatical and stylistic format; in the second rendition punctuation and capitalization are eliminated; and in the final form there is no word division. In his article, "Order and Disorder in Toni Morrison's *The Bluest Eye*," Chikwenye Okonjo Ogunyemi argues that the three paragraphs represent the three family arrangements presented to us in the novel: Geraldine's family, which is closest to the ideal family of the primer, the MacTeers, and finally the Breedloves, who are at the bottom of the social hierarchy. Ogunyemi argues that the "transmutation is Morrison's indirect criticism of the white majority for the black family's situation and for what is taught to the black child in school, as evidenced by the primer paragraph, that in no way relates to the child's reality" (113).[1]

More specifically, the primer's construction of the ideal family enacts the complex relationship between subjectivity, discourse, and ideology. The function of the primer in the educational system is to teach young students how to read. However, in acquiring literacy, the student learns more than language; he or she internalizes the values of the text that is read. In the instance of the primer, while the student learns the workings of nouns and verbs, he or she is also inscribed in the dominant ideology of the family. Critic Donald Gibson elaborates:

> [T]he act of learning to read and write means exposure to the values of the culture from which the reading material emanates. If one wants to read or write, then one must pay for the privilege. The cost of learning to read and write carries with it the necessity to submit to values beyond and other than literacy per se, for words do not exist independent of value. One cannot learn to read without being subjected to the values engraved in the text. (Gates 1993: 160–61)[2]

Gibson's concept here of the "enact[ment] [of] self-oppression" through the internalization of the dominant culture's values echoes the Marxist French philosopher Louis Althusser's theory of hailing and interpellation. Kaja Silverman explains in *Subject of Semiotics*:

> Althusser helps us to understand that discourse may also consist of an exchange between a person and a cultural agent . . . (Althusser isolates priests and education as particularly important cultural agents . . .). The agent addresses the person, and in the process defines not so much its own as the other's identity. . . . Althusser refers to the address as "hailing," and its successful outcome as "interpellation." Interpellation occurs when the person to whom the agent speaks recognizes him or herself in that speech, and takes up subjective residence there. (48–49)

However, the subject position the primer offers is held in sharp contrast to the lived realities of the Breedlove family. Yet, following Althusser, the subject in the text becomes not only more preferable, but also more real. One's own real, lived life becomes, in the words of Pauline, "like the after thoughts one has just before sleep, the early-morning and late evening edges of her day, the dark edges that made the daily life with the Fishers lighter, more delicate, more lovely" (101). The lived, however, does frequently interrupt and disrupt the assumed subjectivity; as with Pauline's tooth, the lived/actual often shatters the illusion.[3]

In a 1978 filmed interview Morrison commented, "I suppose *The Bluest Eye* is about one's dependency on the world for identification, self-value, feelings or worth" (Carmen 1993: 18).[4] In *The Bluest Eye* the original self—that essential "me" Morrison speaks of in her interviews—is displaced through interpellation. As Karen Carmean observes, Pauline conforms "to a role defined by others, and in confusing self with role, Pauline denies any possibility of growth. [She represents] many who, in adopting white values and standards of behaviour, deny their essential value, substituting false—even destructive—standards" (21). In developing the text's theme of false consciousness, several critics have turned to the writings of existential thought, particularly Sartre's notion of the "Look." Critics Wilfred D. Samuels and Clenora Hudson-Weems write: "Pecola, Pauline, and Cholly Breedlove fall victim to their failure to transcend the imposing definition of 'the Other's' look. Reduced to a state of 'objectness' (thingness), each remains frozen in a world of being-for-the-other and consequently lives a life of shame, alienation, self-hatred, and inevitable destruction" (10–11).[5]

Pauline relieves her boredom and loneliness by going to the movies: "The onliest time," Pauline tells us, "I be happy seem like was when I was in the picture show. Every time I got, I went. I'd go early, before the show started. They'd cut off the lights, and everything be black. The screen would light up, and I'd move right in on them pictures" (97). Pauline's experience in the movie house, as with the primer that frames the text, signifies the process of interpellation. Pauline takes on the subject position constructed by the film, "move right in on them pictures," and reads her own life from the perspective of that film narrative: "Them pictures gave me a lot of pleasure, but it made coming home hard" (97). In the darkness of the movie theatre Pauline, as the narrator tells us, is introduced to "probably the most destructive ideas in the history of human thought—romantic love and physical beauty. Both originated in envy, thrived in insecurity and ended in disillusion" (97). *The Bluest Eye* both critiques and challenges that "destructive idea" which "equat[es] physical beauty with virtue" (97).

Critics of *The Bluest Eye* have not considered why Pauline, and later Pecola, are so easily seduced by that master narrative of beauty and romance, while other characters, such as the MacTeers, remain relatively indifferent to it. Part of the answer resides in Pauline's romantic and artistic sensibilities: she has the soul of a poet and the eye of an artist. The narrator tells us that "[d]uring all of her four years of going to school, she was enchanted by numbers and depressed by words. She missed—without knowing what she missed—paints and crayons" (89). In this, she foreshadows Sula in Morrison's second novel: "Had she paints, or clay, or knew the discipline of the dance, or strings; had she anything to engage her tremendous curiosity and her gift for metaphor, she might have exchanged the restlessness and preoccupation with whim for an activity that provided her with all that she yearned for" (105). Patrick Bjork compares Pauline to the grandmothers of Alice Walker's essay "In Search of Our Mother's Gardens" (43), in which Walker talks about "these grand mothers and mothers of ours [who] were. . . . Artists; driven to a numb and bleeding madness by the springs of creativity in them for which there was no release" (233). The black woman artist, Walker goes on to say, "left her mark in the only materials she could afford, and in the only medium her position in society allowed her to use" (239). Black women's creativity then found expression in quilt making or gardening. Separated from her rural roots Pauline lacks even these mediums. Without paints or even a garden to cultivate, the Fishers' kitchen becomes the place of Pauline's art—"here she found beauty, order, cleanliness, and praise" (100). That is why Pauline, as Jacqueline de Weever observes, is so enraged when Pecola spills the cobbler on the floor of the kitchen, her "work of art, and she is ready to beat her daughter Pecola for marring it" (151). Her artistic sensibility causes Pauline to be susceptible to the lure of the beauty myth and makes her later silence and self-abnegation all the more tragic. As Alice Walker, paraphrasing Virginia Woolf, writes: "[A]ny black woman born with a great gift in the sixteenth century . . . would have certainly gone crazed, shot herself, or ended her days in some lonely cottage outside the village, half witch, half wizard . . . feared and mocked at" (1983, 235). What did it mean for a black woman, Walker asks, "to be an artist in our grandmother's time? . . . It is a question with an answer cruel enough to stop the blood" (233).

In *The Dilemma of "Double Consciousness" in Toni Morrison's Novels* (1993), Denise Heinze discusses the loss of Pauline's rainbow: "All of the colors that swirled inside of her—the reds of her sexual passion, the yellows of her boundless joy, and the greens of her quiet moments—have bleached white" (73). "With the rainbow," Heinze continues, "goes . . . [Pauline's] interpretation of life through sensual perceptions" (73). Not only does Pauline's artist soul cause her to succumb to that "most destructive idea"; it also makes the loss of "her rainbow" that much greater and more keenly felt both by Pauline and the reader. Significantly, Pauline's narrative ends with this reflection: "Only thing I miss is that rainbow. But like I say, I don't recall it much anymore" (Morrison 104).[6]

Pauline's susceptibility to the ideologies of the model family and ideal family thus may be attributed to her artistic and romantic temperament. This explanation, however, is only partial. Pauline's life, because of her disconnection from the motherline and its teachings, lacked a proud and strong sense of self that would have enabled her, in the words of the text, "to stand erect and spit the misery out on the street instead [of holding] it in where it could lap into her" (61). In "Eruptions of Funk: Historicizing Toni Morrison," Susan Willis contends that "the problem at the center of Morrison's writing is how to maintain an Afro-American cultural heritage once the relationship to the black rural south has been stretched thin over distance and generations" (Gates 1984: 264). As a young girl in Alabama, Pauline's life was, literally, full of color: "My whole dress was messed with purple, and it never did wash out. Not the dress nor me. I could feel that purple deep inside me. And that lemonade Mama used to make when Pap came in out the fields. It be cool and yellowish. . . . And that streak of green them June bugs made on the trees" (92). Down home, "all of them colors was in [her]" (92). Newly married, she and Cholly move north to Ohio where Pauline experienced, in the words of the text "the lonesomest time of [her] life" (93). Pauline talks about how with moving north "everything changed": "It was hard to get to know folks up here, and I missed my people. I weren't used to so much white folks" (93). The few women she meets snicker at her way of talking and are amused by her unstraightened hair (94). Alone and lonely Pauline turns to her husband Cholly, in the words of the text, for "reassurance, entertainment, for things to fill the vacant places" (93). It would seem that geographical dislocation, and the resulting separation from one's heritage and family, are at the heart of Pauline's emotional estrangement, which drives her to the movies and eventually leads her to a hatred of her black self. Separated from her rural culture and identifying with the values of the dominant one, Pauline loses what is called in *The Bluest Eye* funkiness: "the . . . funkiness of passion, the funkiness of nature, the funkiness of the wide range of emotions" (68). Disconnected from her motherline, Pauline has lost her funkiness and the ancient properties that would have grounded her in the values of her people and enabled her to resist interpellation.

Karen Carmean, however, argues that "Pauline's sense of emotional estrangement has actually been life long" (24). The text tells us that as a child growing up in a large Alabama family Pauline "had never felt at home anywhere or that she belonged any place" (88). Pauline's sense of aloneness and difference is reinforced and demarcated by her deformed foot. "Her general feelings of separateness and unworthiness," the text tells us, "[Pauline] blamed on her foot" (88). Her foot, as Philip Page observes, signifies, as a deficiency, "a lack, a vulnerability, an Achilles' heel, and therefore a sign of her subjugation" (41). Metaphorically, her physical deformity symbolizes Pauline's spiritual and physical alienation from her cultural groundings.[7] Her deformity also signifies her artistic nature: like Sula with her shifting birth mark and Pilate with her smooth stomach, Pauline is an artist without an art form. However, unlike Pilate who conjures, winemakes, prophesizes, sings, and dances, Pauline expresses herself only in her frequent brutal, yet silent, fights with Cholly: "They did not talk, groan, or curse during these beatings. There was only the muted sound of falling things, and flesh on unsurprised flesh" (38). As one of the gossiping woman said of the Breedloves: "Don't nobody know nothing about them anyway. Where they come from or nothing. Don't seem to have no people" (147). "Having no people," Pauline is rendered vulnerable to the seductive myths of the dominant culture (147).

Pauline takes on rather than resists the identity assigned to her by the dominant culture. The narrator comments: "You looked at them and wondered why they were so ugly; you looked closely and could not find the source. Then you realized that it came from conviction, their conviction. It was as though some mysterious all-knowing master had given each one a cloak of ugliness to wear, and they had accepted it without question" (34). The Breedloves, the text emphasizes, are not intrinsically or aesthetically ugly; they are defined as ugly by the dominant culture with its white standards of beauty. "The master had said, 'You are ugly people.' They had looked about themselves and saw nothing to contradict the statement; saw, in fact, support for it leaning at them from every billboard, every movie, every glance. 'Yes,' they had said. 'You are right.' And they took the ugliness in their hands, threw it as a mantle over them, and went about the world with it" (34). The mantle of ugliness the Breedloves wear thus signifies their identification with and internalization of the dominant discourse of beauty. Unable to love themselves, Cholly and Pauline can not love their children because they are made from them and so are reflections of them.

Pauline's relationship with her daughter, her second child, is initially described as a caring and close mother-child attachment. "That second time [pregnant]," Pauline says, "I felt good and wasn't thinking on the carrying, just on the baby itself. I used to talk to it whilst it be still in the womb. Like good friends we was" (98). "Up til the end," Pauline tells us, "(she) felt good about that baby" (99). She also says that "[she'd] love it no matter what it looked like" (98). Once born, the daughter is described as a "big old healthy thing" (99) and is perceived by her mother as a bright and quick child: "They gave her to me for a nursing, and she liked to pull my nipple off right away. She caught on fast. . . . A right smart baby she was" (99–100). Pauline is also attracted to, and fascinated by, her newly born daughter: "I used to like to watch her. . . . Eyes all soft and wet. A cross between a puppy and a dying man" (100). Although, Pauline is impressed by her daughter's health and quickness, and is mesmerized by her facial features, she sees her daughter as ugly: "I knowed she was ugly. Head full of pretty hair, but Lord she was ugly" (100). Pauline can not find in her real flesh-and-blood daughter the unborn child of her imagination: "She looked so different from what I thought. Reckin I talked to it so much I conjured up a mind's eye view of it" (99). Since Pauline spent much of her pregnancy in movie houses, the text suggests her "mind's eye view" of the unborn child was formed in terms of white definitions of beauty and acceptability. The child imagined in the womb is light skinned, fine featured, but the real Pecola is born very dark.

Pauline's birth experience also contributes to Pauline's perception of her daughter as ugly. For the birth of her second child Pauline chooses a hospital over a home birth "so [she] could be easeful" (98). Ironically, though not surprisingly, Pauline's hospital birth is anything but easeful. As a poor, black woman Pauline is treated with contempt and indifference by the medical staff; in the hospital the doctors talk "nice friendly talk" to the white women, but neither speaks to Pauline nor even makes eye contact with her. To the doctors she is merely "[one] of these here women . . . [who] deliver right away and with no pain. Just like horses" (99). While Pauline resists the denial of her subjectivity and the dehumanization of her birth experience by forcing one doctor to look her in the eye and by "moan[ing] something awful . . . to let them know having a baby was more than a bowel movement" (99), her self-perception is, nonetheless, structured through the degradation of her labor experience. So when her child is born, and it is both black and female, Pauline sees it as she herself was seen while in labor as undesirable, irrelevant, and unimportant. Significantly, when Pauline attempts to convey her surprise at seeing her actual daughter, in contrast to the image she had of her while pregnant, she does so by way of analogy to her own

mother and herself as daughter: "So when I seed it, it was like looking at a picture of your mama when she was a girl. You knows who she is, but she don't look
the same" (99). This analogy invokes the theme of the need for the parents to
love themselves if they are to love their children. At the movies and while in labor,
Pauline learns that her blackness renders her undesirable; it therefore is not sur-
prising that when Pauline holds her very black daughter in her arms she perceives
her as ugly.

In "Mothers and Daughters: Another Minority Group," Natalie Rosinsky
argues that "Pauline's transformation is a literary manifestation of Rich's observation that 'power relations between mother and child are often simply a reflection of power relations in patriarchal society. . . . Powerless women have always
used mothering as a channel . . . for their own human will to power'" (282).
"Thus, Pauline," Rosinsky continues, "unable to individually alter the norms
that circumscribe and fragment her existence is capable of moulding her children to fit these norms, and she seizes this opportunity to affirm, through the
exercise of such power, her own self-worth and identity" (282–83, emphasis in
source). I suggest, contrary to Rosinsky, that Pauline's will to power is expressed
not through her mothering role but through her role as a domestic in the Fisher
household. Pauline tells us that "the creditors and service people who humili-
ated her when she went to them on her own behalf respected her, were even
intimidated by her, when she spoke for the Fishers" (101). In the Fisher household "*power,* praise and luxury were hers" (101, emphasis added). And Pauline
affirms her self-worth and identity not in mothering her own children, as Rosinsky argues, but through managing the Fishers' home and raising their child.
Pauline's power is, of course, not real; it is a borrowed power, accorded Pauline
only in her capacity as an employee of the Fishers. Although this power ultimately belongs to the Fishers and not to Pauline, her role as domestic does, as
Samuels and Hudson-Weems have observed, "allow . . . [Pauline] to operate
from a position of strength, compensating for the sense of power she lost with
the deterioration of her sexual life with her husband" (27). In Pauline's mind, as
Gloria Wade-Gayles has pointed out, "she is not yielding to powerlessness; she
is acquiring power" (1984: 141).

Pauline herself contrasts her borrowed power as a domestic to her lived powerlessness as mother. "I loved them and all, I guess, but maybe it was having no
money or maybe it was Cholly, but they sure worried the life out of me. Sometimes I'd catch myself hollering at them and beating them, and I'd feel sorry for
them, but I couldn't seem to stop" (98). Her children, the narrator later tells us,
"she bent toward respectability, and in so doing taught them fear: fear of being
clumsy, fear of being like their father, fear of not being loved by God, fear of
madness like Cholly's mother. Into her son she beat a loud desire to run away,
and into her daughter she beat a fear of growing up, fear of other people, fear of
life" (102). While we may fault Pauline for the way she mothered her children,
her ineffectual mothering (for lack of a better word) originates not from a will to
power, as Rosinsky would have it, but from a despair and resignation that she is

not able, as a black woman in a racist culture, to mother her children well. Pauline is ultimately a victim. As Pettis points out, she was not able to, as the women of Cholly's aunt's generation did, "transform [her] situation . . . and compartmentalize [it], and at the same time uniquely transcend [it]" (28).

The Bluest Eye exemplifies the need for mothers to maintain a strong authentic self so that they may nurture the same in their daughters. In her article, appropriately entitled, "Difficult Survival: Mothers and Daughters in *The Bluest Eye*," Joyce Pettis argues that Pauline fails at nurturing her daughter because she herself is unnurtured; quoting Adrienne Rich in *Of Woman Born* Pettis writes: "The nurture of daughters in a patriarchy calls for a strong sense of self-nurture in the mother" (27). Disconnected from her motherline and in particular the teachings of the ancient properties, Pauline is rendered vulnerable to the dominant white supremacist ideology which results in the effacement and disparagement of her self as a black woman. "It is not simply," to quote Rich again, "that . . . mothers feel both responsible and powerless. It is that they carry their own guilt and self-hatred over to their daughters' experiences" (1986: 224). This generational continuation of female self-hatred explains and is signified by Pauline's inability to love her black female child upon her birth. Pauline is "a mother in a modern industrialized city," who is, as Aoi Mori has argued, "[un]able to find a new sustaining community in the industrialized city, she fallaciously finds her role models in the cinematic world which manipulatively projects only white standards" (104). Cynthia Davis has written that in *The Bluest Eye,* as in Morrison's later writings, "[a] sense of history is not available to women, and without it they have neither the models nor the contextual information to make themselves whole" (1990: 22). Such women have been denied the cultural bearing or motherline mothering that confers affirming images of black people and their history which, in turn, impedes the internalization of the controlling images of blackness put forward by the dominant culture and allows women to develop a strong and authentic selfhood as a black person. While this point is arguable with respect to Morrison's later writings, it seems accurate for *The Bluest Eye.* Having been separated from her people, and interpellated in normative gender discourses, Pauline is disconnected from her motherline and thus she lacks the ancient properties that would afford her a strong sense of self and enable her to foster the same in her children.

Madonne Miner, in "Lady No Longer Sings the Blues: Rape, Madness, and Silence in *The Bluest Eye*," reads the novel as a modern reworking of the myth of Persephone and Demeter. Persephone is abducted by Pluto, God of the Underworld and, in revenge, Demeter withholds the coming of spring. As a compromise, Persephone spends half the year with her mother while the earth yields fruits and flowers and half the year in the underworld with Pluto while the earth is barren. In Homer's telling of the myth, while Persephone is in the underworld: "The Soil did not yield a single seed. / Demeter kept them all underworld" (Pryse 1985: 182). Evocatively, *The Bluest Eye* opens with, "Quiet as it's kept, there were no marigolds in the fall of 1941" (9). As a young girl, Claudia blames herself for the seeds that did not grow; however, the grown Claudia, who is narrating the story, tells us that "[o]ur seeds were not the only ones that did not sprout; nobody's did" (9). "It had never occurred to either of us," she says, "that the earth itself might have been unyielding" (19). In the Demeter-Persephone myth, the unyielding earth signifies the mother's anger at and revenge against her daughter's abduction; by withholding vegetation Demeter protests her daughter's abduction and demands her return. In *The Bluest Eye,* the unyielding earth signifies not the expression of motherlove, but its absence. If we read the seed as representing Pecola, we realize that the child did not grow and blossom because the soil in which she was planted was not rich enough to sustain her. A flower that is planted in shallow, rocky soil and is left without water, fertilization, and sunshine will not grow. Pecola withers and dies because, as a result of her own mother's disconnection from her motherline, she is denied the ancient properties of her motherline that would nurture and sustain her.

Menstruation is the female rite of passage into womanhood and it is usually the mother who guides her daughter through this passing. Pecola begins her "ministration" when she is at the MacTeers. Mrs. MacTeer, we are told, washes Pecola in the bath and Frieda and Claudia can hear "their mother's laughter" (28) behind the closed door and over the gushing water. This important rite of initiation—emphasized by the bath water that signifies rebirth—is left to a neighbor. The bath, characterized by gurgling water and the sound of laughter, is in sharp contrast to the later description of Pauline bathing Pecola: "zinc tub, buckets of stove-heated water . . . tangled black puffs of rough wool to comb" (101). Miner argues that Pecola's menstruation "bonds [her] with her adopted sisters, Frieda and Claudia" (183). While I agree that this event brings the girls closer together, the fact the her first menses takes place in the MacTeer home also underscores the lack of maternal nurturance in Pecola's life. This association between menstruation and mothering is suggested by the imagery of the text. Pecola begins to menstruate, as noted by Donald Gibson, during Mrs. MacTeer's unremitting tirade against the amount of milk Pecola has consumed. "The association of menstruation and lactation, of bleeding and feeding, is," as Gibson emphasizes, "unavoidable and explicit" (165). I would suggest that this reference to milk and, in particular, Pecola's insatiable thirst for it, signifies Pecola's longing to be mothered. In Morrison's fiction, as in much of women's writing, milk is often used as a symbol of motherlove.

Another crucial event in Pecola's maturation occurs in the kitchen of Mrs. Breedlove's employers, the Fishers. Pecola has come by the Fishers to pick up the laundry; waiting for her mother in the kitchen, she touches the berry cobbler and accidentally drops it to the floor. Seeing what her daughter has done, Mrs. Breedlove hits Pecola "with the back of her hand and knocks her to the floor" causing Pecola to "slide in the pie juice." Pecola scolds her daughter with "words that were hotter and darker than the smoking berries" (87), while she soothes the upset "pink and yellow" Fisher girl with "words of honey": "Hush, baby, hush. Come here. . . . Don't cry no more" (87). To her daughter "she spit out words like rotten pieces of apple. 'Pick up that wash and get on out of here'" (87). We learn also that the Fisher girl calls Pauline Polly, while Pecola refers to her own mother as Mrs. Breedlove. As the daughter of the Fishers, the girl exercises authority over Mrs. Breedlove; when she does not find Mrs. Breedlove in the kitchen—which is, of course her place—she calls out, "Polly, come here." From this kitchen, Pecola takes the understanding that the Fisher girl and not herself is the desired and loved child. Significantly, when Mrs. Breedlove sees the spilt cobbler she says, "*my* floor, *my* floor . . . *my* floor," and when the Fisher girl asks who Claudia, Frieda, and Pecola are, Pauline does not answer her. Pauline identifies so completely with the Fishers that she denies her own family; in her eyes the Fisher girl is the beautiful daughter she always wanted and it is she that receives the motherlove that rightly belongs to Pecola.

The final kitchen episode is, of course, Cholly's rape of his daughter Pecola. That this rape occurs in the family kitchen is particularly devastating. Kitchens, particularly in black life and literature, represent a safe haven, a refuge from the racist world outside, a place where the family is replenished and nourished both physically and emotionally.[8] In *The Bluest Eye,* Claudia's Christmas wish is "to sit on the low stool in Big Mama's kitchen with my lap full of lilacs and listen to Big Papa play his violin for me alone. The lowness of the stool made for my body, the security and warmth of Big Mama's kitchen, the smell of lilacs, the sound of music" (21). This warm and secure kitchen is in stark contrast to both the white, sterile, cold kitchen of the Fishers, where Pecola's mother beats her, and the separate back kitchen in her own house where her father rapes her. After the rape, Pecola is found by her mother in the kitchen, tells her mother of the rape, and is not believed and is subsequently beaten. Kitchens, then, are for Pecola not environments of nourishment and love but rather sources of hatred and humiliation, abuse and abandonment. From her kitchen Mrs. MacTeer recalls how Pecola was put "out-of-doors" by her family; Pauline brutally expels Pecola from the Fishers' kitchen; and in the Breedlove kitchen her father rapes her, and her mother denies the rape and does not protect her.[9] Deserted and scorned by those who should love and protect her, Pecola comes to believe that she is not loved because she is not lovable. And so she desires blue eyes; "It had occurred to Pecola . . . that if her eyes were different, that is to say beautiful, she herself would be different. . . . [So] each night, without fail, she prayed for blue eyes" (41). Significantly, she acquires blue eyes, so she believes, by feeding an old dog poisoned meat. The theme of lethal nourishment is finally rendered explicit in the way Pecola achieves her desired transformation.

In *The Bluest Eye,* the significant rites of passage into womanhood—the onset of menstruation and discovery of sexuality—are perverted to emphasize Pecola's motherlessness and her disconnection from the motherline. Likewise, Morrison uses kitchens to emphasize the absence of nourishment in Pecola's life. Finally, the myth of Demeter and Persephone is referenced to underscore Pecola's

motherlessness: Pecola, in contrast to Persephone, has no mother or motherline
to protect her and thus is rendered vulnerable to the racist patriarchal world
which eventually destroys her. In Morrison's next novel *Sula*, the motherline disconnection is also occasioned by and represented through the mother-daughter
relation. *The Bluest Eye* is concerned with a *mother's* loss of the ancient properties
as a result of her identification with the normative discourses of female beauty
and the family and the impact of this on her ability to mother. In contrast, *Sula*,
while signalling motherline disconnection through a mother-daughter split, is
concerned with a *daughters's* identification with a normative discourse, in this
instance, the myth of unconditional motherlove, and how this results in the
daughter's disconnection from her motherline. For Pauline, disconnection occurs
as a result of migration and assimilation, while for her daughter, disconnection
arises from a lack of maternal nurturance. For Sula, disconnection results not
from being separated from the motherline, as with Pauline, or being denied its
teachings, as with Pecola: rather, for Sula, identification with normative ideologies of motherlove causes her to reject the motherline, in particular the values of
the ancient properties.

SULA

Critical commentary on mothers and daughters in Morrison's second novel *Sula*
has focused on the comment Hannah makes about her daughter, Sula: "I love
Sula. I just don't like her. That's the difference" (57). Chikwenye Okonjo Ogunyemi argues that "[Sula's] insecurity and consequent neurosis . . . stem from her
unstable relationship with her mother. Her mother's flippant denial . . . along
with Sula's being unwittingly instrumental in effecting Chicken Little's death, are
crucial events in Sula's life" (130). Samuels and Hudson-Weems agree that "neither Eva nor Hannah served as a positive role model who enforced or exhibited
a lifestyle of domestic tranquillity or security" (36). They continue: "Hannah,
who had not found Eva to be a loving mother, comes up short on the nurturing
yardstick" (36). "Hannah's remark," they continue, "damages Sula's childhood"
and "lead[s] [her] to the independence she strives for" (36).

This interpretation misreads the comment by taking it out of context,
abstracting it from the larger conversation in which it is spoken. The dialogue, in
its entirety, reads as follows:

> "They a pain."
> "Yeh. Wish I'd listened to mamma. She told me not have'em too soon."
> "Any time at all is too soon for me."
> "Oh, I don't know. My Rudy minds his daddy. He just wild with me. Be
> glad when he growed and gone."
> Hannah smiled and said, "Shut your mouth. You love the ground he pee on."
> "Sure I do. But he still a pain. Can't help loving your own child. No mat-
> ter what they do."
> "Well, Hester grown now and I can't say love is exactly what I feel."

"Sure you do. You love her, like I love Sula. I just don't like her. That's
the difference."
"Guess so. Likin' them is another thing."
"Sure. They different people, you know . . ." (56–57)

What Hannah says is that a child is a separate person with her own unique personality. While mothers always love their children—"can't help loving your
own"—they may not like the person their child becomes. A mother may not like
a child at a particular moment, or at a particular stage, or at all, whether because
of differences in personality, lifestyle, beliefs, or values. As children, we want to
believe that our mothers both love and like us unconditionally. The myth that
motherlove is unconditional, as Paula Caplan points out, underpins contemporary ideological constructions of motherhood and is at the heart of mother-
blame.[10] The reality, however, is that mothers do not always like their children or
like them equally. Morrison, herself, when asked about Hannah's comment, said
that it was "an honest statement at any rate."[11] Hannah's comment dispels the
age-old myth that mother love/like is unconditional and guaranteed. Rather than
appreciate Hannah for her honesty and insight—as Morrison does—we pathologize her statement and make it the cause of Sula's so-called "neurosis."[12]

Critics respond to Hannah's comment from the child's point of view: what
concerns them is the effect this statement has on Sula. This child-centered perspective, what Brenda Daly and Maureen Reddy define as daughter-centric, is
"uninterested in the mother's subjectivity" (2). Even those critics who view the
event in a positive way interpret it from the daughter's point of view. Victoria
Middleton, for example, argues that: "Sula becomes hardy and self-reliant
because of her upbringing" (374). "Hannah's candour," Middleton continues,
"helps [Sula] distinguish herself from her mother, giving her the right to live
independently" (375). Middleton proposes that truth benefits Sula, but her concern is still daughter-centric. Rarely noted is that such daughter-centricity begs
the question: "Why does Hannah not like her daughter, Sula?"

Robert Grant, the only critic to my knowledge who asks such a question,
comments, "I think the conventional deterministic search for sociological 'reasons' and environmental 'causes' has been misguided. Rather than view Hannah's
'honest' statement as an etiological solution, the reader should instead see it as a
symptomatic effect, and a confirmation, of Sula's intractable enigma" (98). Grant
goes on to say: "Hannah's attitude inspires not an answer but a question: why
wouldn't a mother (especially one as 'tolerant' and unconventional as Hannah)
like her own daughter?" (98). Why does the mother not like her daughter? Does
she know something we don't? None of the many readings of the novel has asked
these questions, indicating how thoroughly child-centered the scholarship on
Sula has been. We never consider that Hannah may have a good reason for not
liking Sula that readers would be well advised to consider. Instead, the critics
attribute Sula's psychological disease to the way she was mothered; they engage
in mother-blame.

Sula dismisses the teachings of her motherline and decisively breaks her connection to it. The text never fully explains the reason for this dismissal and disconnection nor is one offered by the critics. However, the text does suggest that Hannah's comment, or more precisely Sula's misreading of it, causes Sula's disconnection from her motherline. "[This] pronouncement," the narrator tells us, "sent [Sula] flying up the stairs. In bewilderment, she stood at the window fingering the curtain edge, aware of a sting in her eye. Nel's call floated up and into the window, pulling her away from dark thoughts and back into the bright, hot daylight" (57). Sula interprets her mother's remark as a "pronouncement" of rejection and abandonment because she, as did her own mother when she criticized Eva's preservative love, interprets her mother's words according to the script of normative motherhood that assumes motherlove is unconditional.

After hearing her mother's words, Sula runs with Nel to the river. Once there, the girls partake in a highly symbolic initiation into heterosexuality.

> Sula . . . joined Nel in the grass play. In concert . . . they stroked the blades up and down, up and down. Nel found a thick twig . . . and pulled away its bark until it was stripped . . . Sula . . . found one too. . . . [They] poked [their] twigs rhythmically and intensely into the earth, making a small neat hole that grew deeper. . . . Together they worked until the two holes were one and the same. When the depression was the size of a small dishpan, Nel's twig broke. With a gesture of disgust she threw the pieces into the hole they had made. Sula threw hers in too. Nel saw a bottle cap and tossed it in as well. Each then looked around for more debris to throw into the hole: paper, bits of glass, butts of cigarettes, until all of the small defiling things they could find were collected there. Carefully they replaced the soil and covered the entire grave with uprooted grass. (58–59)

Sula is twelve and stands at the threshold of womanhood. This passage suggests that Sula and Nel enter adult femininity reluctantly. Although they are initially eager to experiment with their soon-to-be heterosexual identity, they eventually join their holes to demarcate the bond of their relationship which will (and does) come to an end when they assume their identities as heterosexual women. Significantly, they throw garbage, defiling things, into the hole and mark it as a grave. Immediately after, Sula and Nel accidentally drown the young boy Chicken Little. This drowning symbolically marks Sula's final rejection of conventional heterosexual femininity, in particular maternity.

Hannah's remark and the drowning of Chicken Little are juxtaposed and structurally and thematically linked through Sula's experimentation with, and rejection of conventional femininity as symbolically conveyed through the hole-digging and twig breaking. This juxtaposition suggests that Sula's rejection of motherhood originates from what she perceived to be her own mother's rejection of her. Both events, as the narrator informs us, shape Sula's developing selfhood:

> [H]ers was an experimental life—ever since her mother's remarks sent her flying up those stairs, ever since her one major feeling of responsibility had been exorcised on the bank of a river with a closed place in the middle. The first experience taught her there was no other that you could count on; the second that there was no self to count on either. She had no centre, no speck around which to grow. (118–19)

Significantly, shortly after the drowning of Chicken Little, Sula's mother burns to death.

At the age of twelve, then, Sula is twice orphaned; first by her mother's comment and later by her mother's death. In patriarchal culture, daughters, as they grow into women, need mothers by their side to keep intact their original self. Sula enters patriarchy, inscribed in the text by the defiling things and grave, alone, without a mother at her side.[13] Disconnected from the motherline and the values of the ancient properties it conveys, she rejects motherhood and embraces dominant standards of female success and well-being. In particular, she fashions a female selfhood modeled on the values of autonomy, independence, and self-sufficiency.

Sula is a hero who lives, as the novel tells us, "an experimental life" (118). Sula "becomes heroic," according to Middleton, "by rejecting the submissive female role approved by the people of her community" (367). Significantly, Middleton's article opens with a quotation from Simone de Beauvoir's *The Second Sex* and a description of de Beauvoir's theory of existentialist feminism. Middleton writes that for de Beauvoir, "a woman's heroism depends on attributes usually thought of as masculine: the freedom to live independently and adventurously, the right to take risks, and the inclination to extend the possibilities of experience . . ." (367). To become an existentialist feminist hero, Sula must renounce the values of the ancient properties of black womanhood as both ship and safe harbor, inn and trail to assume the exclusive masculine role of, to use Morrison's terms, ship and trail. "[Sula's] refusal to be a woman on their terms is," according to Middleton, "the necessary condition of her heroism." Morrison has said of Sula that "[s]he is a masculine character. . . . She's adventuresome, she trusts herself, she's not scared . . ." (367). "[However] that quality of masculinity . . . in a woman at that time is outrage, total outrage. She can't get away with that . . ."[14] Sula claims, according to Middleton, "the kind of freedom and adventurousness [that] Morrison admires in black men" (376),[15] and she refuses the traditional black female role of ship *and* harbor. Sula does not marry or have children and she sends Eva to Beechnut, the white people's nursing home. Although Sula dies young, as she tells Nel, "I sure did live in this world" (143).

Sula, like the character Jadine in *Tar Baby*, seeks to achieve the self-determination and self-definition advocated by existential feminism. As Sula tells Nel: "I got my mind. And what goes on in it. Which is to say, I got me" (143). And when Nel says to Sula: "[Some men are] worth keeping," Sula responds: "They ain't worth more than me" (143). When Sula returns to Medallion after a ten-year absence Eva asks her: "When you gone to get married? You need to have some babies. It'll settle you" (92). To this, Sula responds: "I don't want to make somebody else. I want to make myself" (92). Throughout the text, Sula speaks out against the subservience and, in particular, the self-erasure that traditional motherhood and marriage require of women. "The narrower their lives," Sula says, "the wider their hips" (121). The women with husbands, Sula observes, "had folded themselves into starched coffins, their sides bursting with other people's skinned dreams and bony regrets. . . . [They] had the sweetness sucked from their breath by ovens and steam kettles" (122). Sula and Jadine both want, in Sula's words, to "do it all, why can't I have it all?" (142). In this, Sula and Jadine are the foremothers of what Naomi Wolf has called power feminism.[16] Sula and Jadine seek "[p]ower, power to and power over." They believe, to use the words of power feminism, that they "deserve more of whatever it is they are not getting enough of . . . respect, self-respect, education, safety, health, representation, money" (Wolf 1993, 138).

Morrison, however, does not endorse the existential or power feminism championed by Jadine and Sula (see interview with Judith Wilson [1981] in Taylor-Guthrie 1994: 131). While Morrison allows Sula to voice her criticism of what she perceives to be the oppressiveness of women's traditional ways of being, Morrison herself supports neither existentialist nor power feminism. In an interview with Robert Stepto (1976), Morrison offers this critique of Sula: "[She] knows all there is to know about herself because she examines herself, she is experimental with herself, she's perfectly willing to think the unthinkable thing. But she has trouble making a connection with other people and just feeling that lovely sense of accomplishment of being close in a very strong way" (Taylor-Guthrie 1994: 14). In an interview with Anne Koenen (1980), Morrison calls Sula "the one out of sequence." Morrison explains:

> I thought she had a serious flaw, which led her into a dangerous zone which is . . . not being able to make a connection with other people. . . . Sula's behaviour looks inhuman, because she has cut herself off from responsibility to anyone other than herself. . . . Sula put her grandmother away. That is considered awful because among Black people that never happened. You must take care of each other. That's more unforgivable than anything else she does, because it suggests a lack of her sense of community. Critics devoted to the Western heroic tradition—the individual alone and triumphant—see Sula as survivor. In the Black community she is lost. (Koenen 1984: 207–208)

Sula has cut herself off from her motherline and has lost the ancient properties of black womanhood. Literally and symbolically, Sula kills the ancestor: she puts Eva away and watches as her mother burns to death.[17] It would appear that, in so doing, Sula achieves the independence, self-sufficiency, and agency advocated by existentialist and power feminism. In the eyes of Simone de Beauvoir or Naomi Wolf, Sula is a feminist hero. Morrison, however, sees Sula quite differently. Sula "may have her way" but "she does not understand her past": and for Morrison it is the latter, and not the former, that empowers black women.

"Black women," Denard writes, "always maintain, whether they desire it or not, a connection to their ethnic community" (McKay 1988: 174). The inevitable connectedness that Denard speaks of is manifest in *Sula*. Although Sula attempts to write a life script different from that of her mother and grandmother, her story never becomes more than a subplot of the larger motherline. Sula's life is created from the very history she rejects. Morrison, as Janice M. Sokoloff observes, "goes to great lengths to show how strong, matriarchal lines of temperamental inheritance shape her female characters" (430). In *Sula* the stories of the daughters, Nel and Sula, follow those of the foremothers—Cecile, Rochelle, Helene, Eva, and Hannah. This narrative structure establishes a matrilineal line of descent from which the daughters' lives unfold. In both style and content, Sula's life reenacts the lives of her mother and grandmother. Just as Eva put her leg under a train to collect insurance money, Sula "slashed off . . . the tip of her finger" (54) to frighten off a group of boys. Significantly, Sula maims herself with "Eva's paring knife" (54). Eva bequeaths to her granddaughter a fiery, defiant, "don't-mess-with-me" personality, and Sula inherits from her mother "manlove" and a "pantry" style of loving. The first time Sula has sex with Ajax, as the narrator tells us, "[she] pull[s] him into the pantry. There was no need to go there, for not a soul was in the house, but the gesture comes to Hannah's daughter naturally" (125). Eva outlives her granddaughter, and the memory of Sula lives on through Eva. Whether Sula desires it or not, she is created from, connected to, and sustained by the motherline of her foremothers. Not surprisingly then, when Sula kills the ancestor by putting Eva into a home, she also kills herself. Sula dies shortly after Eva is "put away."

Sula's radical break from her motherline causes Sula to be, in Cynthia Davis's words "centerless" (1984: 22). Sula, as the narrator tells us, "had no center, no speck around which to grow" (119). Children in Morrison receive from their mothers a loved self and from the motherline the ancient properties and funk. Both the funk and the ancient properties are essential for the psychological well-being of African American daughters. Daughters who are orphaned, either literally or psychologically, do not develop a loved sense of self or learn the teaching of the motherline from which to create a strong and proud selfhood as a black woman. Sula is not abandoned by her mother as is Joe in *Jazz,* nor does her mother psychologically desert her as does Pauline in *The Bluest Eye*. Sula is a self-made orphan. Sula presents herself as a self-invented and self-defined woman—"I got me" (143), "Whatever's burning in me is mine!" (93), "My lonely is *mine*" (143)—who forges her own path. However, disconnected from her motherline, she is left, as Marianne Hirsch observes, "[with] nowhere to go" (185).

TAR BABY

Sula's narrative of disconnection foreshadows that of Jadine, the hero of Morrison's fourth novel *Tar Baby* (1981). Jadine, like Sula, is a daughter who identifies

with the modern ideology of female fulfillment. As with Sula, Jadine's disconnection from her motherline originates from the loss of her mother and results
in a disavowal of the ancient properties and a disdain for motherhood. Jadine and
Pecola are also, as Gurleen Grewal comments, "[two] different sides of the same
coin. Pecola is convinced that she is ugly because evidence is everywhere; on bill-
boards, in the eyes of black and white adults, within the home and outside of it.
Jadine has no doubt she is beautiful because the evidence lies in the cover of *Elle*
flaunting her face. But Jadine is no more self-defined than Pecola. . . . [With]
Jadine . . . the hegemonic project of colonization is complete" (81). Similarly, the
narrative of disconnection and loss in *Tar Baby* is signified through female reproductive experiences. Pauline's inability to love Pecola is both caused by and represents Pauline's disconnection from the motherline. Similarly, Jadine's dread and
loathing of motherhood, particularly as it is represented by the fecund maternal
body, both represents her disconnection from the motherline and is what gives
rise to her rejection of the teachings of the motherline.

The central theme of *Tar Baby*, critic Angelita Reyes argues, may be summed
up in Therese's warning to Son: "[D]on't go to L'Arbe de la Croix. . . . Forget her.
There is nothing in her parts for you. She has forgotten her ancient properties"
(305). *Tar Baby* asks, in Reyes words, that "Black people . . . not lose sight of their
African consciousness" (19). Thus, *Tar Baby* can be interpreted, as critic Marilyn
Sanders Mobley observes, as "a modern cautionary tale in which Morrison draws
on the Afro-American oral narrative tradition to expose the pitfalls of white middle-class aspirations for the black woman and to illustrate the consequences of
her social and cultural misbehaviour" (285). The moral story or fable that *Tar
Baby* tells is specifically gendered: a woman, Jadine, rejects the ancient properties
of traditional black womanhood and adopts the values of the dominant white
culture. This rejection causes psychic fragmentation, or in Mobley's words, a
"divided consciousness." *Tar Baby* tells the story of Jadine's quest for wholeness
and its ultimate failure. Mobley attributes Jadine's failure to her "reject[ion] [of]
the very cultural constructions of race and mothering that could heal her and
transform her consciousness" (285–86).

Tar Baby opens with Morrison's dedication to her foremothers: "For [my
foremothers . . . and each of their sisters—and each of their sisters, all of whom
knew their true and ancient properties." The phrase "ancient properties" frames
the novel: it occurs in the dedication and it is mentioned by Therese on the
penultimate page of the novel. We enter the text through this dedication and it
acts as our moral point of reference for our interpretation and judgment of the
novel. "The women of the dedication . . . grandmother, mother, aunts, and sister of [Morrison]," Eleanor W. Traylor writes, "are the guides to whom the narrative voice of the writer is accountable" (McKay 1988: 149). We realize upon
coming to know Jadine that she has, in Karla Holloway's words, "den[ied] [her]
lineage. Instead of Jadine having an inherent self as a Black woman, she has chosen to dispossess herself" (1987: 120). Significantly, we first encounter Jadine as
a disembodied voice overheard by an unidentified man. Her entry into the nar-

rative suggests her aloneness. Her voice and words, "warm on the inside, cold at the edges, or was it the other way around ?": "I'm never lonely. . . . Never" (6), reinforce this sense of herself. In contrast to the dedication, this disembodied voice does not speak the ancient properties. Hers is not the voice of the fore-mothers honored on the opening page of the text. In an interview conducted for *Essence* magazine by Judith Wilson (1981), Morrison says of Jadine:

> She has lost the tar quality, the ability to hold something together that oth-erwise would fall apart—which is what I mean by the nurturing ability. That's what one surrenders, or can surrender, in order to do this other thing—in order to go and get a degree in art history, learn four languages and be in the movies and stuff. That sounds like I'm putting it down; I'm not. I'm saying that the point is to be able to do both. (Taylor-Guthrie 1994: 131)

In contrast, the woman in yellow whom Jadine sees in the market comes to sig-nify and embody those ancient properties:

> The vision itself was a woman much too tall. Under her long canary yellow dress . . . was too much hip, too much bust. The agency would laugh her out of the lobby, so why was she and everybody else in the store transfixed? The height? The skin like tar against the canary yellow dress? . . . Two upside-down V's were scored into each of her cheeks, her hair was wrapped in a gelee as yellow as her dress. . . . The woman leaned into the dairy sec-tion and opened a carton from which she selected three eggs. Then she put her right elbow into the palm of her left hand and held the eggs aloft between earlobe and shoulder. She looked up then and they saw something in her eyes so powerful it had burnt away the eyelashes. (45)

This image of the African woman in the yellow dress is used by Morrison, critic Barbara Christian argues, "as a symbol for the authenticity that the jaded Jadine lacks" (1980, 244). The defiant stance of the woman's body, as Christian observes, is a manifestation of "the woman's inner strength, beauty, and pride" (1980, 144). The woman's Africanness is inscribed in the Vs on her cheeks, while her fertility, like that of Pilate in *Song of Solomon,* is signified by the eggs she car-ries in the curve of her neck. Her beauty, as Jadine tells us, is "unphotographi-cal." She, unlike the Covergirl model Jadine, can not be co-opted by the domi-nant culture. The power, which Jadine tells us burnt her lashes, is the power of the ancient properties of black womanhood. The woman in yellow, Morrison explained in a conversation with Gloria Naylor (1985), ""is somehow transcen-dent and whatever she really was, what she was perceived as by Jadine, is the real chic. The one that authenticates everything. The one that is very clear in some deep way about what her womanhood is" (Taylor-Guthrie 1994: 194). She rep-resents, Morrison explains, further, "a complete individual who owns herself. . . . She is the original self" (194).

In Morrison's fiction, the color yellow, in particular yellow dresses, signify the ancient properties and funk of traditional black womanhood. Creole-speaking

Rochelle in *Sula* wears a canary yellow dress and like the woman in yellow who had "burnt away eye lashes," Rochelle "rubbed burned matches over her eyes" (28). Son, the character whom many critics interpret as Jadine's foil because he embraces, while she denies, the ancient properties, dreams of "yellow houses with white doors which women opened wide and called out, 'Come on in here, you honey you'" (6). He attempts to make his dream become Jadine's: "[While Jadine slept] to insert his own dreams into her . . . [of] yellow houses with white doors which women opened . . ." (119).

Jadine, like the other shoppers in the market, is mesmerized by the "transcendent beauty" of the African woman: "She would deny it now, but along with everybody else in the market, Jadine gasped. Just a little. Just a sudden intake of air. Just a quick snatch of breath before that woman's woman—that mother/sister/she: that unphotographable beauty—took it all away" (46). The African woman, as Samuels and Hudson-Weems observe, makes Jadine "confront her cultural heritage" (80). However, when this African woman finally does make eye contact with the spellbound Jadine, she "looked right at Jadine . . . and, with a small parting of her lips, shot an arrow of saliva between her teeth down to the pavement and the hearts below" (46). The African woman is disgusted by Jadine for she sees in her a black woman who has forgotten her ancient properties.

The "woman's insulting gesture," the narrator tells us, "derailed [Jadine]— shaken her out of proportion to the incident. Why had she wanted that woman to like and respect her? It had certainly taken the zing out of the magazine cover as well as her degree" (47). "The woman," Jadine later reflects, "made her feel lonely in a way. Lonely and inauthentic" (48). "[T]he vision [which] materialized in a yellow dress" functions as an epiphany that awakens Jadine to her inauthenticity. Jadine is awakened to the nothingness of her life. Significantly, the crisis of self-definition caused by the sight of the yellow woman is configured in racial terms. Jadine questions whether she should marry her white lover and wonders "if the person he wants to marry is me or a black girl?" (48). "And then," the narrator tells us, "she ran away because Ryk is white and the woman spit at her and she had to come to see her aunt and uncle . . ." (48).

Shortly after Jadine returns to Isle des Chevaliers she meets Son Green. The text presents, and most readers interpret, Son as the embodiment of essential African American funkiness. In *Toni Morrison's World of Fiction,* for example, Karen Carmean argues that: "Jadine is given a remarkable opportunity to rediscover her 'other' true self when Son arrives at Valerian's estate" (72). Later, it is the mythic tree women who attempt to rescue Jadine and enable her to reclaim her ancient properties:

> They were delighted when first they saw her, thinking a runaway child had been restored to them. But looking closer they saw differently. This girl was fighting to get away from them. The women hanging from the trees were quiet now, but arrogant—mindful as they were of their value, their exceptional femaleness; knowing as they did that the first world of the world had

been built with their sacred properties; that they alone could hold together the stones of pyramids and the rushes of Moses's crib; knowing their steady consistency, their pace of glaciers, their permanent embrace, they wondered at the girl's desperate struggle down below to be free, to be something other than they were. (183)

Jadine, Karla Holloway argues, "is called by this goddess earth who embodies the cosmic life principle. Rejecting the call of the trees she is cut off from the good consciousness—knowledge of the mother" (1987: 118). "[Jadine's] woman-hood," Holloway continues, "is seriously in question in the face of these ancient females who have not lost touch with who they are . . ." (119). Jadine resists the pull of the tar by dancing with the tree in what is portrayed as a heterosexual embrace: "Press together like man and wife" (182–83). Jadine is finally able to pull herself from the swamp when "her right knee grazed something hard and she managed to lift her leg and bend it enough to kneel on the hard thing that seemed to be growing out of her partner the tree" (183). The phallic imagery of this passage does, pardon the pun, noticeably stick out: the "hard thing growing out of the tree" suggests a male erection. Thus, it would seem, as Holloway sug-gests, that "[Jadine] kneels on masculinity and uses it to pull herself out of the earth's tar baby's clutch. This pull toward individuation that scorns and treads on masculinity becomes the basis for her loss" (1987: 119). More specifically, Jadine identifies with male sexuality rather than female fertility as represented by the tree women and the tar. In a 1981 interview with Thomas LeClair (1981), Mor-rison elaborated upon the symbolic significance of tar in African mythology:

> Tar seemed to me to be an odd thing to be in a Western story, and I found that there is a tar lady in African mythology. . . . At one time, a tar pit was a holy place, at least an important place, because tar was used to build things. It came naturally out of the earth; it held together things like Moses' little boat and the pyramids. For me, the tar baby came to mean the black woman who can hold things together. (Taylor-Guthrie 1994: 122)

Morrison's discussion makes sense out of the tree women's statement that they helped build Moses's crib and the pyramids. These women are the tar ladies of African mythology who used the sacred properties of the tar to build civilizations. They are the women of the ancient properties who both build and create, who are ship and harbor. Jadine's problem is that she cannot imagine doing both; for her being a ship and harbor are mutually exclusive. "[He] wanted her to settle for wifely competence when she could be almighty, to settle for fertility rather than originality, nurturing instead of building" (269).

In Eloe at Rosie's, Jadine sleeps in a "little bedroom without windows." Win-dowless and with two doors, one to the living room and one that opened to the back yard, this room suggests a womb-like environment. Significantly, Jadine finds the room "suffocating." To get some air Jadine goes outside only to con-front "the blackest nothing she had ever seen. . . . It's not possible she thought, for anything to be this black" (251). Jadine's unease with the closeness of the room and the darkness outside symbolically mark her rejection of the ancient properties of black womanhood. Significantly, Jadine associates blackness with fecundity: "She might as well have been in a cave, a grave, the dark womb of the earth, suffocating with the sound of plant life moving, but deprived of its sight" (252). In *Tar Baby*, as in *Song of Solomon*, the ancient properties of black womanhood are positioned in opposition to both maleness and whiteness. Jadine shuns the harbor of the ancient properties and desires to be the ship of dominant ideologies of manhood. Pointedly, the text concludes with Jadine returning to Paris feeling "lean and male" (275).

Jadine's rejection of the ancient properties and funk stem specifically from a fear of the maternal, represented in this text by the night women who visit Jadine in the black womb. When she asks: "What do you want with me . . . ?" They reply:

> They looked as though they had just been waiting for that question and they each pulled out a breast and showed it to her. . . . They just stood around in the room, jostling each other gently . . . revealing one breast and then two. . . . (258)

To this Jadine responds: "'I have breasts too,' she said or thought or willed, 'I have breasts too'" (258). However, the night women do not, in the words of the text,

> believe her. They just held their own higher and pushed their own farther out and looked at her. All of them revealing both their breasts except the woman in yellow. She did something more shocking—she stretched out a long arm and showed Jadine her three big eggs. (258–59)

Jadine's rejection of the maternal is clear. The reasons for it, however, are not—leaving much space for critical speculation and debate. Critic Peter Erickson attributes Jadine's fear to her inability to see motherhood as compatible with a career. He writes: "The novel will not allow [Jadine's] avoidance of motherhood to be perceived sympathetically, yet the maternal issue presents itself in the form of a conflict between mutually exclusive imperatives" (305). "[In] the novel," Erickson continues, "there is little suggestion that Jadine could, with complete dignity, choose only 'originality' and 'building.' There is also little suggestion that she could have both 'nurturing' and 'building'" (305). Morrison, however, emphasizes that women of the ancient properties have always been both ship and harbor. Black women, according to Morrison's maternal standpoint, do both build and nurture, but Jadine herself did not know such women because she grew up on the "Streets" separated from her black community.

Jadine attempts, as Karla Holloway argues, "to exist without a discovery of 'whose' child she is" (1987: 119). "She has chosen to dispossess herself" (120). Although Jadine is an orphan, she, as Holloway emphasizes, "had warmth and protection offered her through her extended family, her aunt and uncle" (120). Ondine and Sydney are, according to Holloway, "black folk" who maintain a strong sense of racial identity despite their isolation on Isle de Chevaliers. Ondine, in particular, attempts to impart to Jadine her ancient properties. "Women like Ondine," Holloway contends, "are mothers and daughters and are connected in this way to things past and future" (123). I argue, however, that Ondine does not, as the expression goes, practice what she preaches. Although she espouses black folk values, she identifies with the bourgeois white lifestyle of the Streets. As Samuels and Hudson-Weems observe: "Unlike Pilate, who passes the legacy of her cultural heritage to her nephew, Milkman, Ondine does not perform this function for Jadine" (83). She does not provide the example of folk caring and loving that she talks about. "[Ondine]," Samuels and Hudson-Weems continue, "seem[s] far more interested in the welfare and care of white culture than in [her] own [life]" (83). As Ondine says: "I know my Kitchens. Better than I know my face" (39). And Ondine and Sydney, though well meaning, orphan Jadine a second time when they give her over to the "Streets."

However, Ondine is right when she says to Jadine: "A girl has got to be a daughter first. She have to learn that. And if she never learns how to be a daughter, she can't never learn how to be a woman. . . . [A] real woman: a woman good enough for a child; good enough for a man—good enough even for the respect of other women" (281). What Ondine does not realize until Jadine is grown is that she has not been that mother to Jadine; she has not replaced the mother Jadine lost. Ondine says to Jadine: "I never told you nothing. I never told you nothing at all and I take full responsibility for that. But I have to tell you something now" (281). Ondine, I think, has come to realize that in wanting more for her niece she has alienated Jadine from the black community, and more specifically, has severed Jadine's connection to the motherline.

When Ondine later tells Jadine: "you didn't have a mother long enough" (281), she identifies the source of Jadine's general malaise and her specific anxiety about motherhood. In Morrison, mothering is essential for the psychological well-being of children because it connects the child to the motherline and imparts to that child a loved sense of self. Hudson-Weems and Samuels contend that "Jadine's status as an orphan is significant . . . [at] the crucial age of twelve, a point of transition from childhood to adolescence, she is deprived of parents to nurture and guide her" (83). Jadine loses her mother at precisely the time when a girl becomes a woman.

In Baltimore before her mother's death Jadine comes upon a dog in heat on the streets. She tells us that

> the retired postman [came out] . . . and crack[ed] the bitch over the back and sen[t] her home, she who had done nothing but be "in heat" which she couldn't help but which was her fault just the same so it was she who was beaten and cracked over the head and spine with the mop handle and made to run away and I felt sorry for her and went looking for her to see if she was hurt and when I found her . . . another dog sniffed her ass embarrassing me in the sunlight. (124)

From this, Jadine resolves to never "let the hunger show" (124). "She decided then and there at the age of twelve in Baltimore never to be broken in the hands of any man" (124). "And anybody who wanted nice from this colored girl would have to get it with pliers and chloroform, because Never" (124). Significantly, immediately after this scene, we are told of the mother's death: "When her mother died and she went to Philadelphia and then away to school, she was so quick to learn, but . . . not smile, because Never. . . . [B]eneath the easy manners was a claw ready to rein in the dogs, because Never" (124). Jadine represses the sexual in her self because for her it represents "shame" and a loss of control. In Morrison, the sexual is linked with the funk; "the funkiness of passion, the funkiness of nature, the funkiness of a wide range of emotions." Jadine's repression of the sexual and sensual thus signifies denial of the funkiness of black cultural identity. Jadine must, as the text tells us time and time again, "hold on tight to the leashes." The structural juxtaposition of the story about the dogs and the mention of the mother's death suggest that her denial of sexuality, specifically, and the funk in general, is linked to her mother's death.

The bitch in heat is struck and the mother dies in Jadine's twelfth year, at the threshold of womanhood. Jadine's fear and denial of her developing sexuality may have been negotiated had her mother lived. But without a mother, Jadine is left to enter womanhood alone and unguided.

We have already seen a connection made in Morrison between mothering and the daughter's growing into womanhood. At the age of twelve, Sula is twice orphaned: first by her mother's comments and later by her mother's death. Jadine, too, at the age of twelve, is twice orphaned: first by her mother's death and then by being sent off to school and handed over to the Streets. The loss of the mother causes both girls to become disconnected from their motherline and gives rise to their rejection of the teachings of the motherline. Thus, both Sula and Jadine identify with white, as opposed to black, definitions of female fulfillment. I suggest that both Sula and Jadine's fears about sexuality and intimacy—Jadine doesn't want to lose control/Sula doesn't want to get involved is the same thing—and their rejections of motherhood stem from the loss of their mothers and their disconnection from the motherline. Jadine's loss goes deeper than Sula's, however, because she does not have, as Sula does, a close female friendship which somewhat alleviates the loss of the mother. Sexuality and motherhood are problematic for Jadine because, as Ondine said, "she didn't have a mother long enough." She had no one there to teach her how to be a woman and become a mother.

At the age of twelve, then, Jadine comes up against patriarchy what Elizabeth Debold, Maire Wilson, and Idelisse Malave have called the "Wall."[18] These writers argue that historically there have been two pathways through the wall; the route of conventional femininity and the "girls will be boys" strategy. More recently, they argue, this later strategy has expressed itself as a desire to be one of the guys. They write:

As "one of the guys," girls take a swaggering stance in the face of sexism, a stance that adopts sexism's complete devaluation of femininity and women themselves. The "girls will be boys" strategy involves an understood element of expediency, some internal conflict, an absence of certainty about the complete superiority of all things male, and a lingering appreciation of things feminine. With "one of the guys" strategy girls want to *be* boys. (72, emphasis in original)

Jadine acts out the "one of the guys" strategy. The authors' characterization of this strategy aptly describes Jadine: "[When] faced with the losses at adolescence, [Jadine] idealizes maleness and wants it for [herself]. In self-chosen and self-denying identification with the oppressor, [she] equate[s] male behaviour with honesty, integrity, courage, and strength" (73). The writers emphasize that these so-called "paths of least resistance . . . are short-term survival strategies with enormous costs. All of them require that girls surrender parts of themselves—their agency and compassion. All of these strategies compromise girls' self-love and integrity" (73).

Debold, Wilson, and Malave emphasize, in *MotherDaughter Revolution,* that daughters need their mothers if they are to win against patriarchy and keep their original selves intact. This is particularly so for black daughters whose blackness and femaleness are at risk in a white patriarchal world. Orphaned at twelve, and failed by Ondine who mothered her in ways of assimilation rather than resistance, Jadine must find her own way. Ondine tells Jadine: "You don't need your own natural mother to be a daughter" (281). But you do, I suggest, need a mother figure who protects and fosters a daughter's female and black self by keeping the daughter connected to the motherline. Ondine does not instill in Jadine the ancient properties that would have empowered her as she grew into womanhood. As she says to Jadine: "I thought I was doing right by sending you to all them schools and so I never told you and I should have" (281). Ondine's realization, however, comes too late.

CONCLUSION

The Bluest Eye, Sula, and *Tar Baby* enact and affirm Morrison's theory of the empowerment of women through the motherline by detailing the tragedies of *dis*connection. As a result of Pauline's identification with the normative discourses of the model family and ideal female beauty, she cannot practice cultural bearing to pass on the teachings of the African American motherline. Sula, accepting the dominant definition of motherlove, repudiates her mother and her motherline, leaving Sula bereft of the values of the ancient properties. Finally, Jadine's adherence to Western scripts of female fulfillment causes her to shun the very values of the funk and ancient properties that would give her an authentic selfhood. With each woman's story the narrative and thematic trajectory of assimilation, disconnection, aloneness, and unhappiness is repeated. Detailing the causes of women's disconnection from the motherline and describing the devastating consequences of such for the individual woman, her family, and the larger black culture, Morrison's fiction attests to the critical importance of cultural bearing for the well-being of black women and the families and societies in which they live. "A girl has to be a daughter," as Ondine explains to Jadine, before she can "learn how to be a woman" (281).

chapter three

Ruptures/Disruptions of the Motherline

Slavery, Migration, and Assimilation:
Song of Solomon, Beloved

THE PREVIOUS CHAPTER EXAMINED women's disconnection from the motherline in and through identification with specific normative gender discourses, namely, those of the family, beauty, motherlove, and female fulfillment. This chapter considers how the African American motherline itself is fractured by historical trauma, in particular slavery, migration, and assimilation. Black women, in the task of cultural bearing, pass on to each successive generation the teachings of the motherline, in particular the values of the funk and the ancient proprieties. Individual women, as explored in the previous chapter, may become disconnected from the African American motherline and disavow the values it represents as a result of interpellation in specific hegemonic gender beliefs. While the emphasis in the previous chapter was on individual disconnections, this chapter considers how the line itself is attenuated through historical and cultural change. Migration, assimilation, and slavery seriously impaired black women's ability to perform their maternal function as cultural bearer and hence weakened the motherline in two significant ways. Assimilation, the first theme considered, often results in black families, particularly among the middle class, seeking to emulate the hegemonic script of family relations in which the husband is dominant and the woman subservient and submissive. When African American women assume the traditional (white) role of wife they forsake the funk and in particular the ancient properties of traditional black womanhood because women cannot be both ship and harbor in a patriarchal marriage that assumes women are inferior to men and assigns them exclusively to home and the reproductive realm. This chapter, through a consideration of the character Ruth in *Song of Solomon,* explores how Ruth, schooled in the ways of assimilation, is socialized to be a traditional wife in a patriarchal marriage and how this in turn brings about the loss of the ancient properties and funk and results in Ruth's disempowerment. Consequently, Ruth cannot convey the teachings of the African American motherline.

Migration, the second theme considered, also causes a weakening or more specifically dissolution of the African American motherline. Migration to the urban cities of the North geographically separated women from the rural folk of the South; the place wherein the values of the African American motherline originated and where they are most fully and fastidiously sustained. While cultural bearing, the passing on of the teachings of the motherline, may take place in other times and places, Morrison's fiction attests to the difficulty of such a task, as is made evident with Hagar from *Song of Solomon,* the second woman considered in this chapter. Pilate performs cultural bearing with her nephew, the adult Milkman and, in so doing, becomes a mender of broken motherlines and healer of those wounded by such breakages. Pilate seeks to impart the teachings of the motherline to her granddaughter, Hagar, but she cannot save Hagar as she did Milkman. In the North, the motherline has been worn thin, stretched across time and distance.

Slavery, the final historical event considered, ruptured, as did migration, the African American motherline by separating families through sale. As is made apparent in *Beloved,* slavery, more than any other cultural institution or historical event, damaged the African American motherline by denying African people their humanity and history. In her fifth novel Morrison seeks to symbolize this loss in the character of Beloved and to render it psychologically manifest through the character of Sethe. Morrison's aim here, as with the themes of migration and assimilation, is to render explicit the historical causes of motherline rupture and disruption and to portray the devastating consequence of such for African American people.

RUTH: "CERTAINLY MY DADDY'S DAUGHTER"

Michael Awkward argues that "[Morrison] dissects, deconstructs, if you will, the bourgeois myths of ideal family life. Through her deconstruction, she exposes each individual element of the myth as not only deceptively inaccurate in general, but also wholly inapplicable to Afro-American life" (McKay 1988: 59). But Morrison does more than document the harm that comes with measuring oneself against an ideal you cannot achieve; she also shows the ideal to be an illusion: all is not happy in that green and white house of the primer in *The Bluest Eye.* Awkward argues that the "emotional estrangement of the primer family members (an estrangement suggested by the family's inability to respond to the daughter Jane's desire for play) implies that theirs is solely a surface contentment. . . . [The family is] . . . made up of rigid, emotionless figures incapable of deep feeling" (59). Indeed, no one will play with Jane, not the mother, father, nor the cat or dog. Jane must go outside this so-called perfect family to find companionship in a friend who, significantly, is not named. Neither the mother nor the father speaks to Jane when the request to play is made to them. Although the text says they are "very happy," the grammatical imperative that instructs the mother,

"Laugh, Mother, laugh," and the father, "Smile, Father, smile," undermines the assertion of happiness. The house is introduced before the family, suggesting that property is more important than relationships. As Shelly Wong observes, with the exception of Jane, all the characters "maintain [themselves] in a self-enclosed unity. . . . The short, clipped sentences accentuate their differences." Wong continues, "the child's first lesson in cultural literacy teaches the primacy of the singular and the discrete. The lesson works against memory and history" (471–72). Morrison deconstructs what Wong calls "the metaphysics of isolate unity" through her manipulation of the grammar and structure of the primer. Thus, Morrison does more than critique the bourgeois myth of the ideal family as inappropriate for and inapplicable to African Americans; she also deconstructs the ideal itself to show that it is fraudulent. The Dick and Jane family are not as happy as the primer purports them to be.

A central theme in Morrison's fiction is the emotional barrenness that results when African Americans attempt to realize the illusionary white bourgeois family. In *The Bluest Eye* Geraldine represents those who model themselves on the white family:

> They go to land-grant colleges, normal schools, and learn how to do the white man's work with refinement: home economics to prepare his food; teacher education to instruct black children in obedience; music to soothe the weary master and entertain his blunted soul. Here they learn the rest of the lesson begun in those soft houses with porch swings and bleeding hearts: how to behave. The careful development of thrift, patience, high morals, and good manners. In short, how to get rid of the funkiness. The dreadful funkiness of passion, the funkiness of nature, the funkiness of the wide range of human emotions. (68)

Funkiness, as Elliot Butler-Evans comments, "signifies not merely some primal African-American essence but the feminine ('nature,' 'passion,' and 'human emotions'). These traits are encoded in our society as within the domain of the feminine, and represent what is being repressed" (71). As the text describes how Geraldine represses this funk it effaces the character of Geraldine herself. Geraldine is seen from a male point of view: "Certain men watch them [these type of women]." The woman is thus, as Butler-Evans notes, "erased from the text, or is alternately present and absent" (72). This strategy of representation signifies the self-erasure that happens when black women forsake the funk and structure feminine subjectivity on the white model.

As noted by many critics, Geraldine signifies a denial of blackness. In *Crimes of Innocence in the Fiction of Toni Morrison* (1989), Terry Otten writes, "[Geraldine] represents the sexless, pure, acceptable 'colored' woman who deny their blackness in order to maintain her place in society" (15). Funkiness signifies in Morrison's writing traditional black cultural identity and in particular the ancient properties of traditional black womanhood. Geraldine's "get[ting] rid of the funkiness" (68) thus achieves the repression of both her femaleness and blackness.

Butler-Evans argues that Geraldine's story of the suppression of the sexual/sensual self is part of a larger textual narrative of feminine desire. According to Butler-Evans, the central theme of the novel, namely the conflict between the dominant ideology as represented by the primer, and the lived experiences of the Breedloves, is continuously decentered by what may be called the discourse of feminine desire. He writes: "These dominant narrative themes . . . are subverted by embedded narratives that contribute to the overall effect of the book and simultaneously indicate a departure from the novel's primary focus. . . . [The embedded narratives] disrupt the textual dominant emphasis by introducing the problem of feminine desire" (68). I suggest, with Butler-Evans, that feminine desire originates not from outside the competing cultural discourses as disruption/subversion, but originates from inside it. Feminine desire is structured and negotiated from *within* that ideological struggle.

According to Susan Willis, Morrison "translates the loss of history and culture into sexual terms and demonstrates the connection between bourgeois society and repression" (Gates 1984: 266). In Morrison's work, women such as Geraldine, who are more or less successfully assimilated into the dominant bourgeois culture, are the most alienated from their sexual selves. Pauline comes to lose the colors of her rainbow, her funkiness, when she takes on the identity of the Fishers' domestic and becomes their Polly. Funkiness is lost when girls are socialized into the dominant patriarchal white supremist culture, when they seek to become "male" and "white" identified women. The narrative of desire Butler-Evans identifies in the text is thus woven from the larger script of the white bourgeois family as exemplified in the primer. To be the wife described in the primer, women—whether white or black—must fulfill the ideological role requirements of the wife role discussed in chapter 1. The egalitarian marriages that researchers argue black women have traditionally experienced are disrupted when the black couple attempts to emulate the male dominance of white nuclear family structure. In Morrison's writing, funkiness exists only in female households such as the household of the three whores in *The Bluest Eye,* or in egalitarian marriages, for example, the marriage of the MacTeers, where husband-on-top-heterosexuality is not practised. In female households and egalitarian marriages, black women, not being solely wives, are able to be the women of funk and the ancient properties, and perform the important maternal function of cultural bearing.

More than any other character in Morrison's fiction, Ruth Dead in *Song of Solomon* presents an account of how girls, schooled in the ways of assimilation, are prepared for patriarchal wifedom and prevented from being the culture bearers of the African American motherline. Ruth, rendered susceptible to patriarchal socialization because of her motherless status, is programmed to be a wife through the specific socialization practices of what theorist Miriam Johnson has termed the subject identity of "Daddy's Girl." In *Strong Mothers, Weak Wives* (1990) Johnson argues that women's secondary status originates from their heterosexual identity as wives of men. "It is the wife role," writes Johnson, "and not the mother's role that organizes women's secondary status" (6). The relationship of father and daughter, Johnson asserts, "trains daughters to be wives who are expected to be secondary to their husbands" (8). Johnson argues that fathers often romanticize the father-daughter relationship and interact with their daughter as a lover would. Fathers feminize their daughters: daddies teach their girls to be passive, pleasing, and pretty for men. In Johnson's words, "[The father-daughter relationship] reproduce[s] in daughters a disposition to please men in a relationship in which the male dominates" (184). In other words, "daddy's girls are in training to be wives" (184). Because daddy's girls are trained and rewarded for pleasing and playing up to men, they grow up to be male-defined and male-orientated women. In most so-called normal, that is, male-dominant families, what is experienced is psychological incest. Johnson writes: "The incest . . . is psychological, not overtly sexual. The father takes his daughter over. She looks up to him because he is her father. He is the king and she is the princess. It is all OK because the male is dominant in 'normal' adult heterosexual relations" (173).

Ruth describes herself as "certainly my daddy's daughter" (67) and Dr. Foster's recollections suggest, in Johnson's terms, that their relationship was, at the very least, psychologically incestuous:

> Fond as he [Dr. Foster] was of his only child, useful as she was in his house since his wife had died, lately he had begun to chafe under her devotion. Her steady beam of love was unsettling, and she had never dropped those expressions of affection that had been so lovable in her childhood. The good-night kiss was itself a masterpiece of slow-wittedness on her part and discomfort on his. At sixteen, she still insisted on having him come to her at night, sit on her bed, exchange a few pleasantries, and plant a kiss on her lips. Perhaps it was the loud silence of his dead wife, perhaps it was Ruth's disturbing resemblance to her mother. More probably it was the ecstasy that always seemed to be shining in Ruth's face when he bent to kiss her—an ecstasy he felt inappropriate to the occasion. (23)

Macon is convinced that Ruth and Dr. Foster's relationship had a sexual element to it, but the text is unclear on that point. However, Ruth's love for her father and his love for her expressed itself in a highly romanticized narrative. Ruth tells her son: "I didn't think I'd ever need a friend because I had him. I was small, but he was big. The only person who ever really cared whether I lived or died" (124). Ruth, as Jill Matus observes, "takes her identity entirely from her position in relation to a powerful and respected father. . . . [She] is bred to service and dependency" (82). Ruth, in the words of the text, is "pressed small" by her father (124). Having been "pressed small" by her father, Ruth is well prepared to assume a subordinate wife role in her marriage to Macon.

Dr. Foster is a man who "didn't give a damn about [Negroes]" and when he delivered his own daughter's children "all he was interested in was the color of their skin" (71). Ruth is raised, as were Geraldine in *The Bluest Eye* and Helen in *Sula,* to embrace the values of the dominant bourgeois culture. Such assimilation causes a rupture of the motherline and the loss of the ancient properties and funk. This, compounded with her socialization as a daddy's girl, prepares Ruth for her subordinate position as wife in a patriarchal family structure. The wife role in turn, because it precludes black women's traditional role of cultural bearer, further augments assimilation and the loss of the funk and the ancient properties.

Ruth, like most of Morrison's women characters, is motherless. The frequency of maternal deaths in Morrison, as noted earlier, functions as a metaphor to symbolize the prevalence of motherline disconnections and disruptions and their damaging consequences, particularly for women. At the level of the individual character, being motherless—whether by death of, or separation from the mother—means that the daughter is far more vulnerable to the hurts of a racist and sexist culture, because she has not received the cultural bearing that would give her a strong and proud selfhood. Pauline and certainly Pecola in *The Bluest Eye* are rendered more susceptible to the seductions of the beauty myth because they do not have a mother's love or a motherline to shield them; likewise the novel *Jazz* suggests that Violet would not have been so captivated by the tales of Golden Boy or held hostage by "the tricky blond boy inside her head" (211) had her mother lived. This vulnerability is particularly acute for daughters, such as Ruth, who are not only motherless but who, as a result, are raised as daddy's girls and socialized to be wives.

Women's lack of autonomy, according to Johnson, originates from the daughter's psychological dependency on her father as a male-oriented daddy's girl. "If daddy's girls are to gain their independence," Johnson writes, "they need to construct an identity as the daughters of strong mothers as well" (184). Johnson contends that the mother-daughter relationship is the key to overcoming women's psychological inauthenticity as daddy's girls, and by implication women's social oppression in patriarchy. Thus, the daughter achieves strong selfhood as a woman not through greater involvement with the father, but through a heightened identification with the mother.[1] This identification empowers the daughter in two ways: first, it allows her to step outside her oppressive daddy's girl role; and second, it allows her to identify with an adult woman's strength rather than her weakness. In Johnson's view, women are strong as mothers but made weak as wives. In identifying with her mother as mother the daughter may construct a strong female identity outside of the passive heterosexual one prepared for her by her father and society at large.

Johnson's insights here have particular relevance for motherless daughters in Morrison. While maternal identification is beneficial for all daughters—allowing, as it does, daughters to withstand daddy's girl socialization and hence attain autonomy and authenticity as women—it is crucial for African American daughters. Cultural bearing or mothering from the motherline in Morrison, as we have seen, is the way by which the ancient properties and the funk—that which empowers black women—are passed on generationally. And it is precisely the ancient properties and the funk, acquired through motherline teachings, that immunizes black women from the disempowerment of the wife role. Ruth, because she is motherless and her motherline is severed, is at risk and easy prey for daddy's girl socialization and "wifely" subservience.

Ruth is indeed motherless and without a motherline. Samuels and Hudson-Weems write of Ruth: "The fundamental bond between mother and daughter that Morrison in her work insists is necessary is lacking here. She has not had the luxury of blossoming with her mother's milk; her growth is thus artificial. . . . Although she receives love from her father, Ruth appears psychologically damaged and incomplete" (55). Ruth is thus one of the many motherless daughters in Morrison's fiction who are psychologically scarred by the loss of the mother and are disconnected from their motherline. With Ruth the father does not, as Pilate's father did, take on a nurturing maternal role; rather, Dr. Foster, as the text tells us, is "fond" of his daughter, whom he describes as "useful . . . in the house" (23). The father and daughter relationship of Ruth and Dr. Foster is also, as we have seen, highly problematic in its rendering of the daughter as a daddy's-girl-soon-to-be-submissive-wife. Johnson emphasizes that a positive daughter-mother identification is the foundation for a strong female-defined identity and the key to overcoming women's psychological inauthenticity as daddy's girls and women's social oppression in patriarchy. Had Ruth had a mother she may have been able to develop a strong female-defined self which would have, in turn, empowered her to resist her socialization as a daddy's-girl-soon-to-be-submissive-wife. However, Ruth is offered a surrogate mother with Pilate; a woman who embodies the very funk and ancient properties that would bestow upon Ruth the empowering ancient proprieties and funk denied to her in the wife role. While Ruth does allow Pilate to midwife the conception and birth of her son, she does not allow the same for her own rebirth. Forbidden by her husband to see Pilate, Ruth ultimately disavows Pilate's othermothering and disclaims the values of the ancient properties and funk that Pilate offers to her. This repudiation is symbolically marked by Ruth's refusal to take the peach that Pilate offers her on two separate occasions (132, 139). The peach, with its juice and seed, signifies both the feminine and the masculine, the traditional construct of black womanhood as both ship and harbor. Pilate's offering of the fruit and Ruth's rejection metaphorically represents Pilate's connection to her motherline and Ruth's separation from it.

Pilate and Ruth, as many critics have observed, function as foils of one another. In one instance the narrator comments,

> They were so different, these two women. One black, the other lemony. One corseted, the other buck naked under her dress. One well read but ill traveled. The other had read only a geography book, but had been from one end of the country to another. One wholly dependent on money for life, the other indifferent to it. (139)

Ruth describes herself as a "small woman" (123) while her son Milkman characterizes her "as a frail woman content to do tiny things; to grow and cultivate small life that would not hurt her if it died" (64). Later, contemplating his feelings for his mother, he remarks that "[s]he was too insubstantial, too shadowy for love.

But it was her vaporishness that made her more needful of defense" (75). Pilate, in contrast, is described by Milkman when he first meets her as "sitting wide-legged. . . . [S]he was all angles . . . knees, mostly, and elbows. One foot pointed east, and one pointed west" (36). And later, when Pilate stood up, Milkman, the text tells us, "all but gasped. She was as tall as his father, head and shoulders taller than himself" (38). Critic Karen Carmean elaborates:

> In direct contrast to Pilate, a fully independent woman by the time she becomes sixteen, Ruth remains a child. Ruth's helplessness, domestic inep-titude, and blandness develop to protect her from the men in her life, who consider her only in terms of her usefulness to them. Throughout the novel, Ruth remains a nebulous figure, largely content to assert her indi-viduality in apparently insignificant ways as opposed to Pilate's gigantic presence. (57)

The dissimilarity in the women's presence and stature is further articulated in their contrasting propensities of voice and in particular laughter. Pilate is remembered as a singing woman; Ruth as a silent one. Less acknowledged, how-ever, are their differences with respect to laughter. Milkman, describing "the first time in his life he remembered being completely happy" reflects: "he was sur-rounded by women who seemed to enjoy him and who laughed out loud" (47). Later, speaking to Guitar about the dream he had about his mother, he says, "I've never in my whole life heard my mother laugh. She smiles sometimes, even makes a little sound. But I don't believe she has ever laughed out loud" (194). "Laughter," Morrison has remarked, "is a way of taking the reins into your own hands" (Ross 1995: C1). Violet in *Jazz,* reflecting upon the comfort and insight she obtained through laughter comments, "[She] learned then what she had for-gotten until this moment: that laughter is serious. More complicated, more seri-ous than tears" (113).

These differences in voice, presence, and stature originate from and signify the women's opposing life views or philosophies. Pilate, as noted above and as will be discussed in length in the following chapter, is a woman who fully and completely embraces the ancestral memory, ancient properties, and funk of the motherline while Ruth, disconnected from her motherline and schooled as a daddy's girl in the ways of assimilation, has disavowed the traditions of her fore-bears. Their contrasting life values give rise to and are represented in opposing motherhood practices and philosophies.

Adrienne Rich distinguishes between two meanings of motherhood "the potential relationship of any woman to her powers of reproduction and to chil-dren; and the institution, which aims at ensuring that that potential—and all women—shall remain under male control" (1986: 13). I use the term *mother-hood* to refer to the institution of motherhood, which is male defined and con-trolled, and *mothering* to refer to experiences of mothering, which are female defined and centered. Ruth mothers in the patriarchal institution of motherhood while Pilate engages in gynocentric mothering, or, more specifically, she mothers against motherhood. Motherhood, according to Morrison's maternal philosophy, means to mother in the ways of assimilation; while mothering, for Morrison, signifies mothering by way of the values—funk, ancient properties, and ancestral memory—of the motherline. *Song of Solomon* presents Pilate as an "outlaw of the institution of motherhood." Pilate, like Hannah and Eva in *Sula,* resists the patriarchal script of motherhood that demands women mother children in a nuclear family in which the mother is subservient/inferior to the husband; economically, psychologically, and so forth. Pilate also, as did Eva and Hannah, refuses the patriarchal dictates of "good" motherhood, namely, that mothers are to be respectable, moral, chaste, passive, obedient, controlled, altruistic, selfless, and domestic. In defiance of these patriarchal imperatives, Pilate mothers in accordance with the values of the funk and the ancient properties (29). Later, Ruth describes Pilate's house as "a haven . . . an inn, a safe harbor" (135); a particularly revealing image given the centrality of the concepts of inn and harbor in Morrison's maternal standpoint theory of the ancient proprieties.

Macon's description of the "effortless beauty of the women singing in the candlelight" (30) is contrasted to his own Dead household, "his wife's narrow unyielding back; his daughters, boiled dry from years of yearning; his son to who he could speak only if his words held some command or criticism. . . . There was no music there" (28–29). In contrast to Pilate, Ruth is characterized as the "good" mother of patriarchal ideology. And while she may lack the requisite culinary ability of good motherhood, Ruth, in every other way, performs the quiet, obedient, passive, motherhood role well.[2] Ruth is also, though such is seldom acknowledged by critics, a battered wife who is abused by her husband in every manner possible: sexually, emotionally, and physically. The text tells us that "his wife, Ruth, began her days stunned into stillness by her husband's contempt and ended them wholly animated by it" (10–11). Milkman knocked his father "into the radiator" to stop him, in the words of the text "[from] smash[ing] his fist into [his mother's] jaw" (67). As the hegemonic script of patriarchal motherhood requires the subservience Ruth enacts and normalizes the violence she experiences, it also defines the parent-child relationship as exclusively a biological relation in which children are regarded as both the property and responsibility of the parents. Ruth's love for her son is described as a "possessive love" (79) and later when Pilate interrupts Ruth and Hagar's quarrelling about Milkman she says, "[You] talkin 'bout a man like he was a house or needed one. He ain't a house, he's a man, and whatever he need, don't none of you got it" (138). In contrast to Ruth's possessive love, Pilate's mothering is presented as expansive and emancipatory.

Pilate engages in the African American custom of othermothering. "Nurturing children in black extended family networks," writes Patricia Hill Collins, "stimulates a more generalized ethics of caring and personal accountability among African-American women who often feel accountable to all the Black community's children" (1991: 129). Pilate is such an othermother to Milkman. The potion Pilate prepares enables Ruth to become pregnant with Milkman, and

Pilate's voodoo practices and warning to Macon keep Milkman alive in the womb. Ruth's labor begins outside of Mercy Hospital where Pilate is singing the Song of Solomon; and Pilate refers to Milkman as Hagar's brother. Pilate is also, as her name phonetically signifies, the pilot of Milkman's quest. Like Connie in *Paradise,* Pilate is a healer. Her healing, however, is not only physical or emotional; it is most powerfully a spiritual healing. Finally, Pilate engages in what was described in the introduction as communal mothering; a concern and caring for people who are spiritually troubled. Pilate heals Milkman by returning him to his community and history. Trudier Harris writes: "Pilate can do for Milkman what no one in *The Bluest Eye* could do for Pecola Breedlove and Lorain, Ohio. Not only does she sing the lore of her culture, she lives it as well" (115). And upon her death, Pilate's only regret is that "I wished I'd a knowed more people. I would of loved 'em all. If I'd a knowed more, I would a loved more" (340).

HAGAR: "SHE NEEDED WHAT MOST COLORED GIRLS NEEDED: A CHORUS OF MAMAS"

Through the character Pilate, *Song of Solomon* celebrates the redemptive powers of mothering from the motherline or mothering against motherhood. In particular, and as will be discussed at length in the following chapter, Pilate, in imparting the teachings of the motherline to her nephew Milkman, mends broken motherlines and heals those wounded by such breakages. However, as various critics have pointed out, the power of such restorative love is qualified or at the very least problematized by Pilate's inability to save her own granddaughter from the destructiveness of the consumerist and patriarchal culture in which she lives. Wendy Harding and Jacky Martin write of Pilate's household: "Although it offers an attractive option to the oppressiveness and sterility of conventional models, Pilate's way of life does not represent a lasting alternative" (73). Pilate, they continue "protects her family as a big tree protects small ones, but she allows them to remain weak" (74). According to many readers of *Song*, Pilate is responsible for Hagar's death. Stephanie Demetrakopoulos writes: "[M]issing in her life are male relatives to help build her animus" (1987: 97). Hagar, she continues "has been terribly 'over-mothered'" (98). Samuels and Hudson-Weems also argue that "[t]o some degree . . . they are responsible for Hagar's inability to accept Milkman's rejection. She was not accustomed to being told no. . . . We may," they write, "conclude in the end that such untrammelled maternal love is as destructive as Macon's blind materialism" (75).

These critics argue that too much mothering and not enough fathering is what occasions Hagar's vulnerability to Milkman. This interpretation resembles the mother-blaming stance found in many of the psychoanalytic approaches to Morrison's literature. However, the text refuses this reading:

> Neither Pilate nor Reba knew that Hagar was not like them. Not strong enough, like Pilate, nor simple enough, like Reba, to make up her life as they had. She needed what most colored girls needed: *a chorus of mamas,*

grandmamas, aunts, cousins, sisters, neighbours, Sundays school teachers, best girl friends, and what all to give her the strength life demanded of her—and the humor with which to live it. (311, emphasis added)

Here we are told that it was not male absence, as Demetrakopoulos theorizes, but a scarcity of othermothers that rendered Hagar susceptible to the hegemonic discourses of romantic love and female beauty. "Modern urban and industrialized life," writes Aoi Mori, relegate "black mothers to the margin. Since only those mothers who can locate the basis of their strength in their foremothers can pass on the knowledge of survival to daughters, the absence of mothers unavoidably brings about a weakening of the next generation" (104). This absence of othermothers, which limits and weakens the cultural bearing function, is a consequence of migration to a Northern urban environment.

Terry Otten writes that "*[Song of Solomon]* shifts from a rural setting, emphasizing the pronounced racial dislocation of blacks transported from a nature-bound community to the more materialistic dominance of white urban culture" (45). Had Hagar grown to maturity in a rural village, she would indeed have been raised among a community of black women who would have instilled in her pride for her black female self. In the rural South, Hagar would have been less susceptible to what Susan Willis calls, in "I Shop Therefore I Am," "the mutila[tion] [of] black personhood [through] commodity consumption" (179). Pilate, Reba, and Hagar, as Karla Holloway observes, "gain strength from each other" and "fiercely protect their solidarity." "Insulated in Pilate's fertile home," Holloway continues, "their strength is intact." Only one person is able, in Holloway's words, "to break . . . their unit" (1987: 111). That person is, of course, Milkman. Holloway argues that Milkman was able to gain entry into their circle because of his "feminine potentia," the result of his being breastfed so long. If blame is to be laid it must rest principally with Milkman and the consumerist culture in which Hagar lived.

Morrison has commented that the writing of *Song* had much to do with the death of her father: "For the first time I was writing a book in which the central stage was occupied by men, and which had something to do with my loss . . . of a man (my father) and the world that disappeared with him." (1987: 123). This, I think, helps to explain Morrison's preoccupation in *Song* with men generally and fathers specifically. In this text, unlike any of her others, Morrison stresses the importance of fathers and fathering for the psychological well-being of children. But in *Song* fathers are not scripted as the saviors of daughters, rescuing them from the mother. Rather, fathers are seen as an integral part of the larger nurturant community. Their role is that of a communal othermother. In an interview with Samuels and Hudson-Weems, Morrison commented on the importance of Pilate's father in her upbringing: "Pilate had 12 years with her father and a meaningful relationship with brother and father. Her daughter had less, the daughter's daughter had none. So her relationship to men was curious and destructive, possessive . . . the stuff that Pilate has is not transmitted by DNA"

(75). For Morrison, as Hudson-Weems and Samuels argue, "there must be shared responsibility, for the child to begin to approach wholeness" (75). Morrison goes on to emphasize:

> [Pilate's intimate relationship with her father and brother during those twelve years] gave her a ferocity and some complete quality. Hagar had even less and was even more frail. It's that world of women without men. But in fact a woman is strongest when some of her sensibilities are formed by men at an early, certainly at an important age. It's absolutely necessary that it be there, and the farther away you get from that, the possibility of distortion is greater. By the same token, Milkman is in a male macho world and can't fly, isn't human, isn't complete until he realizes the impact that women have made on his life. It's really a balance between classical male and female forces that produces, perhaps, a kind of complete person. (106–107)

In her interview with Nellie McKay (1983), Morrison explained that

> Hagar does not have what Pilate had, which was a dozen years of a nurturing, good relationship with men. Pilate had a father, and a she had a brother, who loved her very much, and she could use that knowledge of that love for her life. Her daughter Reba had less of that, but she certainly has at least perfunctory adoration or love of men which she does not put to very good use. Hagar has even less because of the absence of any relationships with men in her life. She is weaker. . . . Strength of character is not something one can give another. It is not genetically transferred. (Taylor-Guthrie 1994: 144)

Morrison's emphasis here on the importance of the fathers is not to be read, I believe, as a criticism of mothers. Rather, Morrison is speaking from a specific African American belief best summed up in the African proverb: "It takes a village to raise a child." Communal or surrogate mothering is central both to African American culture and Morrison's own views on the best way to parent children.

Thus, while Pilate's mother died in childbirth, Pilate was not an unmothered daughter, as was Pecola in *The Bluest Eye*. Unlike Ruth, Pilate was nurtured by a loving and devoted father. Pilate also loved and was loved by the farm animals, and thus experienced nurturance and learned how to nurture (150). Throughout the text, Pilate is described as smelling like a forest and looking like a tree. "Pilate is," as Samuels and Hudson-Weems observe, "literally the daughter of Nature: motherless, she was nurtured by the forest during her childhood" (62). The text also links Pilate to Singing Bird, the mother who died before she herself was born. Sing is the name of Pilate's mother, and by singing people know Pilate. The mother's last name was Bird and when Pilate dies we are told that birds are awakened by Milkman's song and "[t]wo of the birds circled round them. One dived into the new grave and scooped something shiny in its beak before it flew away" (340). In contrast, the nurtured self of Macon dies when his own father is killed. Just as Cholly became dangerously free when he was rejected by his father, so Macon becomes obsessively materialistic when his father is killed defending his property. Macon Sr. was, Valerie Smith writes, "an American Adam, a farmer who loved the land and worked it profitably. Moving North cost Macon, Jr. some of the talent he had inherited from his father: still able to manipulate cold cash, he lost his father's organic connection to the soil" (282). Both Cholly and Macon lose their fathers at the onset of adolescence when they are assuming a masculine identity; their loss causes them to sever their connection to their own motherline.

Hagar's death must then be attributed to a rupture of the motherline as a result of the family's migration to the North. Moreover, once North there are not enough othermothers—women and men—to pass on the teachings of the motherline to the next generation, in particular the values of the funk, ancestral memory, and the ancient properties. While Pilate does her best, she cannot mend the motherline for her granddaughter or heal the vulnerabilities occasioned by the breakage. Pilate, as Philip Page observes, "[while she was able to] form her own successful identity, despite the violent break-up of her own family, she is unable to transmit her strengths to her daughter and granddaughter" (85). Consequently, Hagar, having no motherline and/or othermothers to immunize her, is rendered susceptible to the ills of assimilation.

BELOVED AND SETHE: "I AM BELOVED AND SHE IS MINE"

Beloved, a novel of slavery and its aftermath, shows that slavery, more than any other cultural institution, severed the African American motherline by separating families through sale and by commodifying African Americans as property, robbing them of their subjectivity and history. With the characters Ruth and Hagar in *Song of Solomon,* Morrison details how assimilation, in the instance of Ruth, and migration, in the case of Hagar, rupture the motherline. While her first four novels may be read as sociological exposés of the causes and consequences of motherline disconnection and disruptions for individual women, with *Beloved* Morrison reflects upon the representation of this loss and considers how this loss, in turn, becomes psychologically manifest. The historical trauma of motherline loss is represented through the character of Beloved while the psychological trauma of this loss is conveyed through the character Sethe.

The characterization of Beloved as a flesh and blood personification of the motherline, or more appropriately, given that she is a spirit, a "beyond-the-grave" reincarnation of it, is developed and sustained throughout the text. However, the metaphorical dimension of the Beloved character has been largely missed by readers of the text. Beloved is analyzed as if she were a real character rather than the ghost or the metaphor that she is. Beloved's relationship with her mother, in turn, is analyzed as an actual mother-daughter relationship. Consequently, most critics read this relationship as highly problematic if not pathological.[3] According to psychoanalytic interpretation, Sethe and Beloved are trapped in the pre-Oedipal mother-daughter symbiosis where differentiation between self and other is not possible: Sethe over-identifies with her daughter and does not allow her psychic individuation.[4]

The portrayal of Sethe and Beloved's relationship in the final section of the book seems to support the psychoanalytic conclusion that the mother-daughter bond is indeed "dangerous," "devouring," and "destructive."[5] Beloved says: "I am not separate from her there is no place where I stop" (210, spacing in original), and Sethe: "You are my face; I am you" (216). The mother and daughter are, as the text tells us, "locked in a love that wore everybody out" (243).

The psychoanalytic approach posits too literal a reading of Sethe and Beloved's relationship. Beloved is not a "real" human being but the ghostly reincarnation of Sethe's murdered baby girl and more importantly a symbolic representation of the broken motherline—the "sixty-million and more" to whom the book is dedicated.[6] She is the "flesh and blood" embodiment of the African American motherline, signifying both its rupture and its healing.

Elizabeth House (1990) convincingly argues that Beloved is *not* the reincarnated baby girl. Piecing together the fragments of Beloved's stream-of-conscious rememberings, we learn the story of a young girl who is captured with her mother by the "men without skin," brought over in an overcrowded slave ship— "there will never be a time when I am not crouching and watching others who are crouching" (210)—and witnesses the suicide of her mother—"they do not push the woman with my face though she goes in they do not push her" (212, spacing in original). Beloved is then separated from the other slaves and becomes a sex slave for an unidentified white master—"he puts his finger there" (212). In all likelihood, Beloved is the girl Stamp Paid mentions who "was locked up in the house with [the] whiteman over by Deer Creek" (235). When Beloved awakens and sees Sethe, she mistakenly assumes that Sethe is her long-lost mother. At the end of the novel, Beloved mysteriously disappears, "all trace is gone" (275), only to reappear, as Wild, the mother of Joe Trace in *Jazz*.[7]

But the text also certainly does invite us to see Beloved as the flesh and blood reincarnation of Sethe's murdered baby girl. When Beloved is introduced in the story she is described as a newborn baby: we are told she is unable to hold up her head and that "[e]verything hurt but her lungs most of all" (50). Beloved comes from the water, the amniotic sac of the womb, and Sethe voids endless water upon seeing Beloved; "But there was no stopping water breaking from a breaking womb and there was no stopping now" (51). It would seem then that Beloved is simultaneously Sethe's daughter from beyond the grave and the captured and orphaned African daughter from "the other side."

Beloved is both Sethe's daughter and the daughter of the "woman who picks flowers": she is the embodiment of all the "disremembered and unaccounted for" daughters whose "stories have not been passed on." Beloved, as Deborah Horwitz argues, "is the haunting symbol of the many Beloveds—generations of mothers and daughters—hunted down and stolen from Africa" (157). She embodies each and every woman of the African American motherline. Beloved also comes to represent, as Brooks Bouson has argued, "the collective suffering and shame-rage of the 'black angry dead'" (198) as well as "the psychic woundedness of those who survived the middle passage and were victimized by slavery" (152). Beloved, as Gurleen Grewal writes, "is the very embodiment of pain" (1998, 114).

Beloved is also linked to Sethe's own mother who, like the murdered granddaughter, remains nameless. Throughout the text the voice or presence of the daughter Beloved triggers Sethe's "rememory" of her own mother. Significantly, when Sethe first sees Beloved she remembers herself as the daughter of her mother: "Not since she was a baby girl, being cared for by the eight-year-old girl who pointed out her mother to her, had she had an emergency that unmanageable" (51). Beloved's questions about Sethe's mother—"Your woman she never fix up your hair?" (60)—cause Sethe to speak about her mother for the first time and "remember[ing] something she had forgotten she knew" (61). Denver, too, is symbolically identified with her maternal grandmother: when Sethe is pregnant with Denver she calls her an antelope, which is the name of the dance Sethe's mother performed before she lived at Sweet Home.

In a reversal of roles, the daughter, Beloved, engages the mother, Sethe, in "rememory," a journey into self and back through time. Beloved prompts Sethe to remember all that she was resolved to forget. Similar to Milkman in *Song of Solomon,* who recovers his history and discovers his identity through a spiritual return home to the place of his ancestors, Sethe, in *Beloved,* learns to live with the past and to accept herself through a psychic journey of remembering. And it is the daughter who enables the mother to remember, accept, and forgive. Thus, the mother-daughter relationship both represents and achieves an identification with, and an acceptance of, the past. Thus, in and through her relationship with Beloved, the embodiment of the African American motherline, Sethe finds her own lost motherline.

The matrilineal heritage metaphorically represented by Beloved is a radical reclamation of the mother and daughter bond that was denied and severed under slavery. Reconnecting Sethe to her own mother, and embodying the murdered baby, the one of the future, and the "sixty million and more," those of the past, Beloved emerges as Morrison's most powerful representation of the African American motherline.

As Beloved represents the African American mother line—both its historical rupture in slavery and its repair through mother-daughter connection—the character Sethe represents the psychological trauma of motherline rupture. In her study of matrilineal heritage in African American women's writing, Missy Dehn Kubitschek explores the duality of Sethe's subjectivity. Sethe is both mother and daughter: she occupies that "double position" of mother-daughter described by Marianne Hirsch.[8] Kubitschek emphasizes that Sethe's maternal identity is inseparable from her identity as daughter. She writes: "Beneath Sethe's passionate commitment to motherhood lies an equally passionate desire to be mothered, to be a daughter to her mother" (170). Significantly, Sethe identifies and articulates this longing to be a daughter in communication with her own daughter, Beloved:

> My plan was to take us all to the other side where my own ma'am is. They
> stopped me from getting us there, but they didn't stop you from getting here.

> Ha ha. You came right on back like a good girl, like a daughter which is what
> I wanted to be and would have been if my ma'am had been able to get out of
> the rice long enough before they hanged her and let me be one. (203)

This yearning to be a daughter originates from Sethe's own displaced identity.
Her self has no familial or ancestral grounding. Sethe longs to have a historical
and communal identity, to fulfil the role of daughter described in *Tar Baby:* "I'm
just saying what a daughter is. A daughter is a woman that cares about where she
come from and takes care of them that took care of her" (281). Kubitschek
emphasizes that it is "this unsatisfied hunger in Sethe [which] conditions her own
extremely possessive definition of motherhood" (171). It is as if Sethe compen-
sates for not being mothered herself by overmothering her own children.

Beloved makes clear the need for mothers to have their motherline. In a conversation with Paul D., Sethe details how difficult it was to mother her young
children at Sweet Home without a community of elder women to turn to for
guidance and support:

> So there wasn't nobody. To talk to, I mean, who'd know when it was time
> to chew up a little something and give it to em. Is that what makes the teeth
> come on out, or should you wait till the teeth came and then solid food? . . .
> I wish I'd a known more, but, like I say, there wasn't nobody to talk to.
> Women, I mean. So I tried to recollect what I'd seen back where I was
> before Sweet Home. (160)

Sethe recognizes that daughters learn "how to mother" from the knowledge and
example of their foremothers. In other words, daughters learn how to be mothers through the teachings of the motherline. Cut off from her motherline, Sethe
is unsure how to mother.

Sethe also realizes that mothers bequeath more than practical advice to their
daughters. In loving her daughter, the mother enables the daughter to love when
she herself becomes a mother; motherlove fosters self-love. Mothering is thus
essential for the emotional well-being of children. To be a loving mother, a
woman must first be loved as a daughter. As Kubitschek concludes: "Only by
remembering one's history as a loved daughter . . . and excavating history for
empowering female role models can one become a complete woman" (170).

Nancy Chodorow (1978) has argued that girls acquire a relational sense of
self from the intense and prolonged pre-Oedipal symbiosis with their mothers.
Women recapture the pre-Oedipal oneness through a maternal intimacy; they
become mothers where once they were daughters. Hence, the reproduction of
mothering. A scenario not fully considered by Chodorow and of utmost importance here in this reading of the motherline is the sociohistorical displacement of
the mother-child relationship. If the ability to mother is developmentally built
into the daughter's personality through the mother-daughter bond—she acquires
a relational self, which in turn becomes a maternal self—what happens when that
crucial bond is denied, damaged, or destroyed as it was in slavery? If a daughter

is prevented from bonding with her mother, is she then without the relational sense of self required to mother? How does she then mother her children?

Such questioning helps to clarify Sethe's own maternal stance. As a child, Sethe is told that she is the chosen one: "[Your mother] threw them all away but you. . . . Without names she threw them. You she gave the name of the black man. She put her arms around him. The others she did not put her arms around. Never. Never" (62). Sethe is also the archetypal motherless child, emotionally and physically orphaned, with no family or history to call her own. Separated from her mother at the tender age of three weeks, Sethe was left in the care of an eight-year-old child. She received her nursing milk from another woman's breast "that never had enough for all" (203), and recognized her mother only by the hat she wore in the rice field (30). The adult Sethe is haunted by the possibility that her mother abandoned her as a child: "I wonder what they was doing when they was caught. Running, you think? No. Not that. Because she my Ma'am and nobody's ma'am would run off and leave her daughter, would she?" (30). The only memory Sethe retains from the place of her birth—Carolina maybe? or was it Louisiana?—is the singing and dancing women who spoke in a "code she no longer understood" (63). The song, laughter, and the "different words" suggest the primordial mother tongue of the pre-Oedipal realm, the maternal semiotic that exists outside of, and in opposition to the symbolic language of the Father. "[The] world of cooing women, each of whom was called Ma'am" refers also to the ancient motherline. Sethe's request of her mother, "Mark me too," signifies her need for a communal identification and historical continuity, a connection to the motherline of her foremothers.[9]

It would seem that Sethe is denied that crucial bond that engenders the relational sense of self from which a maternal subjectivity is formed. However, several psychoanalytical readings of the novel diagnose Sethe as suffering from a subjectivity that is too relational. Sethe's overidentification with her returned Beloved however cannot be attributed to a relational subjectivity engendered by mother-daughter attachment, because Sethe did not experience such a relationship.[10] Sethe's excessive relationality with her returned daughter should be read metaphorically. If Beloved signifies the African American motherline, the merging of Sethe with Beloved—"they were the same, had the same face" (241)—thus signifies Sethe's own longing to connect with her own lost motherline. Sethe wants to be a daughter to her mother, and a mother to her daughter. Her unsatisfied yearning, and the guilt that accompanies it, causes Sethe to connect with Beloved, who, as the personification of the African American motherline, is both Sethe's mother, her daughter, and her own self as daughter-mother.

Chodorow's theory of the reproduction of mothering offers us an explanation for why women must be loved as a daughter before they are able to love as mothers: the pre-Oedipal bond engenders a relational sense of self from which a maternal sense of self is formed. However, I suggest that the daughter's eventual maternal subjectivity is determined less by the way she was mothered and more by how she perceived her own mother. A daughter acquires the selfhood needed to mother only by recognizing selfhood in her own mother.

In *The Bonds of Love* (1988), Jessica Benjamin advances a theory of inter-subjectivity to analyze and account for structures of domination in Western culture. Benjamin argues that the child's selfhood develops in relation to the autonomous subjectivity of the mother. She writes:

> The intersubjective view maintains that the individual grows in and through the relationship to other subjects. Most important, this perspective observes that the other whom the self meets is also a self, a subject in his or her own right. It assumes that we are able and need to recognize that other subject as different and yet alike, as an other who is capable of sharing similar mental experience. Thus the idea of intersubjectivity reorients the conception of the psychic world from a subject's relation to its object toward a subject meeting another subject. (19–20)

What is of importance here is Benjamin's insistence on "the need for mutual recognition, the necessity of recognizing as well as being recognized by the other" (23). The child must be able "to recognize the mother as a person in her own right" in order to recognize his/her own subjectivity. "[The mother's] recognition [of the child]," Benjamin writes, "will be meaningful only to the extent that it reflects her own equally separate subjectivity" (24).

In her "The Bonds of Love and the Boundaries of Self in Toni Morrison's *Beloved*," Barbara Schapiro reads Morrison's *Beloved* by way of Benjamin's theory of intersubjectivity. Schapiro uses Benjamin's psychoanalytic model of intersubjectivity to understand the sociohistorical depiction of slave motherhood in Morrison's text. Schapiro writes:

> For Morrison's characters, African-Americans in a racist, slave society, there is no reliable other to recognize and affirm their existence. The mother, the child's first vital other, is made unreliable or unavailable by a slave system which either separates her from her child or so enervates and depletes her that she has no self from which to confer recognition. (194)

The development of the child's selfhood is contingent upon the mother already having a clearly defined sense of self from which to confer recognition. When that mother is denied her own subjectivity, lack of self is reproduced with the next generations. Schapiro asks: "How can a child see self or mother as subjects when the society denies them that status?" (197) "[In *Beloved*]," Schapiro continues, "Sethe's mother, deprived of her authentic selfhood, her status as a human subject, can not provide the recognition and affirmation that her child craves. The cycle is vicious, and thus Sethe's children, Beloved and Denver, will suffer the same loss" (201). Sethe's weak sense of self is not reproduced through the mother-daughter identification, as Chodorow would argue; but rather through her own mother not having a strong sense of self from which the daughter could form her own selfhood. Under slavery black women are viewed as object and breeder; this denies slave women their own subjectivity, the very requirement for an attainment of selfhood in children. Sethe, however, powerfully resists the displacement of her maternal self and the denial of her identity as mother; a topic that will be explored in chapter 5.

As the character Beloved represents the motherline, its historical loss and return, the character Sethe conveys the psychological wounding that occurs when there is this loss. And while the text does not psychologically dramatize the healing as it does the wounding, healing is suggested in Sethe's reconnection to the motherline. Healing is also signified in Sethe's eventual understanding and acceptance of her own motherlove, as will be discussed in chapter 5.

CONCLUSION

The ruptures and disruptions of the motherline occasioned by assimilation, migration, and slavery described by Morrison in *Song of Solomon* and *Beloved* attest to the significance of the motherline for female empowerment by describing the disempowerment that results from loss of the motherline. Whether the line be severed as in slavery, impoverished or diluted as in the instance of migration, or displaced as in the case of assimilation, these breakages prevent women from engaging in the essential and central task of cultural bearing and passing on the teachings of the motherline that make possible a strong and proud selfhood. For Ruth, Hagar, and Sethe the motherline is never restored nor are its psychological/cultural tatters repaired. However, as *Song of Solomon* and *Beloved* describe the psychological and cultural disarray of motherline fissures, they do suggest, with Sethe's reconnection to the motherline, a way that motherlines may be mended. This strategy of reconnection or return to the motherline is most fully developed in *Song* and *Tar Baby* and is the subject of the following chapter.

chapter four

Reconnections to the Motherline

Deliverance and Exile: *Song of Solomon, Tar Baby*

DISCONNECTIONS FROM, AND DISRUPTIONS OF the motherline were explored in the last two chapters: here the theme of reconnection is investigated. Surveying Milkman's successful quest in *Song of Solomon* and Jadine's failed quest in *Tar Baby,* this chapter will consider Morrison's reflections on the theme of reconnection in terms of two interrelated questions: How is reconnection made possible and by whom? More than any of Morrison's other novels, *Song of Solomon,* as critics have argued, affirms and celebrates the African American motherline, detailing how African Americans may reconnect back to their lost motherline and reclaim the ancient properties, ancestral memory, and funk of their forbears. "In many ways," as Karla Holloway observes,

> *Song of Solomon* is a beginning book. It places value, establishes identity, and unequivocally shows us point-of-origin. If later we suffer as Pecola suffers, or lose touch as Nel and Sula and Jadine did, then *Song of Solomon* is there to tell why and remind us of where we were before the destructiveness of Western civilization corrupted and displaced our African selves. This book is a whole and it fills in all gaps and all questions and compels our attention to its quintessential song of African individuation patterns that underlie Black Americans' quests for survival. (1987: 103–104)

Song provides us with a trajectory of the African American motherline at its "point-of-origin," describing the way it was, and the way it may be again.

This chapter delineates Milkman's return to his motherline. It also asks, as few critical readings have done, what enables this man to return to his motherline while Jadine does not. Milkman's return is made possible, this chapter will argue, because the person who guides his quest is a cultural bearer who embodies the ancient properties, ancestral memory, and funk of the motherline. As a cultural bearer of the motherline, Pilate becomes Milkman's spiritual midwife

93

and is able to deliver his rebirth, his return to the motherline. The chapter will then go on to ask why Jadine's search miscarries while Milkman's does not. Jadine's failed quest, this chapter will argue, results from Son's inability to fulfill the function of cultural bearer as Pilate did in *Song*. The question the text asks us to consider is: Why is Son not able to be a Pilate for Jadine? *Tar Baby* ultimately argues that Son, though embodying African American funk, cannot be a cultural bearer of the motherline and hence return Jadine to her motherline because of his identification with patriarchal masculinity, which in turn is predicated upon mother-son separation.

MILKMAN'S DELIVERANCE: "WITHOUT EVER LEAVING THE GROUND, [HE] COULD FLY"

Song of Solomon differs from Morrison's other novels in its use of a male central character. In a 1980 interview with Anne Koenan, Morrison explained why the protagonist is male:

> [I]t had to be a man. Men have more to learn in certain areas than women do. . . . I wanted . . . a character who had everything to learn, who would start from zero, and had no reason to learn anything, because he's comfortable, he doesn't need money, he's just flabby and pampered. Well, that kind of character, a sort of average person who has no impetus to learn anything—to watch that person learn something was fascinating to me as opposed to watching the man who already was that perfection. . . . And the men have more places they can hide and not learn. They don't have to learn anything, they can always be men. So that's why it had to be a man for me. (Taylor-Guthrie 1994: 75–76)

Morrison goes on to say, "In the beginning I was a little scary *[sic]* about that [the character's being male], until I realized how much he had to learn from women, which is part of what he had to learn. This man, Milkman," Morrison continues, "has to walk into the earth—the womb—in that cave, then he walks the surface of the earth and he can relate to its trees—that's all very maternal—then he can go into the water . . . then he can get to the air" (Taylor-Guthrie 1994: 76). Specifically, Milkman must come to see his disconnection from the motherline and the absence of the funk and ancestral memory in his life. *Song of Solomon* centers upon Milkman's return to the funk of his black cultural identity. *Song* thus works as a traditional Bildungsroman or apprenticeship novel, which, in accordance with the definition of this genre, "recounts the youth and young adulthood of a sensitive protagonist who is attempting to learn the nature of the world, discover its meaning and pattern, and acquire a philosophy of life and 'the art of living'" (Holman 1980: 33).

In keeping with this genre, the novel opens with the birth of Milkman and ends with what is presumed to be his death. However, this novel is less about acquiring a philosophy of life than it is about *un*learning meanings and patterns in order to acquire a new philosophy of life. In this way, *Song* is closer to a spiritual quest than to a traditional Bildungsroman. A spiritual quest, as the feminist theologian Carol Christ describes it, concerns "a woman's awakening to the depths of her soul and her position in the universe" (8). The spiritual quest moves the woman toward self-integration while the ambition of the Bildungsroman or social quest is integration with society. The spiritual quest usually takes place later in life, during the adult years, and is characterized by four distinct stages that Christ defines as Nothingness, Awakening, Insight, and New Naming. At the beginning of her spiritual quest the woman experiences "emptiness" which gives rise to a "questioning of the meaning of [her] li[fe]." This, according to Christ, engenders "an awakening, similar to a conversion experience, in which, the powers of being are revealed." Awakening "grounds her in a new sense of self and a new orientation in the world" (13). This awakening often takes place in nature. The new naming of self and world that is achieved through the spiritual quest "reflect[s] wholeness, a movement toward overcoming the dualism of self and world, body and soul, nature and spirit, rational and emotional, which have plagued Western consciousness" (13–14).

Of interest to us in our reading of *Song* are the differences Christ identifies between the male and female spiritual quest:

> The experience of nothingness often has a different quality for women than for men. Men are not conditioned to think of themselves as worthless. For them the experience of nothingness often comes after they have taken their place in the world of male power and joined the traditional hierarchies that support men's dominance in family and society. After achieving power and respect, men may come to experience their power as illusory. They may then open themselves to a deeper experience of power "not as the world knows it." (17)

Awakening is also experienced differently by men and women:

> "[C]onversion" for men means giving up conventional . . . power and trusting that genuine power rooted in union with the powers of being. For women, awakening is not so much a giving up as a gaining of power. Women often describe their awakening as a coming to self, rather than a giving up of self, as a grounding of selfhood in the powers of being, rather than a surrender of self to the powers of being. (18–19)

Christ's observation echoes Morrison's thoughts on how men have more to learn and how they have available to them more places to hide.[1]

The opening chapters of this text follow the traditional pattern of the Bildungsroman. However, Milkman's search for identity soon takes the shape of a spiritual quest because it is guided by a woman, Pilate, and it moves toward embracing the funkiness of black cultural identity. By the fourth chapter Milkman has "taken his place in the world of male power"; he has defied and struck his father, been told his father's story—"You want to be a whole man, you have to deal with the whole truth" (77)—he has rejected his mother in response to his father's story and his own remembering of her late nursing of him. Significantly, after his discussion with his mother he goes in search of Guitar and finds him in a company of men. From chapter 4 on we witness Milkman's growing dissatisfaction with his masculine identity. He decides to end his relationship with Hagar because she has become, in his words, "the third beer. Not the first one, which the throat receives with almost tearful gratitude; nor the second, that confirms and extends the pleasure of the first. But the third, the one you drink because it's there, because it can't hurt, and because what difference does it make?" (91). He experiences the nothingness identified by Christ:

> Maybe I should [get married]. . . . There were lots of women around. . . . Maybe he'd pick one—the redhead. Get a nice house. His father would help him find one. Go into a real partnership with his father and. . . . And what? There had to be something better to look forward to. He couldn't get interested in money. . . . Politics . . . Everybody bored him. The city was boring. (107–108)

Although he does not yet realize it, the nothingness Milkman experiences is the result of his disconnection from the motherline. He believes that Pilate's gold will free him and allow him to create a new identity out of the nothingness of his current one. Hearing Guitar talk about the gold, "[h]e felt a self inside himself emerge, a clean-lined definite self" (184). As he leaves for Pennsylvania he tells Guitar: "I just know that I want to live my own life. I don't want to be my old man's office boy no more. And as long as I'm in this place I will be. Unless I have my own money. I have to get out of that house and I don't want to owe anybody when I go" (223). In pursuit of gold, Milkman goes in search of his "own life."

Milkman's departure from the city marks the end of his social quest—integration with society—and the beginning of his spiritual one; the shift is symbolically marked by the flight of the airplane and textually delineated by the opening of the second section of the novel. The self he finds, however, is not the one of which he has gone in search. At the start of his spiritual quest, Milkman is like the white peacock he and Guitar see at the used car lot. Guitar explains to Milkman that "[t]he male is the only one got that tail full of jewellery." And this is why the male bird is unable to fly: "Too much tail. All that jewellery weighs it down. Like vanity. Can't nobody fly with all that shit. Wanna fly, you got to give up the shit that weighs you down" (179–80). Before Milkman can be awakened, he must, like the male peacock, "give up the shit that weighs him down."

Upon arriving in Danville, the home of his paternal grandparents, he checks his bag at the diner, a symbolic beginning to renouncing his old self. Struggling across the creek on his way to the cave, Milkman ruins his shoes and breaks his watch. When he finds nothing but blackness in the cave we are told that he "leaped to his feet, whereupon the sole of his right shoe split away from the soft cordovan leather" (255). Upon returning to the diner/bus station he learns that his suitcase has been misplaced (258). When he arrives in Shalimar in a beat-up old car that, significantly, breaks down right in front of Solomon's General store, all he brings with him are the clothes on his back.

The nothingness Milkman experiences in his life is reflected by the dark and empty cave: "There was no fat little pigeon-breasted bags of gold. There was nothing. Nothing at all. And before he knew it, he was hollering a long *awwww* sound into the pit" (255). The cave itself is represented as a womb. When he first sees it Milkman describes it as a "black hole in the rock" (224). Later, when he enters the cave, Milkman tells us he was "blinded by the absence of light." The entrance of the cave, we are told, has "several boulders standing around . . . one with a kind of V-shaped crown" (254). The interior walls of the cave gradually come closer together to form a narrow passage and at the end of the cave is the pit where the gold is supposed to be buried. The cave, as it is described, closely resembles the reproductive organs of the female body; the boulders suggest the labia majoria, the V-shaped boulder the clitoris, the narrow passage, the birth canal and, the pit the womb. His entry then is the passage of birth experienced in reverse. Similar to Plum in *Sula* and later Joe in *Jazz,* Milkman returns to the womb so that he may be reborn. Significantly, when Milkman discovers that there is no gold he lets out a long *awwww* sound which signifies the cry of the infant at birth. Upon leaving the cave, "Milkman began to shake with hunger. Real hunger" (255). The womb-like cave, Milkman's cry, and his hunger symbolically mark a rebirth and prepare Milkman for the next stage of his spiritual quest.

Milkman's quest thus far has been guided by women. His search for Pilate's gold is what brings Milkman to Danville and it is Circe who tells him how to find the cave. Circe also tells Milkman the name of his paternal grandmother, a revelation that will later enable him to decode the children's song, learn the legend of his ancestors, and become reconnected to the motherline. The next two significant occurrences in Milkman's quest take the form of rites of initiation and are performed by men. The first of these is the fight at Solomon's store.

Not sensitive or perceptive enough to see that he has offended the men with his arrogant city ways, Milkman finds himself involved in a knife fight that leaves his face slit and his "pretty beige suit" bloodied. At this point, as Dorothy H. Lee observes, "the older men take over the initiation rite from the youths. The names of the men—Omar, King Walker, Luther Solomon, Calvin Breakstone, and a giant called Small Boy—seem to indicate that Milkman has entered the circle of village elders, of poets, kings, and men of God" (69). The names Luther and Calvin in particular, as Samuels and Hudson-Weems comment, are "associat[ed] with reform and rebirth" and thus signal the metamorphosis of self Milkman will undergo during the hunt (66). Milkman's awakening to his new sense of self occurs in a natural environment, as described by Christ in her plotting of the spiritual quest. It also takes place in a Southern state, near the home of Milkman's paternal great-grandparents. This is of crucial importance because the new self that Milkman achieves at the conclusion of his spiritual quest is one formed from the values of the ancestral memory of his African American motherline.

During the hunt, Milkman's fatigue and lack of physical fitness cause him to become separated from the other men. Tired and alone, Milkman's feelings turn, as they do throughout the novel, to self-pity: "What kind of savages were these people. . . . He had done nothing to deserve their contempt. Nothing to deserve the explosive hostility. . . . He didn't deserve . . ." (279). However, in this instance and for the first time in Milkman's life, the self-pity gives way to a decentering of the self:

> They were troublesome thoughts, but they wouldn't go away. Under the moon, on the ground, alone, with not even the sound of baying dogs to remind him that he was with other people, his self—the cocoon that was "personality"—gave way. He could barely see his own hand, and couldn't see his feet. He was only his breath, coming slower now, and his thoughts. The rest of him had disappeared. So the thoughts came, unobstructed by other people. . . . There was nothing here to help him—not his money, his car, his father's reputation, his suit, or his shoes. . . . Except for his broken watch, and his wallet . . . all he had started out with on his journey was gone. . . . (280)

With his self displaced, Milkman is able to truly connect with the natural environment that surrounds him:

> Little by little it fell into place. The dogs, the men . . . were talking to each other. In distinctive voices they were saying distinctive, complicated things. . . . No, it was not language: it was what there was before language. Before things were written down. Language in the time when men and animals did talk to one another, when a man could sit down with an ape and the two converse . . . when men ran with wolves not from or after them. (281)

With this realization he is open to the teachings of nature:

> Down either side of his thighs he felt the sweet gum's surface cradling him like the rough but maternal hands of a grandfather. Feeling both tense and relaxed, he sank his fingers into the grass. He tried to listen with his fingertips, to hear what, if anything, the earth had to say, and it told him quickly that someone was standing beside him and he had just enough time to raise one hand to his neck and catch the wire that fastened around his throat. (282)

Nature, in this instance, delivers nurturance because it is the earth that saves Milkman from the death clutch of Guitar. Leaving the forest Milkman was "[l]aughing too, hard, loud, and long. Really laughing, and he found himself exhilarated by simply walking the earth. Walking it like he belonged on it; like his legs were stalks, tree trunks, a part of his body that extended down down down into the rock and soil, and were comfortable there—on the earth and on the place where he walked. And he did not limp" (284).

Milkman is now prepared for his new self. Samuels and Hudson-Weems write:

> Milkman's experiences in the Blue Ridge Mountains and Shalimar allow
> him to finally divest his fostered self, the life that has become a burden; like
> the peacock's vanity, it had weighed him down. Like an African initiate who
> enters the forest at puberty, symbolically dies through the act of circumci-
> sion, and returns to his village a man, Milkman enters the woods of his par-
> ents' youth and there, stripped of his social trappings, completes his rite of
> passage. He leaves the forest a new man, one who has been shaped not
> solely by the environment but also by his distinct choices and actions: by
> his decision to live, to walk the earth as "Self." (67)

More specifically, as Demetrakopoulos observes, the hunt occasions the death of
[Milkman's] masculine ego, which is signified by Guitar's attempts to kill him by
strangulation—a decapitation. Significantly, upon leaving King Walker's gas station Milkman sees "[a] peacock soar away" (286).

The next rite of passage Milkman undergoes returns him to a female space.
Having accepted Milkman and initiated him into their male culture, the men
offer Sweet to Milkman. He learns from her reciprocity in male and female relations. We are told that

> [s]he put salve on his face. He washed her hair. She sprinkled talcum on his
> feet. He straddled her behind and massaged her back. She put witch hazel
> on his swollen neck. He made up the bed. She gave him gumbo to eat. He
> washed the dishes. She washed his clothes and hung them out to dry. He
> scoured her tub. She ironed his shirt and pants. He gave her fifty dollars.
> She kissed his mouth. He touched her face. She said please come back. He
> said I'll see you tonight. (288–89)

With Sweet, as Carmean observes, Milkman learns "the joy of sharing" (61).
Doreatha Drummond Mbalia points out, "[I]t is not until after Milkman has
revolutionized his consciousness in regard to race oppression and class exploitation that he sheds his sexist views on women" (61); only then can he "see women
as his equals." With Milkman, Mbalia continues, Morrison has created "a male
as protagonist, one who must first become conscious of himself in relationship to
his people; then and as a consequence, reject the individualistic, vulturistic class
aspirations of his oppressor before experiencing a wholesome relationship with a
woman" (65). Milkman's rejection of these white middle-class values enables him
to change. As a growing boy and a young man, Milkman is an unrepentant male
chauvinist: he is spoiled, smug, and self-centered in his demeanor and dismissive
and contemptuous in his treatment of women. Milkman's sexism is summed up
nicely for us in Lena's speech to her brother:

> Our girlhood was spent like a found nickel on you. When you slept, we were
> quiet, when you were hungry, we cooked; when you wanted to play, we
> entertained you; and when you got grown enough to know the difference

between a woman and a two-toned Ford, everything in this house stopped
for you. You have yet to wash your underwear, spread a bed, wipe the ring
from your tub, or move a fleck of your dirt from one place to another. And
to this day you have never asked one of us if we were tired, or sad, or wanted
a cup of coffee. You've never picked up anything heavier than your own feet,
or solved a problem harder than fourth-grade arithmetic. Where do you get
the *right* to decide our lives? . . . I'll tell you where. From the hog's gut that
hangs down between your legs. (216–17)

Milkman is indeed, in the words of Lena, "a sad, pitiful, stupid, selfish, hateful
man" (218).

Unlearning sexism, stripping away the masculine self, begins in the maternal cave at Danville and concludes in the Blue Ridge mountains. During the
hunt Milkman experiences "his self—the cocoon that was 'personality'—[giving]
way." As he loses his masculine self Milkman gains insight into how horribly he
has treated others, particularly Hagar: "And if a stranger could try to kill him,
surely Hagar, who knew him and whom he'd thrown away like a wad of chewing
gum after the flavor was gone—she had a right to try to kill him too" (280). Here
Milkman is able, at last, to see and name the self-centeredness of his masculine
identity. "Apparently he thought he deserved only to be loved—from a distance,
though—and given what he wanted. And in return he would be . . . what? Pleas-
ant? Generous? Maybe all he was really saying was: I am not responsible for your
pain; share your happiness with me but not your unhappiness" (280). It is no
coincidence that Milkman's awareness of his connectedness to and responsibility
for others comes with the loss of his masculine self. In white Western culture the
masculine self is defined as autonomous, separate, and individuated, as contrasted to the feminine sense of self that is experienced relationally and in a web
of interdependence. Although not white, Milkman has been socialized to
embrace the values of the dominant culture, predicated on masculine individualism and separateness. Only when Milkman relinquishes that masculine self of
white Western culture is he able to experience and value connectedness.

In Morrison, women are the cultural bearers of the funk of black cultural
identity. Thus, it makes sense that Milkman would first experience his new connected sense of self with a black woman. Significantly, it is a bath that Milkman
first requests when he arrives at Sweet's, signifying his baptism into a new self.
While staying at Sweet's, he has "a warm dreamy sleep all about flying, about sail-
ing high over the earth" (302); the dream signifies the legend of Solomon, which
Milkman will use to decode the children's song. As he stands and listens to the
children's song the day after his night with Sweet, Milkman, for the first time,
comes to see the women in his life—his mother, Pilate, and Hagar—as real people. Reflecting upon the celibacy of his mother's life Milkman realizes that "[h]e
hadn't thought much of it when she'd told him, but now it seemed to him that
such sexual deprivation would affect her, hurt her in precisely the way it would
affect and hurt him" (303). This is contrasted to his earlier thought that he had

"[n]ever . . . thought of his mother as a person, a separate individual, with a life apart from allowing or interfering with his own" (75). Regarding Hagar, he understands that "[h]e had used her—her love, her craziness—and most of all he had used her skulking, bitter vengeance. It made him a star, a celebrity . . ." (304). Milkman's realization shows him to be a connected and caring person who feels empathy for, and responsibility to, others. This relational sense of self enables Milkman to truly listen to and interpret the children's song and discover his heritage. *Song of Solomon* thus makes explicit the interconnectedness of relational subjectivity and ancestral memory—and so explains the reason women, in Morrison's fiction, assume the role of culture bearers. This chapter ends, significantly enough, with a mirrored, doubled image of Milkman. "[He] caught a glimpse of himself in the plate-glass window. He was grinning. His eyes were shining. He was as eager and happy as he had ever been in his life" (308). This image of Milkman contrasts with an earlier one in which his self is "lack[ing] coherence, a coming together of the features into a total self" (69–70).

Upon his return from Susan Byrd's house, Milkman demands of Sweet that they go swimming: "He almost broke her door down. I want to swim! . . . Come on, let's go swimming. I'm dirty and I want waaaaater!" When Sweet suggests a bath Milkman responds: "Don't give me no itty bitty teeny tiny tub, girl. I need the whole entire complete deep blue sea!" (330). Milkman's swim in the quarry is another baptism, one of greater importance than the earlier bath at Sweet's home. His born-again self emerges when Milkman learns of his great-grandfather, Solomon, the man who flew back to Africa leaving his wife and twenty-one children behind. He tells Sweet: "The son of a bitch could fly! You hear me, Sweet? That motherfucker could fly! Could fly! He didn't need no airplane. Didn't need no fuckin tee double you ay. He could fly his own self!" Milkman's excitement over "his great-granddaddy [who] could flyyyyyy" suggests that the relational sense of self Milkman has recently acquired has given way to an individuated and separate sense of self. When Sweet asks him, "Who'd he leave behind?" Milkman responds, "He left everybody down on the ground and he sailed off. . . . Solomon done gone/Solomon cut across the sky, Solomon gone home!" (332).

Milkman's excitement over "his granddaddy [who] could fly" and Sweet's question "Who'd he leave behind?" underscore the centrality of flight metaphor in this novel. In an interview with Thomas LeClair (1981), Morrison commented:

> If it [the flying myth] means Icarus to some readers, fine; I want to take credit for that. But my meaning is specific: it is about black people who could fly. That was always part of the folklore of my life; flying was one of our gifts. I don't care how silly it may seem. It is everywhere—people used to talk about it, it's in the spirituals and gospels. Perhaps it was wishful thinking—escape, death, and all that. But suppose it wasn't. What might it mean? I tried to find out in *Song of Solomon*. (Taylor-Guthrie 1994: 122)

In an earlier interview with Mel Watkins (1977), Morrison spoke of her fascination with flight, particularly as it is experienced by black men:

> That's why flying is the central metaphor in *Song*—the literal taking off and
> flying into the air . . . is everybody's dream. . . . I used it not only in the
> African sense of whirling dervishes and getting out of one's skin, but also in
> the majestic sense of a man who goes too far, whose adventure takes him
> far away . . . black men travel, they split, they get on trains, they walk, they
> move. I used to hear those old men talk about traveling—which is not get-
> ting from here to there, it's the process. . . . It's a part of black life, a posi-
> tive, majestic thing, but there is a price to pay—the price is the children.
> The fathers may soar, they may triumph, they may leave, but the children
> know who they are; they remember, half in glory and half in accusation . . .
> it is the children who remember it, sing about it, mythologize it, make it
> part of their family history. (Taylor-Guthrie 1994: 46)

Flight in *Song* thus signifies both freedom and abandonment; while Solomon
may have freed himself from enslavement, he left others, his family, behind.
Critic Patrick Bjork (1992) argues that these two meanings of flight as "both
destabilizing and as liberating" are introduced to us at the beginning of the text
with Mr. Smith's death. In Morrison's writing, Samuels and Hudson-Weems
argue, flight is "a trope for achieved selfhood." "Flight also," as they quote Morrison as saying, "has that other meaning in it; the abandonment of other people."[2] Flight is, thus, in Hudson-Weems and Samuels's words, both "triumph and
risk—tragedy and triumph." Nonetheless, Samuels and Hudson-Weems conclude that "what seems to matter to Morrison is not the violation ('you do leave
other people behind'), but the willingness to become exceptional, to take the
leap" (69–70).

While I would agree with Hudson-Weems and Samuels's contention that
Song of Solomon celebrates the transcendence and freedom of flight, I would
argue that more central to the novel is a reconfiguration of the meaning and
experience of flight. In Morrison's fiction it is young black men who yearn for
flight. In *Sula*, we are told of Ajax, "airplanes . . . he thought of airplanes, and
pilots, and the deep sky that held them both" (126). One of the first things we
learn about Milkman is that "when the little boy discovered, at four, the same
thing Mr. Smith had learned earlier—that only birds and airplanes could fly—he
lost all interest in himself" (9). These men also shun commitment in human relationships; Ajax leaves for the Dayton airshow the moment "he detected the scent
of a nest," and Milkman regards Hagar as nothing more than "his private honey
pot, not a real or legitimate girl friend—not someone he might marry" (91).

Stephanie Demetrakopoulos argues that in *Song of Solomon*, Morrison
"broaden[s] and complicate[s] the myth [of masculine flying] by looking at if
from an outsider's vantage point" (1987: 87). This text, Demetrakopoulos contends, emphasizes the cost of this freedom: "The children of the flying men suffer discontinuity of every kind. They lose their homes, a sense of their fathers, a

sane and stable mother, and even their racial roots in this case of the boy raised by the Indian" (88). Susan Byrd tells Milkman that while the myth says Ryna lost her mind because she couldn't live without her man, Byrd thinks "it was trying to take care of children by [herself]" that caused Ryna's despair and eventual insanity. In Morrison children need to be parented so that they may know their history and grow up with a strong and proud sense of self. By flying back to Africa, Solomon not only abandons his children, but he also breaks the children's connection to the motherline and ancestral memory.

The trope of flight also, as Demetrakopoulos observes, signifies "men [being] out of touch with the ground" (1987: 86). Demetrakopoulos argues that "the loss to the men's own soul development is perhaps an even more devastating result of [masculine flying]." Morrison values connectedness and community—markers of the ancestral memory and the funk—and sees them as essential for the psychological well-being of African Americans. Men, such as Milkman, who choose autonomy over attachment, individualism over connectedness, live a life bereft of meaning or purpose; their selves have no core or ground—for example, Milkman's image as "lack[ing] coherence" (75). The flying men in *Song of Solomon*—I include among them Solomon, Macon, Milkman, Guitar, Henry Porter, Robert Smith—are emotionally cut off and thus are unable to nurture themselves or others.[3]

When Milkman learns that his granddaddy could fly he becomes once again one of Morrison's flying men. He sees Solomon's flight as triumph and transcendence and does not concern himself with those that were left behind. It is not until Milkman returns to Pilate that his relational sense of self is restored. When Milkman comes to after being knocked unconscious by Pilate he realizes that Hagar is dead:

> He had hurt her, left her, and now she was dead—he was certain of it. He had left her. While he dreamt of flying, Hagar was dying. Sweet's silvery voice came back to him: "Who'd he leave behind?" He left Ryna behind and . . . children. . . . And Ryna had . . . lost her mind. . . . Who looked after those . . . children? Jesus Christ, he left twenty-one children! Guitar and the Days chose never to have children, Shalimer left his, but it was the children who sang about it and kept the story of his leaving alive. (336)

This passage is important because it shows that Milkman accepts responsibility for Hagar's death and that, in taking on this responsibility, he identifies with those that were left behind. He realizes, in Pilate's words, that "[y]ou just can't fly on off and leave a body" (336). "Under the tutelage of Pilate and other women," Wendy Harding and Jacky Martin write, "Milkman comes to learn of the limitation of flight as a mode of survival." *Song of Solomon,* they continue

> represents a reconsideration of the male adventure story, the Ulysses theme, from a woman's perspective. In a teasing allusion to Homer's epic, Morrison recreates Circe as an ancient survivor before whom Milkman appears

like a little boy. . . . From Sweet who responds . . . "Who'd he leave behind?"
Milkman learns to take into account other people's part in the conventional
heroic quest. After his quest Milkman returns not to a loyal and loving
Penelope but to a dead Hagar and an angry Pilate. By the end of the novel,
Milkman is beginning to remake himself as a new kind of man. (74)

His new connected and caring self is signified by the box of Hagar's hair that Milkman takes home. As Pilate did with what she believed to be the murdered white
man's bones, Milkman brings home the box of hair to mark both his commitment
to, and responsibility for the life that he had taken. The hair is also an "icon," as
Terry Otten observes, "of [Milkman's] black consciousness and his love" (60).
Trudier Harris argues that "when Milkman . . . discover[s] . . . his great-grandfather's
flying abilities, he has two options. He can continue the path of Solomon (celebration without commitment), or he can use the kinship as a sign to renew his ties to
his family" (1991: 106). I suggest that when Milkman accepts Pilate's teachings that
"you just can't fly on off and leave a body" he has chosen kinship over flight.

Significant for the theme of flight, Milkman and Pilate return to Shalimar
by car: "She wouldn't set foot on an airplane, so he drove" (338). There Guitar
shoots Pilate as she buries her father's bones. As she lies dying, Pilate says to Milkman: "I wished I'd a knowed more people. I would of loved 'em all. If I'd a
knowed more, I would a loved more." Moments before her death Pilate asks
Milkman to "'Sing,' she said. 'Sing a little something for me'" (340). Harding
and Martin argue that this episode suggests that "flying, the heroic act of detach-
ing oneself from the community, is not as vital as singing, defining a harmonious,
vital community by uniting singers in performance" (74). Milkman's singing thus
signifies that the self he has claimed at the conclusion of the novel is a communal one, connected to the motherline.

With Pilate's death, Morrison reconfigures the meaning of flight. Milkman
says of Pilate: "Now he knew why he loved her so. Without ever leaving the
ground, she could fly" (340). This truth is symbolized by the bird that flies away
with her name. Pilate flies, achieves transcendence if you will, not through a taking off but in relationships with others and through responsibility to others.
Pilate has, as Bjork points out, "combined the best aspects of self, place, and
motion" (109). With *Song*, Morrison radically alters notions of flight and freedom: displacing the masculinist impulse toward separateness and detachment,
Morrison positions relationships and responsibility as the way to be free and to
take flight. Milkman's decision to give himself to Guitar is predicated on this realization. Terry Otten writes, "The only 'flight' possible to Milkman is also symbolic, a spiritual and psychological flight assured when he no longer evades but
offers himself to his brother: 'You want my life? . . . You need it? Here'" (62).

Pilate, as noted in the previous chapter, embodies the ancient properties,
funk, and ancestral memory of African American culture and serves as the midwife for Milkman's birth and rebirth. In an interview with Nellie McKay (1983),
Morrison explains that Pilate is a step beyond:

Not Sula, but Eva. Pilate is a less despotic Eva. Eva is managerial. She tells
everybody what to do, and she will dispute everybody. Pilate can tell everybody what to do, but she's wide-spirited. She does run anybody's course.
She is very fierce about her children, but when she is told by her brother to
leave, she leaves, and does not return. She is wider scaled and less demand-
ing about certain things. She trusts certain things. She does behave in a protective way with her children, but that's purely maternal. This strong maternal instinct is part of her otherworldliness. Eva was this-worldly. She
wanted to arrange everybody's life and did so—and was generally liked.
(Taylor-Guthrie 1994: 144)

More specifically, Pilate is a personification of Morrison's maternal standpoint; namely, that black women are ship and harbor, inn and trail. As noted in
chapter 1, the funk is often conveyed through the metaphor of food: raw foods
represent the funk while commercially prepared foods such as candies signify the
capitalistic/materialist values of the dominant culture. Likewise, Pilate's ancient
properties are developed through food imagery. The imagery of fruit and eggs—
suggestive as they are of fertility—express Pilate's role as nurturer and cultural
bearer. When Milkman first meets Pilate it is the orange she is peeling that cap-
tures and holds his attention: "He kept on staring at her fingers, manipulating
the orange . . . he knew he could have watched her all day: the fingers pulling
thread veins from the orange sections . . ." (36–37). Later, however, he rejects the
soft-boiled egg Pilate offers to him. His refusal of the egg signifies that he is not
yet ready for Pilate's cultural bearing which will return him to the ancient properties, ancestral memory, and funk of his motherline.

The fruits associated with Pilate—oranges, peaches, and grapes—composed
as they are of both seed and juice, couple the feminine and masculine principles
to convey the ancient properties of ship and harbor, inn and trail of Pilate's character. Critics Wendy Harding and Jacky Martin argue that Morrison, with Pilate,

imagines an alternative to the dominant ideals of femininity that prove so
restrictive to her imitative women characters. Confounding stereotypes of
female fragility, Pilate is as strong as any man. She can knock Milkman
down a flight of stairs or boil him a perfect egg. Unique as she is, Pilate represents the type of self-invented black woman that Morrison celebrates not
only in her novels . . . but also in her nonfictional writings. (72)

Morrison, in an interview with Jones and Vinson (1985), says of Pilate: "She is
very sweet and nurturing and also very fierce. And she really does combine for
me, and I think that is what makes her unique, some male and female characteristics blended so they work" (Taylor-Guthrie 1994: 185). A spiritual healer and
nurturing mother for Milkman, Pilate is also a bootlegger. As her female avoca-
tion delivers nurturance, her male vocation requires independence. The tree
imagery associated with Pilate unites these two dimensions of her personality.
Macon chose the name for his daughter because the word suggested, in its visual

configuration, the shape of a tree: "confused and melancholy over his wife's death in childbirth, [Macon] had thumbed through the Bible, and since he could not read a word, chose a group of letters that seemed to him strong and handsome; saw in them a large figure that looked like a tree hanging in some princely but protective way over a row of smaller trees" (18). Milkman also describes Pilate as looking "like a tall black tree" (38). Like the princely and protective tree her name majestically creates, Pilate is both strong and nurturing.

In contrast to her brother, who is the self-made man of white American capitalist ideology, Pilate is a self-invented, self-created woman of the ancient proprieties. As the midwife Circe explains, Pilate "[b]orned herself. I had very little to do with it. I thought they were both dead, the mother and the child. When she popped out you could have knocked me over. I hadn't heard a heartbeat anywhere. She just came on out" (246). In an interview with Anne Koenen (1980), Morrison spoke about how, with *Song of Solomon,* she became "interested in a woman producing a woman producing a woman in a kind of non-male environment . . ." (Taylor-Guthrie 1994: 78). Pilate's giving birth to herself is, of course, symbolized by the absence of her navel. Ostracized by others because of this "deformity," Pilate was compelled to invent her own life, continue the self-creation that began in birth. As the text tells us:

> [W]hen she realized what her situation in the world was and would probably always be she threw away every assumption she had learned and began at zero. First off, she cut off her hair. That was one thing she didn't want to have to think about anymore. Then she tackled the problem of trying to decide how she wanted to live and what was valuable to her. When am I happy and when am I sad and what is the difference? What do I need to know to stay alive? What is true in the world? (150)

We are told that Pilate "acquired a deep concern for and about human relationships" and that "most important, she paid close attention to her mentor—her father who appeared before her sometimes and told her things" (150).

Signified here is a communal and ancestral connection that is predicated on a specific interpretation of time. Pilate experiences time as cyclical and expansive while Macon experiences it as linear and exclusive. Macon's conception of time always looks to the future while Pilate always returns to the past. Pilate is the quintessential cultural bearer. She sings the song of Solomon which tells the history of her ancestors. The stories she tells keep alive the memory of her family. "Storytelling is," as Joseph T. Skerrett observes, "the primary folk process in Toni Morrison's fictional world." Pilate is the central storyteller in *Song,* and in Skerrett's words, she is, "[the most] effective informant." Macon and Ruth tell their life stories to justify, excuse, or explain their behavior. Macon's story of his marriage, told immediately after he struck his wife, is a gesture of rationalization and justification. Ruth's story, told to her son after he finds her in the cemetery, is also motivated by the need to explain and account for what is perceived to be inappropriate behavior, her love for her father and the late nursing of her son. "It is

only Pilate," as Skerrett points out, "for whom storytelling is *not* self-dramatiza-
tion, self-justification, or ego-action" (Pryse 1985: 93–95). Pilate's stories are told
not to justify, explain, or even to amuse, but to educate and enlighten. Milkman
first learns the story of his paternal grandfather from Pilate; it is a narrative so
compelling that, in the words of the text, "the boys watched, afraid to say anything lest they ruin the next part of her story, and afraid to remain silent lest she
not go on with its telling" (43). Critic Deborah McDowell writes in her review
of *Jazz* that "Morrison's entire oeuvre has involved a studied effort . . . to make
the dry and disconnected bones of the black historical past live." In her storytelling Pilate is also engaged in narrative excavation.[4]

Karla Holloway suggests "there are archetypal children's needs, and these
show in Black children's special need for memory" (1987: 104). If black children
are to survive, Holloway continues, "they must come to know the stories, legends
and myths of their ancestors" (104). In *The Song of Solomon,* Milkman's survival
is made possible through Pilate's function of cultural bearer; she not only embodies, in her connection to the motherline, the ancient properties, funk, and ancestral memory of her people, she also conveys these values to her people, through
the stories she tells and the songs she sings. Scholars have long argued that this
novel provides those stories, legends, and myths of the ancestors needed for the
continuation of the motherline. In so doing, the novel explicates, for African
Americans who have lost their way, the route by which they may find the lost
funk, ancient properties, and ancestral memory of their tribe, to use Morrison's
terms. Toni Morrison once commented that she "wrote the books . . . I wanted
to read" (Russell 1988: 43). However, what has been less recognized is that it was
Pilate who piloted Milkman's journey home and who midwifed his rebirth. Had
it not been for Pilate, it is doubtful that Milkman would have been reconnected
to the motherline. The novel, as Holloway writes, "affirms our past and promises
us a future" (1987: 104). However, it does so both by mapping the route back to
the motherline *and* by describing for us the type of person qualified to lead us on
this journey. Ultimately, the novel shows that the former depends on the latter:
you can only find your way back if you have the right person to lead you. And
for Morrison, the only person able to do this is someone—man or woman—of
the ancient properties, funk, and ancestral memory; a cultural bearer who
embodies and delivers these values to his or her people.

JADINE'S EXILE AND THE
PROBLEMATIC OF MALE MOTHERING

Pilate is recognized, in the words of Joseph Skerrett, as "Morrison's most complex and concentrated image of an African-American in touch with the spiritual resources of Afro-American folk traditions" (263). Son, in Morrison's
fourth novel, is also portrayed, as Elliott Butler-Evans has observed, "[as] a
Black male whose existence is informed by an ideal and authentic Black culture" (158). In *Song of Solomon,* healing is made possible in an aunt/nephew
relationship in which the woman, Pilate, heals a man by returning him to his

motherline. Many critics see Son as a type of Pilate figure who offers healing
to Jadine in a heterosexual relationship.

Jadine, writes Marilyn Mobley, "remains a cultural orphan, in a state of permanent motherlessness" (291). Moreover, there is, as Samuels and Hudson-
Weems observe, "no Pilate in [Jadine's] life" (83). The novel, however, does position Son—"the man who valued fraternity over industry"—as a type of healer
who seeks to return Jadine to her motherline as Pilate did with Song. However,
as examined in chapter 2, Jadine's quest is ultimately a failed one. At the conclusion of the text occurs a particularly telling image given the above discussion
about flight and Pilate's fear of planes: Jadine, on a plane returning to France, is
described as "feeling lean and male" (275).[5] Thus, while the novel presents Son
as a cultural bearer and though he is frequently read as a healer in the style of
Pilate, he ultimately cannot save Jadine as Pilate does with Milkman. The text
asks us to consider why Son is not able to be a Pilate for Jadine. *Tar Baby* ultimately argues that Son, though embodying African American funk, cannot
restore Jadine because of his identification with patriarchal masculinity.

In her book *Archetypal Patterns in Women's Fiction*, Annis Pratt argues that
in women's novels of rebirth and transformation, there is often the archetype of
what she calls the green world lover. The green world lover, Pratt explains, "is an
ideal, nonpatriarchal lover [who] sometimes appears as an initiatory guide and
often aids at difficult points in the [woman's] quest" (140). This figure, Pratt
continues, "leads the hero away from society and towards her own unconscious
depths" (140). As a guide, the green world lover delivers the hero to her own
unconscious self where she, in the words of the feminist theologian Carol
Christ, "discovers a new naming of self and world." Significantly, the green
world lover is, in Pratt's words, "matrilinear . . . and suggests a realm of inherited feminine power quite different from patriarchal culture" (141). Son is often
seen by critics as such a green world lover archetype, a reading underscored by
Son's last name—Green. Son certainly is identified with the feminine. He is
introduced through images of birth: "[He immersed himself] in water so soft
and warm" (3). The narrator tells us that "[Son] floated as best he could in water
that heaved and pulsed in the ammonia-scented air." This image suggests the
amniotic waters of the womb, while the, "bracelet tighten[ing]" and the
"whirling . . . vortex," suggest the labor contractions of birth. Son attempts to
make it to shore, but is held back by the "gentle but firm" push of the water:
"Like the hand of an insistent woman it pushed him. He fought hard to break
through, but couldn't. The hand was forcing him away from the shore. The man
turned his head to see what lay behind him. All he saw was water, blood tinted
by a sun sliding into it like a fresh heart" (4). The shore, in this description, in
particular the pier, suggests the male realm of culture while the blood-tinted sea
implies the maternal space of the womb.

Significantly, the "water-lady cup[s Son] . . . in the palm of her hand, and
nudge[s] him out to sea" (5). While Son initially resists the water lady he eventually decides to let her "carry him for awhile" (4). The text thus positions Son

as a pre-Oedipal son. Like Plum in *Sula,* Son is identified with the feminine and the maternal. Therese, the woman with the magic breasts, "adopts" Son as her own and provides him with both food and counsel. At the conclusion of the novel, Therese returns Son to the horse men whose nakedness and blindness signify the maternal space of the pre-Oedipal. Significantly, Therese calls Son "small boy" and instructs him to "crawl" along the rocks to the shore and tells him to "don't see; feel . . . you can feel your way . . ." (304).

Son is also associated with nature and fertility. He causes Valerian's plant to blossom. A moment before Son "flicked the stem of the cyclamen" we are told that "his kimono came undone at the belt and fell away from his body . . . [exposing] his genitals and the skinny black thighs" (148). Significantly, Son's sexuality is specifically linked with fertility, an association usually reserved for female sexuality. Peter Erickson argues in "Images of Nurturance in *Tar Baby*" that "[t]he images of fruitfulness and birth associated with Son are designed to win our approval, while the corresponding negative images for Jadine neatly undercut our sympathy" (Gates 1993: 301). Jadine's admiration for the coat made of "ninety baby seals stitched together so nicely you could not tell what part had sheltered their cute little hearts and which had cushioned their skulls" is contrasted to Son's memory of live seals "gliding like shadows in water off the coast of Greenland." Son's sexuality is thus portrayed as fertile, life-giving, while Jadine's sexuality is seen as sterile. As his name suggests, Son is also a man defined through his family and ancestral relations. He thus possesses a relational sense of self that is usually seen as a feminine subject position.

Son's connection to ancestors, community, and family signifies the ancient properties and ancestral memory of black womanhood. In each of Morrison's novels, there is a clearly demarcated opposition between the values of the African American worldview and that of the dominant white culture. Whether symbolized by opposing households, as in *Song of Solomon,* or by individuals, the texts juxtapose cultural values. In *Tar Baby,* Son embraces the ancient properties, while Jadine denies them.

Like Pilate in *Song of Solomon,* Son is also a spiritual guide, who summons Jadine upon a journey into self and back through time. Through him, as Holloway observes, "Morrison gives Jadine the ultimate opportunity to confront her past as well as her femininity" (1987: 121). As Mbalia argues in *Toni Morrison's Developing Class Consciousness,* Son struggles to make Jadine aware of capitalist values and practices that divide her from her heritage. Mbalia writes: "[Son] attempts to kill Jadine's old capitalist-class affiliations and instill new people-orientated ones. And while he never gets her to forsake her capitalist ideology, [he] does help [Jadine] become more conscious of herself as an African" (79).⁶ What Son demands of Jadine is nothing less than a new self, formed in and through the ancient properties and funk of her motherline.

When Son first meets Jadine she aligns herself with the white Street family: "It depends on what you want from us." To which Son responds: "Us? You call yourself 'us'" (118). Although Jadine is not, as Son points out, "a member of the family," she assumes kinship with her white benefactors, the Streets. She dines with the Streets and is waited upon by Sydney, her uncle. She sleeps upstairs in what is textually demarcated as white space, while Ondine and Sydney, and later Son, stay downstairs.[7] Later, when Jadine accuses Son of being a rapist, he responds: "Rape? Why you little white girls always think somebody's trying to rape you?" When Jadine protests that she is not white, Son says: "Then why don't you settle down and stop acting like it" (121).

Son is the only major character in the book who embodies the funk, and who voices criticism of the values of the white dominant culture. He is also, arguably, the least selfish, least pretentious, and most decent character in the novel. He is the one who returns to Yardman his humanity and dignity: "It bothered him that everybody called Gideon Yardman, as though he had not been mothered" (161). And he also honors women in their humanity and dignity: "Anybody who thought women were inferior didn't come out of north Florida" (268). For these reasons many readers of *Tar Baby* interpret Son as Morrison's spokesperson or, at the very least, the embodiment of the values she holds dear. Moreover, Son's presence in the text certainly allows Morrison to critique Jadine's denial of her ancient properties.

However, the above reading of Son as the embodiment of the ancestral memory cannot explain why Son fails at saving Jadine. A close reading of the text shows that the reason Son cannot save Jadine or ultimately himself is because Son, despite his maternal sensibilities, lives his life and defines himself in accordance with the script of traditional patriarchal masculinity. Son's views and beliefs are more often than not sexist. His behavior is consistently arrogant and aggressive, domineering and dismissive. And despite his stance to the contrary, he has divorced himself from his motherline and disavowed his family, and in particular his mother. Finally, Son is indisputably violent: he murdered one woman and battered another.

Some critics have called attention to the several sexist comments made by, or attributed to, Son in the narrative. In the greenhouse with Valerian, Son remarks: "I know all about plants. They like women, you have to jack them up every once in a while" (148). In Eloe, Drake says about Son: "[He] knows people. He just gets confused when it comes to women. With most everything else he thinks with his heart. But when it comes to women he thinks with his dick . . ." (255). These two statements tell us that Son objectifies woman as Other. To him, women are "not people," they are "like plants." Moreover, interwoven with these obvious—and often-quoted—examples of Son's sexism are other, more subtle sexist sentiments and statements.

Son first "meets" Jadine when she is asleep. We are told that he enters—a clearly phallic connotation—her room and watches her sleep in the predawn light. She is for him the fairy tale Sleeping Beauty waiting to be woken by her prince. Significantly, as Son watches her sleep, the narrator tells us:

> [He] thought hard . . . in order to manipulate her dreams, to insert *his* own dreams into her so she would not wake or stir . . . and dream steadily the

dream he wanted her to have about yellow houses with white doors which women opened and shouted Come on in, you honey you! and the fat black ladies in white dresses minding the pie table in the basement of the church and white wet sheets flapping on a line. . . . (119, emphasis added)

No critic, to my knowledge, has examined Son's wish "to press his dreams . . . into hers." Patrick Bjork acknowledges that Son does attempt "to impart to [Jadine] his dream, [his] rural folk consciousness" (121). However, Bjork does not view this desire as at all problematic. Yet Son wants Jadine to forgo her dreams and fulfil his. "Insert[ing] his dreams into hers," Son redesigns, in Pygmalion fashion, another Jadine, one crafted from his idealized and romanticized view of blackness. His male imposition invokes a very conventional patriarchal assertion of the husband-on-top heterosexuality, theorized by Miriam Johnson and discussed earlier.

The town of Eloe signifies and embodies for Son the funk values of traditional black culture. Craig H. Werner argues in "The Briar Patch as Modernist Myth: Morrison, Barthes, and Tar Baby As-Is" that Son's ideal of essential blackness as represented by Eloe is a "romantic counter myth" which "evades reality by dehistoricizes experience." Werner continues, "by embracing [this myth, Son] dehistoricizes Jadine's complex history as a black woman" (McKay 1988: 164–65). Indeed, by mythologizing Jadine and making her an archetype of black womanhood—fat black lady minding the pies—Son robs Jadine of her own specific and individual identity. Significantly, when Son first meets Jadine he cannot look at her; he chooses instead to look at her pictures because they are "easier . . . they don't move" (119). This, I argue, indicates Son's refusal to see Jadine as a real and so a changing person and his wish to fix her in a mythological narrative.[8]

His statement about Florida women notwithstanding, Son subscribes to sexist categorizations of gender difference. When Son sees Margaret and Jadine leaving the boat, he tells us that: "It amused him that these tiny women had handled that big boat" (133). Later, in New York City, Son reflects upon Jadine "having *his* baby" and wonders about "What would he name his son? Son of Son?" (219). With these words, Son expresses a patriarchal reproductive consciousness that regards, as Barbara Katz Rothman writes, "children [as] being born to men, out of women" (30). In keeping with patriarchal reproductive consciousness, Son sees the male seed as the defining and original essence of identity, one planted by the father in the mother's body. Equally problematic is Son's assumption that the child will be male. With these views, Son expresses the age-old patriarchal preference for sons and maintains the patriarchal practice of patrilineal descent—"he will be the son of son."

In reading Son as a maternal and feminine figure, critics ignore the phallocentric discourse by which he is also delineated. In the scene where Son first takes a shower in Jadine's bathroom, the language, pardon the pun, pulsates with phallic imagery. We are told that "[Son] squeezed [the sponge] . . . again, but lightly this time, loving the juice it gave him." He pumped the spout, and later pumped the bath gel. The water spray is "too hard" so Son "fiddled with the head until he got mist instead of buckshot." After getting some lather in his mouth Son is "reminded of a flavor he could not name. He sprayed more and swallowed it. It did not taste like water, it tasted like milk. He squirted it all around in his mouth before pressing the button to shut off the water" (131–32). While the reference to the milk suggests the maternal and supports the interpretation of Son as the pre-Oedipal son, the many references to male sexuality and anatomy here also characterize Son as a male whose sexuality is expressed in a highly phallocentric manner.

A few pages before the shower scene occurs the brilliant and often quoted description of Son's hair: "Here, alone in her bedroom . . . his hair looked overpowering—physically overpowering, like bundles of long whips or lashes that could grab her and beat her to jelly. And would. Wild. Aggressive, vicious hair that needed to be put in jail. Uncivilized, reform-school hair. Mau Mau. Attica, chain-gang hair" (113). Son's dreadlocks are a trope for his sexuality and presage the phallocentricism suggested in the shower scene. The text thus characterizes Son's sexual self as overpowering, wild, aggressive, vicious, and uncivilized. His presence, as the text tells us time and time again, unsettles the otherwise cool and calm Jadine, causing her to "grab the leashes" to keep the "dark dogs" at bay. The aggressiveness and phallocentricism of Son's sexuality is part of his larger masculine propensity for violence.

Son is a murderer. When he found Cheyenne in bed with another man, he murdered her by driving his car through the house causing it to explode and the house to catch fire. He tells Jadine that he "meant the killing but . . . didn't mean the death" (175). Significantly, when Son tells Jadine of the murder, he does not name his wife. In his narrative, Cheyenne has no identity or history: she is presented only as a statistic, yet another faceless victim of domestic violence. In *Mythmaking and Metaphor in Black Women's Fiction* (1991), Jacqueline de Weever observes that: "no records attest to [Son's] existence, except those that show his arrest and charge for murder" (38). While many critics make reference to Son's murder of Cheyenne, they read the killing as an isolated event, an unfortunate accident. I suggest that the killing is part of Son's larger pattern of violence. Later, when Son tells Jadine about the murder of Cheyenne he realizes that "[Jadine] is scared. . . . In the company of a killer on an island . . . she is too scared. *Suddenly he liked it. Liked her fear.* Basked in it like a cat in steam-pipe heat and it made him feel protective and violent at the same time" (177, emphasis added). Jadine's fear, in the words of the text, "alarmed and pleased" him. Son is also comforted by Jadine's fear: he basked in it like a cat in steam pipe heat. A disturbing association is made between care and harm; in this passage Son feels both protective of and violent toward Jadine. Not surprisingly, Son says to her: "I won't kill you, I love you" (177), a blurring of love and hate common to situations of domestic violence. There is also the suggestion that Son is sexually aroused by Jadine's fear. Son recognizes that he frightened Jadine and caused her to tuck her legs under her skirt. Son pleads with Jadine in highly sexualized language to "unfold" her legs—"Come on. . . . Show me. Please?" Once her foot is revealed, the narrator tells us that: "Son did it. Put his forefinger on her sole and held it and held it and held it there" (179). Son's desire originates from Jadine's fear; his violence is linked with eroticism.

After Son's return from Eloe, the violence, which the text earlier represented through metaphor and suggestion, is expressed through actual physical aggression. During one fight the narrator tells us that:

> [Jadine] slapped [Son] and before he could turn his head back she was choking him with both hands around his neck, screaming all the while. . . . He pulled her hair until she let go and when she tried another blow, he dropped her as carefully as he could. She fell back on her behind, turned over and crawled on all fours to jump him again. He held her arms behind her back and she bit him to his teeth. The pain was so powerful he had to put out her light with his fist. (263–64)

This fight can be interpreted in several ways. One could argue that the violence described here is simply a lover's quarrel gone too far, a case of the lovers' emotions getting the better of them: regrettable but understandable. Or the violence is nothing more than a good old-fashioned fist fight, a duel among worthy equals: she bit and choked him, he dropped and punched her. Perhaps one might argue that Son had no choice but to punch Jadine, after all she was "bit[ing] him to the teeth." Or maybe the b____ simply had it coming. These explanations, I argue, are rationalizations that attempt to justify, trivialize, or naturalize Son's violence. What this passage describes is nothing less than spousal assault. Son knocks Jadine unconscious. He does not leave the room or attempt to calm Jadine when, in anger, she turns on him; rather, he uses his greater physical strength to end the dispute by way of physical violence. What Son does is wrong. It is also illegal.

Son's crime of spousal assault is never acknowledged as such by Jadine, Son, or the narrator. Rather, the crime is trivialized and made into a joke. After the assault, we are told that "Jadine dressed the bite marks on his face; and they said, 'Ollieballen,' laughing as best they could with the bruises." It is interesting to note that only Son's injuries are specifically mentioned and actually tended, although Jadine is also injured. Also significant is Son's response to Jadine's injuries. The narrator tells us that "When [Jadine] came to and touched her jaw [Son] went wild thinking he had loosened one of the side teeth so precious *to him*" (264, emphasis added). Son does not show remorse for his violence or concern for Jadine's suffering.

In the following scene Son also resorts to violence to end, in that instance, a verbal argument between Jadine and himself. The narrator tells us that

> Son picked her up and took her to the window. After a violent struggle he actually held her out of it by her wrists. . . . It was only ten feet off the ground and she wet her pants but still she hollered loud enough for him to

hear as well as the few people gathered on the side walk to watch. "You want to be a yardman all your life?" . . . When he pulled her back in, her arms were so sore she could not move them. (264–65)

In this passage, violence is again trivialized: an assault is turned into a farcical slapstick adventure, a freak sideshow. We are told Son calls her an "educated nitwit" and that "Jadine wet her pants though she was only ten feet off the ground." The language undercuts the seriousness of the incident. If we ignore the farcical language, the seriousness of the event becomes apparent: Jadine wetting herself reveals that she was genuinely afraid; she would have sustained injuries had she been thrown to the pavement ten feet below. We do not see Jadine's legitimate fear and the real likelihood of harm because of the farcical tone of the passage. The truth is that Jadine and Son are engaged in what the text itself describes as "a violent struggle." In the following paragraph the narrator tells us that

> [w]hen he [Son] pulled her back in, her arms were so sore she could not move them. But she was curled up teary-eyed in his lap an hour later when the doorbell rang. Son was massaging her shoulder, and begging forgiveness. They both went to the door and looked so lovey-dovey the police thought they had the wrong apartment, it must have been somebody else throwing a woman out of the window. (265)

The police, we are told, arrive an hour after the incident was reported. The lengthy delay in response time suggests that the police do not regard Son's assault of Jadine as a crime. The police only recently have come to view domestic violence as a serious crime. The police, as African American singer/song-writer Tracy Chapman reminds us, "always come late if they come at all." While the delay referred to in this passage may be only an accurate reflection of the racism and sexism of a 1970s New York City police force, nonetheless, it contributes to the overall trivializing and naturalizing of violence in the text. The arrival of the police, however, does suggest that at least one person saw Son's treatment of Jadine as a crime and reported it.

What is most disturbing in this passage is Jadine's forgiveness of Son. Domestic violence follows a cyclical pattern: episodes of escalating violence culminate in a particularly bad assault. This is followed by a period of calm and renewed love, the so-called honeymoon phase, during which the man pleads for forgiveness and promises never to do it again. Jadine and Son are described as looking "lovey-dovey" and Son, we are told, begs for forgiveness. The description suggests that the cycle is about to repeat itself.

Violence against women in *Tar Baby* is trivialized and naturalized. The murder of Cheyenne and the battering of Jadine do not receive the same serious attention as the rape in *The Bluest Eye*. Only one critic, to my knowledge, calls Son a murderer and a batterer.[9]

Jadine and Son's relationship, rather, is typically analyzed in terms of the folktale of Tar Baby, an organizing theme of the narrative explicitly mentioned by Son during an argument with Jadine in New York. After accusing Jadine of "taking care of white babies and turning black babies into white ones" and seeing the disgust in Jadine's eyes, Son tells her the story of Tar Baby. What Son emphasizes in his story is that the tar baby is made by the white farmer in order to trap the rabbit—"He made him a tar baby. He made it, you hear me? He made it!" (270). Allegorically, the tar baby is Jadine, who is made by her white benefactor, Mr. Street. Son, of course, is the rabbit about to be ensnared in the white man's trap. In *Fiction and Folklore: The Novels of Toni Morrison,* Trudier Harris argues that Jadine is both trickster and tar baby: "Her femininity makes her a tar baby, but her color makes her a trickster (identified with the white farmer to whom Son refers)" (125–26). Son calls her: "Gatekeeper, advance bitch, house-bitch, welfare office torpedo, corporate cunt, tar baby side-of-the road whore trap . . ." (219–20). She traps him with her beauty and, in Harris's words, "[s]he wants to trick Son into acceptance of the emasculating (for black men) values of American economic and social system" (125). But Son, Harris goes on to emphasize, is also a tar baby figure. Indeed, one could argue, as the critic Bjork does, that "the entrapment more fully resides in Son's own desire for and possession of Jadine" (126). Son, as we have seen, attempts to define, own, and control Jadine, "[to] insert his dreams into hers."

But even if we interpret Son as the ensnared rabbit, as do most of the critics, the characterization of Son as the tricked/wronged one in the story, I argue, actually serves to emphasize Son's aggressive masculinity and the violence associated with it. Significantly, in Joel Chandler Harris's version of the tale, Uncle Remus refers to the tar baby as "she." Brer Rabbit, so the story goes, attempts to get the Tar Baby to speak to him:

> You er stuck up, dat's w'at you is . . . I'm gwine ter larn you how ter talk ter 'spectubble folks . . . ef you don't take off dat hat en tell me howdy, I'm gwine ter bus' you wide open . . . Brer Rabbit keep on axin' im, en de Tar-Baby, she keep on sayin' nothin, twel present'y Brer Rabbit draw back wid his fis', he did, en blip he tuck 'er side er de head. Fight dar's whar he broke his merlasses jug. . . . Ef you don't lemme loose I'll knock ou agin . . . en wid dat he fotch'er a wipe de udder han' . . . Tu'n me loose, fo' I kick de natchul stuffin' out'n. . . . (7)

The rabbit is angered when the tar baby does not show respect and deference toward him, just as Son is angered by Jadine. Both Brer Rabbit and Son threaten and resort to violence when a female does not respond as they wish. Both also take their anger and frustration out on a woman.

In all, Son is not an unproblematic character. More particularly, Son's sexism, and in particular his arrogant, aggressive, and abusive behavior toward women prevents him from being a male mother and providing the maternal nurturance that makes healing possible. Moreover, although Son does seem to represent the funk and seeks to return Jadine to her motherline, he does not practice the maternal philosophy that he preaches. Son is said to value fraternity above all else: "He could not give up the last thing left to him—fraternity" (168). However, we are told, time and time again, that he is a loner who has wandered from place to place—"In those eight homeless years he had joined that great underclass of undocumented men" (166). While Son condemns Jadine for having no communal/familial grounding, it is Son, and not Jadine, who fails to write home to his folks—"How come you never put no note or nothing in them envelopes? I kept on looking for a note" (120). For all his talk of his love for his people, Son's treatment of Alma is dismissive for he forgets to bring the wig that he had promised and which meant so much to her. Son's sense of self is expressed as the separate, individuated, autonomous, self-sufficient, alone sense of self championed by the normative ideology of patriarchal masculinity. Most significantly, Son makes little mention of his mother or his own motherline. This disconnection from kin and in particular his mother and motherline, signifies that Son's funk values are more preached than practiced. Men and women, according to Morrison, acquire the funk, ancestral memory and ancient properties in and through connection with the motherline. Son is not and cannot be a cultural bearer of the African American motherline. Because his patriarchal masculinity is predicated upon disconnection as opposed to relationality and is manifested in aggression, arrogance, and abuse, Son cannot be, as Pilate was for Macon, Jadine's cultural bearer or healer.

CONCLUSION

Morrison's reflections on reconnection to the motherline in *Song of Solomon* and *Tar Baby* both complicate and clarify her maternal philosophy. While *Song* maps a clear trajectory of return, it qualifies or problematizes this trajectory by insisting that the success of such a quest is contingent upon the individual characteristics of the person who initiates and directs the protagonist's journey. Milkman's deliverance is made possible by Pilate who, unlike Son, truly and authentically guides, mentors, and heals in accordance with the values of the African American motherline. Likewise, Son, despite his and the critics' claims to the contrary, exiles Jadine from her motherline because he embodies and enacts patriarchal masculinity, the values of which stand in sharp contrast to those of the motherline. However, in complicating the conditions of motherline reconnection, Morrison clarifies her maternal standpoint through the characterization of Pilate and Son. Through Pilate, Morrison makes flesh the philosophical abstractions of her maternal standpoint of black woman as ship and harbor, inn and trail. In so doing, *Song* provides not only a detailed map of the route back home, as the critics have long pointed out, but also *Song* and *Tar Baby* describe who may be qualified to guide people on this journey. In this, the novels make clear that such a guide, whether male or female, must model and mentor the teachings of the motherline. Son fails not because he is man but because he is not truly a son of the motherline.

chapter five

Maternal Interventions

Resistance and Power:
The Bluest Eye, Sula, Song of Solomon, Tar Baby,
Beloved, Paradise

THE RUPTURE AND REPAIR of the motherline were examined in the previous three chapters. This chapter emphasizes how mothers themselves seek to sustain the motherline and empower their children through the maternal tasks of preservation, nurturance, and cultural bearing. Black mothers are the cultural bearers who model and mentor the ancient properties and the funk of the motherline. Likewise, black mothers, through both preservation and nurturance, seek to ensure the physical survival and psychological well-being of their children. In each of these functions—cultural bearing, preservation, and nurturance—mothering is represented in Morrison as a site of resistance, or more specifically an act of intervention against racist practices that cause injury to both the African American motherline and its people. As chapters 2 and 3 observed disconnections and disruptions of the motherline and chapter 4 looked at how one may be returned to the motherline, this chapter examines how mothers seek to prevent motherline loss and the psychological wounding it occasions by claiming maternal power and performing the maternal functions of cultural bearing, preservation, and nurturance.

Chapter 1 argued that black mothers, by way of preservative love, keep children alive in a world hostile to their well-being. Through maternal nurturance, black women seek to immunize their children from racist ideologies: in loving her children, a mother instills in them a loved sense of self that enables children to resist and refuse internalization of racist ideologies. Finally, through cultural bearing, the mother imparts to her children the African American values of the funk and the ancient proprieties that enable them to form a proud and strong African American identity. These three strategies—preservation, nurturance,

117

cultural bearing—of maternal intervention are explored in the first section of this chapter through a consideration of the preservative love of Mrs. MacTeer and Eva Peace, the cultural bearing of Mrs. MacTeer, and the maternal nurturance of Sethe. In each of these three tasks, mothers seek to protect their children and empower them so that they may grow whole and strong in a world destined to harm and maim them.

The second section of this chapter considers the theme of failed maternal nurturance. Ruth in *Song,* Margaret in *Tar Baby,* and the women in *Paradise* all display problematic, and in the case of Margaret, abusive maternal behavior. Ineffectual or failed mothering, as noted in chapter 1, signifies in Morrison's fiction, an act of resistance against patriarchy and in particular the patriarchal institution of motherhood. Mothers in Morrison, as they confront racism on behalf of their children, also challenge their own oppression in the patriarchal institution of motherhood. Patriarchal motherhood is oppressive to both white and black mothers but it is particularly harmful to black women because, as noted in chapter 1, it prevents black women from fulfilling their essential cultural bearing function. Resistance to patriarchal motherhood is conveyed in the many instances of failed maternal roles and fractured relationships in the novel *Paradise,* Ruth's "deviant" maternal practices, in particular the "late" nursing of her son, and Margaret's abuse of her son Michael.

Mothering as resistance—whether to be conveyed against white supremacy or patriarchal motherhood—challenges the normative discourse of motherhood that configures mothering as simply and solely private and emotional. Motherhood in the dominant culture has frequently been regarded as the cause of women's oppression in patriarchal culture. Mothers are understood to be powerless and disempowered. In contrast, African American motherhood, as explained in chapter 1, allows mothers, as Nina Jenkins explains, "to develop a belief in their own empowerment [while] providing a base for self-actualization" (206). Building upon this theme, Morrison developed the maternal standpoint of black mothers as ship and harbor, inn and trail, a standpoint that defines motherhood as a site of power for black women. From this position, black women seek to empower their children.

However, in Morrison's fiction, as explained in chapter 1, black mothers, despite the power of their maternal standpoint, must mother their children in a world hostile to them and often must battle to provide the preservation, nurturance, and cultural bearing necessary for the empowerment of their children. Morrison's fiction affirms and confirms the importance of motherwork by detailing the personal and cultural suffering that occurs when it is absent. Likewise, Morrison's fiction bespeaks the despair and rage of mothers who, in the face of racism and poverty, are not able to fulfill these essential tasks of motherwork. Morrison's novels often center upon a mother's desperate, frequently heroic, struggle to provide preservation, nurturance, and cultural bearing for her children. At times, as with Sethe in *Beloved,* a mother must resort to extreme measures, the murder of her child, in order to provide protection. The final section of this chapter will examine the mother Eva in *Sula* and her murder of her adult son Plum. Eva, recognizing that she cannot save her son from his drug addiction and imminent death, decides to end his life. In making this decision, Eva acts upon a maternal power that society denies to her as a black mother. From Eva's perspective, the murder of her son is done through love and as an act of preservation. This final section, as it argues that this murder, for Eva, is an act of preservative love, will explore why readers fail to consider the murder from the mother's perspective and instead condemn Eva for it. The murder distresses readers, I will argue, precisely because Eva claims a maternal power that upsets comfortable notions of maternal powerlessness, particularly as such pertains to black women, who are expected to be powerless in a racist and sexist culture. However, while such expressions of maternal power may disturb readers, maternal power, according to Morrison, is essential for black mothers to perform the necessary tasks of motherwork. This section will argue that Eva acted upon her power as a mother to do what she believed was best for her child. This, according to Morrison's maternal standpoint and theory of motherwork, *is* what black mothers should do. The issue for readers of *Sula* should not be that Eva acted upon maternal power; but rather that murder was the only way she could nurture and protect her beloved child.

RESISTANCE AGAINST RACISM

PRESERVATIVE LOVE: "THIS CHILD'S GONNA LIVE"

Mariah Upshur, the African American mother in Sara Wright's novel *This Child's Gonna Live* (1986), declares, "Don't care how much death is in the land, I got to make preparations for my baby to live" (Wright 143). "Preserving the lives of children," as noted earlier is "the central constitute, invariant aim of maternal practice" (Ruddick 1989, 19). Though maternal practice is a response to two other demands—nurturance and training—this first response, what Ruddick defines as preservative love, is what describes much of economically disadvantaged African Americans' motherwork. Mothering for many black women, particularly among the poor, is about ensuring the physical survival of their children and those of the larger black community. Securing food and shelter, struggling to build and sustain safe neighborhoods, is what defines both the meaning and experience of black women's motherwork and motherlove. However, normative discourses of motherhood, particularly in its current configuration as sensitive mothering, define motherlove and motherwork solely as nurturance. "Physical survival," writes Collins, "is assumed for children who are white and middle class. The choice to thus examine their psychic and emotional well-being . . . appears rational. The children of women of color, many of whom are 'physically starving' have no such choices however" (Forcey 1987: 49). While exclusive to middle-class white women's experiences of mothering, the normative discourse of mothering as nurturance, as noted in chapter 1, has been naturalized as the universal normal experience of motherhood. Preservative love, such as that practiced by

Mrs. MacTeer in *The Bluest Eye* and Eva in *Sula,* is not regarded as real, legitimate, or "good enough" mothering. For Morrison, this pathologizing of preservative love is particularly problematic because only by way of preservative love can black women keep alive their children in a world hostile to their well-being. Preservative love is at the heart of black women's motherwork.

Mrs. MacTeer in *The Bluest Eye* expresses her motherlove through the practices of preservative love. This love however has seldom been acknowledged by the critics. While Marco Portales, for example, does concede that Claudia had "the essential support, [to withstand] the ubiquitous daily messages which tell her that she is a 'nothing,'" he goes on to argue that the way Mrs. MacTeer introduced her children to the boarder Mr. Henry ("here is the bathroom; the clothes closet is here; and these are my kids, Frieda and Claudia; watch out for this window; it don't open all the way") (16) reveals, in his words, "[that] although she does love her girls, Mrs. MacTeer doesn't really know better—she has had little schooling and this is the forties" (495–96). Michael Awkward argues that each black family in *The Bluest Eye* seeks to be the desired family of the primer and that "[t]he first such apparent failure chronicled in the text involved the MacTeer home's state of physical and emotional disrepair. In direct contrast to the primer house which is 'green and white', 'has a red door,' and is 'very pretty' is the 'old, cold, green' MacTeer house. The structure's physical disrepair is symbolized in its inability to protect its inhabitants from cold (and cold germ-bearing winds). Its apparent emotional impoverishment is exemplified for the novel's first person narrator by her mother's apparently insensitive reaction to her daughter's contraction of a cold and her resultant vomiting" (1993: 93).[1] The passage to which Awkward refers reads as follows:

> My mother's voice drones on, she is not talking to me. She is talking to the puke, but she is calling it my name: Claudia. She wipes it up as best she can and puts a scratchy towel over the large wet place. I lie down again. The rags have fallen from the window crack, and the air is cold. I dare not call her back and am reluctant to leave my warmth. My mother's anger humiliates me; her words chafe my cheeks, and I am crying. I do not know that she is not angry at me, but at my sickness. I believe she despises my weakness for letting the sickness "take holt." By and by I will not get sick; I will refuse to. But for now I am crying. I know I am making more snot, but I can't stop. (13–14)

Claudia realizes that her mother is speaking not to her but to her illness, as represented by the puke, and from her adult perspective Claudia further realizes that her mother is angry not at her but at the sickness which causes her daughter's suffering and threatens her life. As an adult Claudia reflects:

> But was it really like that? As painful as I remember? Only mildly. Or rather, it was productive and fructifying pain. Love, thick and dark as Alaga syrup, eased up into that cracked window. I could smell it—taste it—sweet,

musty, with an edge of wintergreen in its base—everywhere in that house. It stuck, along with my tongue, to the frosted windowpanes. It coated my chest, along with the salve, and when the flannel came undone in my sleep, the clear sharp curves of air outlined its presence on my throat. And in the night, when my coughing was dry and tough, feet padded into the room, hands repinned the flannel, readjusted the quilt, and rested a moment on my forehead. So when I think of autumn, I think of somebody with hands who does not want me to die. (14)

Claudia's adult perspective shifts Awkward's interpretation of Mrs. MacTeer. He writes: "This passage suggests Claudia's rejection of white evaluative standards vis-a-vis Afro-American life. Thus, her childhood, formerly conceived in a vocabulary of pain—her mother's droning voice, the scratchy wet towel, the coldness of the air—has been reconceptualized as filled with protective, 'sweet,' 'thick and dark' love of a mother 'who does not want me to die'" (1993: 93). Awkward only values Mrs. MacTeer's mothering when the adult Claudia "reinterprets" it. However, from the perspective of Morrison's theory of motherwork and her emphasis upon the importance of preservation, the droning voice and scratchy towel are to be seen as real and legitimate gestures of maternal love; we should not need the adult Claudia to explain this for us. This critic relies on Claudia's adult perspective because he measures Mrs. MacTeer's mothering against the dominant discourses of "good mothering."

In descriptions of Mrs. MacTeer's caretaking of Claudia, her hands are often emphasized. We are told, in a passage Awkward does not quote: "Her hands are large and rough, and when she rubs the Vicks salve on my chest, I am rigid with pain. She takes two fingers' full of it at a time, and massages my chest until I am faint. Just when I think I will tip over into a scream, she scoops out a little of the salve on her forefinger and puts it in my mouth, telling me to swallow" (13). This passage describes a genuine concern; although contemporary readers may not see Mrs. MacTeer's actions as soft or sensitive enough, they do denote love. That this caretaking is conveyed through hands is also significant. In Morrison's writing, hands signify care and concern. When the women tend to Cholly's aunt Jimmy who is dying, their care is expressed through their hands.[2] M'Dear's hands, like those of Mrs. MacTeer, thus both comfort and diagnose; they provide healing through love and knowledge.

Claudia's father, Mr. MacTeer, also plays a crucial role in the successful raising of his daughters. Trudier Harris calls Mr. MacTeer a "provider, loving parent, protector" and argues that "although [he] has a less conspicuous place in the novel than his wife, his concern for his daughters equals hers, and he works equally hard to ensure their moral development" (1991: 41). Mr. MacTeer is described as "[w]olf killer turned hawk fighter, he worked night and day to keep one from the door and the other from under the windowsills" (52). When Mr. MacTeer learns that Frieda has been sexually molested by Mr. Henry, the boarder, we are told that he "threw [the] old tricycle at his head and knocked him off the porch" and then chased him down the street with a shotgun (80). Given that girls typically are not believed when they report incest and/or sexual assault, Mr. MacTeer's swift and forceful response is all the more commendable. It is, of course, in stark contrast to Pauline's response to Pecola. There is no doubt that this father seeks to protect his daughters, believes them, and avenges any wrong done to them.[3]

Preservative love is also a central theme in Morrison's second novel, *Sula*. At issue, however, are not only the critics' views on this topic but also those of the characters themselves, particularly as they are debated in the oft-cited dialogue between Eva and Hannah on the meaning of motherlove. Prior to this conversation we were told that the mother, Eva, in 1895 was left by her husband with "$1.65, five eggs, three beets," and three children to feed. After her baby son nearly dies from constipation, Eva leaves her children in the care of a neighbor, saying she will be back the next day, only to return eighteen months later with money and one of her legs gone. It was rumored that Eva placed her leg under a train in order to collect insurance money to support her children. The conversation in question reads as follows:

> "Mamma, did you ever love us?" . . .
> "You settin' here with your healthy-ass self and ax me did I love you? Them big old eyes in your head would a been two holes full of maggots if I hadn't."
> "I didn't mean that, Mamma. I know you fed us and all. I was talkin' 'bout something else. Like. Like. Playin' with us. Did you ever, you know, play with us?"
> "Play? Wasn't nobody playin' in 1895. Just 'cause you got it good now you think it was always this good? 1895 was a killer, girl. Things was bad. Niggers was dying like flies. . . ."
> "Mamma, what you talkin' 'bout?"
> "I'm talkin' 'bout 18 and 95 when I set in that house five days with you and Pearl and Plum and three beets, you snake-eyed ungrateful hussy. What would I look like leapin' 'round that little old room playin' with youngins with three beets to my name?"
> "I know 'bout them beets, Mamma. You told us that a million times."
> "Yeah? Well? Don't that count? Ain't that love? You want me to tinkle you under the jaw and forget 'bout them sores in your mouth? Pearl was shittin' worms and I was supposed to play rang-around-the-rosie?"
> "But Mamma, they had to be some time when you wasn't thinkin' 'bout . . ."
> "No time. They wasn't no time. Not none. Soon as I got one day done here come a night. With you all coughin' and me watchin' so TB wouldn't take you off . . . what you talkin' 'bout did I love you girl I stayed alive for you can't you get that through your thick head or what is that between your ears, heifer?" (67–69)

Much has been written on this conversation between mother and daughter. Dayle DeLancey argues that "Eva must withhold some love from her children because she has neither the time nor the energy to give it." "The rigors of improving her family's existence," DeLancey continues, "have led Eva to adopt a severe manner that distances her children from her. The struggle for survival has given Eva's love for her children a hard edge which has nearly destroyed her relationship with them" (17). Patrick Bryce Bjork calls Eva a "pragmatic, possessive, and domineering Matriarch." Eva, in his words, "has been driven to a state of unnaturalness; there is 'no time' for anything but to 'stay alive,' to survive . . . she sacrifices love for some sense of order and continuity within [her] household" (67). While Trudier Harris argues that "Eva . . . starts out as a traditional mother. Her redefinition of role begins with her depositing her three children with a neighbor. . . . She chooses self over sacrifice, borders on immorality, and therefore becomes free" (1991). Karen Carmean describes Eva as having a "twisted sense of responsibility, a sense warped by dire circumstance" (34). Whether the critics condemn Eva or pity her, her mothering is regarded as somehow unnatural (Bjork) and untraditional (Harris).

The words *unnatural* or *untraditional,* however, acquire meaning only if both the speaker (writer) and listener (reader) know what is meant by their opposites, the normative terms—in this instance, natural or traditional. When the critic DeLancey laments that Eva has "no time to lavish traditional displays of affection upon her children" or that "she has to work for the survival of her offspring at the expense of having fun with them," she is working from a very specific definition of what constitutes good mothering. The two questions Hannah asks of her mother are: "Did you ever love us? Did you ever play with us?" For Hannah, loving your children means playing with your children; she cannot imagine an expression of motherlove other than that sanctioned and rendered natural by the normative ideologies of motherhood, in particular the discourse of sensitive mothering.[4] Readers of *Sula* also define sensitive mothering as the natural, normal motherhood experience. What the critics argue is that Eva would have loved her children—i.e., would have played with them—if there had been "more time" (Bjork) or she had "more energy" (DeLancey). While Eva is usually not blamed for the lack of "affection" and "fun" in her mothering, her motherlove is nonetheless regarded as somehow deficient or lacking. The critical stance is either a patronizing one: we feel sorry for Eva and curse the poverty and ignorance that kept her from being a true good—i.e., sensitive—mother. Or the critics pathologize this difference as deviance as evidenced by the words *neglect* and *immoral.*

Eva does not mother according to the script of sensitive mothering. Eva's motherlove, as the critic DeLancey describes it, "is hard edge[d] and severe." Hannah and most readers of the novel do not see "[sitting] in a house with three beets" and "[staying] alive for [your children]" as maternal love because motherlove is defined as sensitive mothering. Mother-daughter relationships in Morrison, as Phil Page has observed, "appear to lack closeness [but] only in comparison to a traditionally white ideal." "As with *The Bluest Eye,*" Page continues, "where imposed white standards of beauty and value are set against contrasting black standards, here white stereotypes of parent-child harmonies are implicitly contrasted with more fluid communal values. Mothers may not love, or like their daughters in the ideal of the Dick-and-Jane myth, but through belief in communal values, even though such values are not ideal, mothers endure, holding their households and the community together" (67). Morrison asks, in Eva's own words, "Don't that count? Ain't that Love?" In a 1980 interview with Koenen, Morrison commented:

> [I]t's problematic playing with children when you don't know how to stay alive. The children are always hostile about it, but then they carry the same thing on. That kind of sentimental love for the children is not possible except in a certain kind of loving society, where you can relish it. Children are easy marks in aggressively oppressive societies. (Taylor-Guthrie 1994: 69–70)

With this novel Morrison deconstructs normative ideologies of motherhood, in particular the discourse of sensitive mothering, and inscribes mothering as a culturally determined experience. Reflecting upon the questions Hannah asks, we realize that preservative love is both an act of motherwork and an expression of motherlove.

The novel redefines the meaning of motherlove by foregrounding preservative love as an expression of mothering. Feminist theorists on motherhood argue that normative discourses of good mothering distance daughters from their mothers and the motherline. Whether the ideologies of "good" mothering result in the disparagement of mothers (who aren't good), or the idealization of mothers (those who are), it drives a wedge between mothers and daughters. In the first instance, the daughter blames her mother for her "deficient, deviant" mothering, and in the second instance the mother raises her daughter inauthentically in accordance with patriarchal discourse. In *Sula*, Hannah interprets Eva's motherlove through the normative discourse of sensitive mothering; yet her funk remains intact. In this instance, the motherline withstands the normalizing practices of sensitive mothering that distance daughters from their mothers. And yet, Hannah does die before her mother, and her death, along with the later one of her daughter, brings an end to this motherline.

CULTURAL BEARING, MOTHERING FROM THE MOTHERLINE: MENTORING THE ANCIENT PROPERTIES

According to Morrison's maternal standpoint, preservative love, such as that practised by Eva and Mrs. MacTeer, is an act of resistance because it keeps children alive and well in a world that is at best indifferent to, and at worst hostile to, the survival of black children. But Morrison is equally concerned about the psychological well-being of blacks in America. And just as mothering, through preservative love, ensures physical survival, cultural bearing makes possible psychological survival. By way of cultural bearing, the mother imparts to her children African American values of the funk and the ancient properties that become for them strategies for survival. However, as noted in chapter 1, the significance of cultural bearing is made manifest in Morrison by detailing the suffering that occurs in its absence. In particular, and as was examined in the three previous chapters, Morrison's fiction describes the disconnections and disruptions to the motherline that arise when cultural bearing does not take place. While this strategy—to affirm importance through absence—describes how Morrison portrays cultural bearing in her fiction, we do find in her first novel, *The Bluest Eye,* a glimpse of cultural bearing in the mothering of Mrs. MacTeer.

Trudier Harris has written that "Mrs. MacTeer is the model for parenting and caring in Morrison's wasteland" (1991: 41). Mrs. MacTeer emerges as a model of resistant mothering because she engages in preservative love and practices cultural bearing. Mrs. MacTeer, through song and story, imparts to her daughters the values of the funk and the ancient properties.

> If my mother was in a singing mood, it wasn't so bad. She would sing about hard times, bad times, and somebody-done-gone-and-left-me times. But her voice was so sweet and her singing-eyes so melty I found myself longing for those hard times, yearning to be grown without "a thin di-i-ime to my name." I looked forward to the delicious time when "my man" would leave me, when I would "hate to see that evening sun go down . . ." 'cause then I would know "my man has left this town." Misery colored by the greens and blues in my mother's voice took all of the grief out of the words and left me with a conviction that pain was not only endurable, it was sweet. (24)

Significantly, Mrs. MacTeer's songs bespeak the sensuality—note the reference to colors—that Morrison associates with the funk. The daughters also learn from their mother's songs how to survive and endure: "her voice took the grief out of the words." Claudia relates how she and her sister were spellbound by her mother's female talk:

> Their conversation is like a gently wicked dance: sound meets sound, curtsies, shimmies, and retires. Another sound enters but is upstaged by still another: the two circle each other and stop. Sometimes their words move in lofty spirals; other times they take strident leaps, and all of it punctuated with warm-pulsed laughter—like the throb of a heart made jelly. The edge, the curl, the thrust of their memories is always clear to Frieda and me. We do not, cannot, know the meanings of all their words, for we are nine and ten years old. So we watch their faces, their hands, their feet, and listen for truth in timbre. (16)

Mrs. MacTeer's language is also specifically feminine: it bespeaks the fluid, bodily "language" of the maternal in which, in the words of Barbara Hill Rigney, "sound is more important than the sense" (11). In its emphasis on the sensual, it signifies the funk. By eavesdropping on their mother's conversations the sisters are also made aware of the centrality of female friendship, community, and neighborhood in black women's lives, the importance of which is emphasized in Morrison's writings.

Discussing Mrs. MacTeer's songs and soliloquies, notably her kitchen tirade against Pecola, Karla Holloway argues that "[l]anguage becomes a means of catharsis and, following an ancient ritual from field days, song becomes a signal for many things unexpressible by action direct or indirect" (1987: 39). "The girls," Holloway continues, "learn from their mother, learn of their Blackness and their femaleness by listening to these sung messages and understanding better how to cope" (40). In *The Bluest Eye* the narrator tells us that "[Mrs. MacTeer] would go on like that for hours, connecting one offence to another until all of the things that chagrined her were spewed out. Then, having told everybody and everything off, she would burst into song and sing the rest of the day" (23).[5] Mrs. MacTeer speaks her grievances; she is not silenced by them, as is Mrs. Breedlove. Frieda and Claudia learn from their mother's songs, soliloquies, and conversations that women have a voice and that through the speaking, singing, and sharing of experiences women can claim and take control of their lives.

As Mrs. MacTeer passes on the values of the funk and the ancient properties to her daughters through song and storytelling, these values also inform her mothering practices. Although we are afforded only glimpses of her mothering, the text suggests that Mrs. MacTeer practices as well as teaches the values of the ancient proprieties and the funk in her mothering. What Claudia desires for Christmas, the text tells us, is not the white blue-eyed doll, which revolted and frightened her, but the "security and warmth of Big Mama's kitchen," a signifier of the ancient properties. Although Mrs. MacTeer does give her daughters white baby dolls at Christmas as other black mothers did at that time, black dolls being unavailable, Claudia is not punished when she destroys them.[6]

Mrs. MacTeer is the only mother in Morrison's fiction who practices cultural bearing for children, and the portrayal of such mothering is suggested rather than fully described. Similarly, the importance of nurturance for children's survival and resistance is shown not by way of descriptions of nurturance but through depictions of mothers' attempts to provide this care.

THICK LOVE: MATERNAL NURTURANCE

The aim of black mothering, once preservation has been ensured, is to nurture children so that they may transcend the maiming of racism and grow into adulthood whole and complete. Black women immunize their children from racist ideologies by raising them in accordance with the values—the funk and ancient properties—of the African American motherline and by loving them so that they may love themselves in a culture that defines them as not deserving or worthy of love. In her last three novels, Morrison has become increasingly preoccupied with how mothers through maternal nurturance protect their children from the emotional hurts of racism and how they heal these wounds once inflicted. While her two most recent novels are concerned with healing, Morrison's fifth novel, *Beloved,* considers how mothers through the maternal task of nurturance challenge the cultural denial and disparagement of black motherlove. In *Beloved,* maternal nurturance is situated as a political act that seeks to defy two different, although intersecting, ideologies: the first deems black children as nonsubjects and the second defines slave mothers as breeders and so not mothers. This section of the chapter will explore how Sethe claims a maternal subjectivity in defiance of the construction of slave mothers as breeders, in order to instill in her children a loved sense of self so that they may be subjects in a culture that commodifies them as objects. Sethe's interpretation of her motherlove as resistance will be contrasted to Paul D.'s and the critics' view that Sethe's love is indeed "too thick."

Adrienne Rich's *Of Woman Born* opens with this observation: "We know more about the air we breathe, the seas we travel, than about the nature and meaning of motherhood" (11). While Rich's statement is true for all mothers, it is particularly true for slave mothers who were denied the very experience of motherhood. *Beloved* speaks the hitherto silenced maternal narrative of slave women. In *Beloved,* one slave woman's "disremembered and unaccounted for" story of motherhood is told; and, like the voices of the thirty neighborhood women who came to exorcise Beloved, Sethe "searched for the right combination, the key, the code, the sound . . . until she found it, and when [she] did it was a wave of a sound wide enough to sound deep water and knock the pods off chestnuts trees." In this voice, "that broke the back of words" (261), Sethe brings to history and language the story of slave motherhood.

In 1851 Sojourner Truth, former slave, preacher, orator, abolitionist, and mother, deconstructed the dominant ideology of normative femininity and foregrounded her own subjectivity as a Black Woman:

> That man over there says that women need to be helped into carriages, and lifted over ditches, and to have the best place everywhere. Nobody ever helps me into carriages, or over mud puddles, or gives me any best place! And ain't I a woman? Look at me! Look at my arm! I have ploughed and planted, and gathered into barns, and no man could head me! And ain't I a woman? I could work as much and eat as a man—when I could get it—and bear the lash as well! And ain't I a woman? I have borne thirteen children, and seen them most all sold off to slavery, and when I cried out with my mother's grief, none but Jesus heard me! And ain't I a woman? (Gilbert 1985: 253)

History tells us that a man once accused Sojourner Truth of being a man in disguise: in response she bared her breast asking the same question, "ain't I a woman?"

With the Industrial Revolution there emerged an elaborate cultural discourse of femininity that came to be called the Cult of True Womanhood. A "good" woman, in this discourse, possessed the virtues of piety, purity, and passivity; to be otherwise she was not a woman. This ideological construction of femininity as an innate gender difference included a specific cultural discourse around women's reproductive identity. Alternatively called the cult of mother worship, the empire of the mother, and the cult of domesticity, the nineteenth-century ideology of moral motherhood put mothers on a pedestal and placed a halo over their heads. Mothers were by definition naturally pure, good, chaste, altruistic, and morally superior to men. In her informative work *The Empire of the Mother: American Writing about Domesticity 1830–1860* (1985), Mary Ryan explores how women appropriated this ideology of moral motherhood to endorse feminine activism.[7] Ryan writes:

> Under the banner of the cult of motherhood, women participated in the creation, circulation, and generational transfer of social values. . . . With motherhood their symbolic crown and the home the functional centre of their empire women, did, in fact, command a critical social position. They were the special agents of what has been called the relations of social reproduction. (18)

The ideology of moral motherhood, however, was race and class specific: only white and middle-class women could wear the halo of the Madonna and transform the world through their moral influence and social housekeeping. In her book, *Reconstructing Womanhood: The Emergence of the Afro-American Woman Novelist* (1987), Hazel Carby explores the formulations of this gender ideology in the antebellum South. Carby writes: "[T]wo very different but interdependent codes of sexuality operated in the antebellum South, producing opposing definitions of motherhood and womanhood for white and black women which coalesce in the figures of the slave and mistress" (20). As the white woman was revered as a virgin, the black woman was scorned as a whore. And as the white mother was worshipped on a pedestal as a Madonna, the slave mother was auctioned on a block as a breeder.[8]

The ideology of black woman as breeder produced and justified many of the horrific practices of slavery. The disruption of families through sale was rationalized by this ideology, as was the practice of forced pregnancy through studding or rape. This ideology also defined the very meaning of motherhood for black women and thus determined the actual material conditions of their mothering.[9] Slave women were defined as not-mothers and thus denied the right to mother their own children. Viewed only as breeders, slave women were separated from their own children and forced to work the fields or on behalf of the master's children. In the words of Barbara Hill Rigney: "The disintegration of family, the denial of a mother's right to love her daughter . . . is perhaps the greatest horror of slavery" (68). The discursive and material erasure of the slave women's motherlove served the economic interests of slavery and ensured its continual reproduction. *Beloved* gives voice to slave women's stories of motherhood and thus creates an alternative, subversive, discourse of black motherhood. Just as Sojourner Truth challenged the dominant discourse of womanhood to claim her own identity as a woman, Toni Morrison deconstructs the racial/gender ideology of black woman as not-mother by grounding Sethe's subjectivity in her mother role.

Beloved powerfully—and painfully—describes one woman's determined fight to break through her silencing and speak as mother.

The text tells us that slaves must, in the words of Paul D., "protect . . . yourself and love . . . small . . . a big love . . . would split you wide open" (162). Sethe's mother-in-law, Baby Suggs, bore eight children but saw only her youngest grow into adulthood. With the other seven children, "she didn't know . . . what their permanent teeth looked like; or how they held their heads when they walked" (139). The two eldest girls were gone before Baby Suggs even knew of their sale, and her first boy who was promised to Suggs in exchange for sex with her master, was sold for lumber the following spring. "Anybody, Baby Suggs knew, let alone loved, who hadn't run off or been hanged, got rented out, loaned out, bought up, brought back, stored up, mortgaged, won, stolen or seized" (23). "Don't love nothing," Ella advises Sethe upon her arrival in the North (92). With your children "moved around like checkers" it was, as Paul D. warns, "risky . . . and dangerous to love [too] much." Or in the words of Sethe, "Unless carefree, mother love [is] a killer" (132).

With the children who were not traded, sold, or killed, the slave woman had to struggle against her society's denial of her maternal feelings, the definition of her children as property, and the master's demand that her time and energy be spent elsewhere in order to give them the love and attention they needed for basic survival. As a baby, Sethe was separated from her own mother at the tender age of three weeks and left in the care of another woman. With her own children, Sethe, as she explains to Paul D., "couldn't love 'em proper . . . because they wasn't mine to love" (162). When Sethe speaks of her early mothering at the ironically named Sweet Home, she emphasizes how difficult it was to provide a safe and nurturing environment for her young children: "[The] children cannot play in the kitchen anymore, so she is dashing back and forth between house and quarters—fidgety and frustrated trying to watch over them. They are too young for men's work and the baby girl is nine months old" (223). Slave culture vehemently denied black children their basic humanity and actively prohibited slave mothers from loving their children and being attentive to them. Under such historical circumstances it was both dangerous, as Paul D. claimed, and almost-beyond-hope difficult "to love your children proper."

The commodification and appropriation of slave mothering is symbolically dramatized in *Beloved* through the white men's brutal taking of Sethe's breast milk. In "The Nursing Mother and Feminine Metaphysics" (1982), Stephanie Demetrakopoulos argues that in much of women's writing "milk is the symbol for the essence of mother love" (439). In *Beloved,* the taking of breast milk through the practice of wet nursing signifies the appropriation and commodification of slave women's motherlove. A slave mother was seldom allowed to nurse her babies and, when she was, they received milk only after the white babies had suckled. Rehearsing in her mind what she will tell Beloved to explain the murder, Sethe reflects upon the relationship between nursing milk and motherlove:

Nobody will ever get my milk no more except my own children. I never had to give it to nobody else—and the one time I did it was took from me— they held me down and took it. Milk that belonged to my baby. Nan had to nurse whitebabies and me too because Ma'am was in the rice. The little whitebabies got it first and I got what was left. Or none. There was no nurs- ing milk to call my own. I know what it is like to be without the milk that belongs to you; to have to fight and holler for it, and to have so little left. I'll tell Beloved about that; she'll understand. She my daughter. The one I managed to have milk for and get it to her even after they stole it. . . . (200)

Even after the children are weaned, Sethe describes her motherlove metaphori- cally as breast milk and interprets her relationship to the children as a physical nursing bond: "sure enough, she had milk enough for all" (100); "Nobody will ever get my milk no more except my own children" (200); "I have your milk/ . . . I brought your milk" (216).

That is why the white men's theft of her breast milk so devastates Sethe: her "stolen milk" metaphorically signifies the motherlove that is denied to her as a slave woman. When Sethe tells Paul D. about the "two boys with mossy teeth, one sucking on [her] breast the other one holding [her] down, their book-read- ing teacher watching and writing it up" (70), and the later beating which "opened up [her] back" (17), she emphasizes that what was intolerable was not the pain of the beating, but the loss of her babies' nursing milk:

> "They used cowhide on you?"
> "And they took my milk."
> "They beat you and you was pregnant?"
> "And they took my milk!" (17)

When Sethe says, "Nobody was going to nurse her like me. Nobody was going to get it to her fast enough, or take it away when she had enough and didn't know it. Nobody knew that she couldn't pass her air if you held her up on your shoulder, only if she was lying on my knees. Nobody knew that but me and nobody had her milk but me" (16), the word, *nurse,* takes as its referent not just the physical act of nursing but all dimensions of Sethe's motherlove. Sethe is saying that she is the only one who knows "how to love her children proper" and that her children need her, Sethe, to be their mother. Sethe recognizes that children depend on motherlove for psychological well-being. When Sethe resolves to "get milk to her [children]" (161), she refuses the ideological defin- ition of herself as not-mother by giving to her children the love they need for emotional health.

Sethe is the archetypal "outraged mother" who defies the prohibition against black motherhood and actively mothers her own children.[10] The novel is rich with descriptions of Sethe's motherlove. The few fond memories Sethe holds of Sweet Home involve her love for the children. She says of her sons: "That's the way I used to see them in my dreams, laughing, their short fat legs running up the hill" (192); and of Beloved: "I wanted to pick you up in my arms and I wanted to look at you sleeping too. Didn't know which; you had the sweetest face" (192). Sethe attentively and protectively watches over children to keep them from harm. She shares with Paul D. her memory of the time:

> [Buglar] got up on the well, right on it. I flew. Snatched him just in time. So when I knew we'd be . . . smoking and I couldn't see after him well. I got a rope and tied it round his ankle. . . . I didn't like the look of it, but what else could I do. It's hard, you know what I mean? by yourself and no woman to help you get through. (160)

In an earlier discussion with Paul D., Sethe struggles to convey to him, who is neither a woman nor a mother, the depth and strength of her commitment to, and protection of her children. The dialogue is worth citing in its entirety because the passage is crucial to our understanding of Sethe's motherlove and is not often cited by the critics. The discussion develops in response to Denver's rudeness to Paul D.

> "Excuse me, but I can't hear a word against her. I'll chastise her. You leave her alone." . . .
> "Why you think you have to take up for her? Apologize for her? She's grown."
> "I don't care what she is. Grown don't mean nothing to a mother. A child is a child. They get bigger, older. But grown? What's that suppose to mean? In my heart it don't mean a thing."
> "It means she has to take it if she acts up. You can't protect her every minute. What's going to happen when you die?"
> "Nothing! I'll protect her while I'm alive and I'll protect her when I ain't."
> "Oh well. I'm through . . ."
> "That's the way it is, Paul D. I can't explain it to you no better than that, but that's the way it is. If I have to choose—well, it's not even a choice." (45)

Here Sethe struggles for words to express the intense devotion and immense depth of her maternal love. Later, I will consider whether such maternal love is indeed "too thick," as Paul D. charges. What must be emphasized here is that Sethe is passionately committed to, and fiercely protective of, her children, and that her nurturance is a radical act of defiance against the prohibition against slave motherhood.

When Sethe is reunited with her children her motherlove is portrayed as all-encompassing: "Sethe lay in bed under, around, over, among but especially with them all. The little girl dribbled clear spit into her face, and Sethe's laugh of delight was so loud the crawling-already? baby blinked. Buglar and Howard played with her ugly feet. . . . She kept kissing them. She kissed the backs of their necks, the tops of their heads and the centers of their palms" (93). "I was big," Sethe tells Paul D., "and deep and wide and when I stretched out my arms all my children could get in between. I was *that* wide" (162). Indeed, "she had milk enough for all" (100).

Sethe not only speaks as a mother, she secures subjectivity through her mothering. As she explains to Paul D.: "I did it. I got us all out. Without Halle too. Up till then it was the only thing I ever did on my own. Decided. And it came off right, like it was supposed to. . . . I birthed them and I got em out and it wasn't no accident. I did that. . . . Me having to look out. Me using my own head. . . . It was," Sethe continues, "a kind of selfishness I never knew nothing about before. It felt good" (162). The courage and intelligence Sethe discovers through her mothering recalls that expressed by Harriet Jacobs in the slave narrative *Incidents in the Life a Slave Girl.* Both Sethe and Harriet interpret their maternal love as a powerful and empowering stance of resistance. After Harriet learns that she and her young children are to be sent to the plantation she proclaims to the reader: "I had a woman's pride, and a mother's love for my children; and I resolved that out of the darkness of this hour a brighter dawn should rise for them. My master had power and law on his side; I had determined will. There is might in each" (85). The love for their children motivates both Sethe and Harriet to seek freedom. Jacobs writes: "[I]t was more for my helpless children than for myself that I longed for freedom" (89). The concern for her unborn child is what keeps Sethe from despair and resignation: "[I]t didn't seem such a bad idea [to die], all in all . . . but the thought of herself stretched out dead while the little antelope lived on—an hour? a day? a day and a night?—in her lifeless body" (31).

Both mothers recognize, in the words of Jacobs, that "[s]lavery is terrible for men; but it is far more terrible for women." "Superadded to the burden common to all," Jacobs continues, "*they* have wrongs, and sufferings, and mortifications peculiarly their own" (77). Women's desire and determination for freedom is thus particularly acute when they reflect upon their daughters' lives as slaves. Jacobs writes: "I knew the doom that awaited my fair baby in slavery, and I determined to save her from it, or perish in the attempt" (90) and "I thought of what I had suffered in slavery at her age, and my heart was like a tiger's when a hunter tries to seize her young" (199). Sethe explains to Beloved:

> No undreamable dreams about whether the . . . bubbling-hot girls in the colored-school fire set by patriots included her daughter; whether a gang of whites invaded her daughter's private parts, soiled her daughter's thighs and threw her daughter out of the wagon. *She* might have to work the slaughterhouse yard, but not her daughter. And no one, nobody on this earth, would list her daughter's characteristics on the animal side of the paper. No. Oh no. (251)

Both mothers love their children more than life itself. Jacobs says to her readers: "I loved them better than my life" (92); Sethe tells Beloved: "I wouldn't draw breath without my children" (203). Jacobs shares with Sethe the belief that death is preferable to slavery and both mothers would rather see their children dead in the grave than watch them grow up in slavery. "I would rather see them killed than have them given up to his power" (80), writes Jacobs; and

Sethe explains, "[I]f I hadn't killed her she would have died and that is something I could not bear to happen" (200).[11]

In *Women, Race & Class* (1981), Angela Davis examines how the racial ideologies of white and black motherhood influenced the representations of maternal heroism in nineteenth-century women's writing. In particular, Davis examines the mother figure Eliza in Harriet Beecher Stowe's *Uncle Tom's Cabin.* Davis argues that Stowe presents Eliza as "white motherhood incarnate" to accommodate a smooth transference of the white woman reader's sensibilities. Davis writes: "It may have been Stowe's hope that the white woman reader of her novel would discover themselves in Eliza. They could admire her superior Christian morality, her unfaltering maternal instincts, her gentleness and fragility—for these were the very qualities white women were being taught to cultivate in themselves" (27). Stowe passionately believed in the nineteenth-century cult of mother-worship, so writes the romantic tale of Eliza's flight from this perspective.

Eliza's melodramatic story of escape is, as Davis emphasizes, a travesty of slave mothers' very real resistance against slavery: "Countless acts of heroism carried out by slave mothers have been documented," writes Davis. "These women, unlike Eliza, were driven to defend their children by their passionate abhorrence of slavery. The source of their strength was not some mystical power attached to motherhood, but rather their concrete resistance to slavery on behalf of themselves and their children" (29).

Davis's reading of Stowe's mother-figure Eliza offers us an illuminating perspective from which to analyze the maternal heroism of Sethe. Both Eliza and Sethe flee slavery with child—Sethe is pregnant and gives birth en route—and both manage, against all odds, to cross the seemingly impassable Ohio River. Sethe's determination is seen as larger than life, "She would get that milk to her baby girl if she had to swim" (83), and the birth of her child on the wrong side of the Ohio River is indeed a miracle. However, Sethe's determination, unlike that of Eliza's, is not divinely ordained or religiously inspired. Rather, Sethe's numerous maternal feats, from escape to infanticide, are planned acts of resistance grounded in her abhorrence of slavery.

An equally compelling reading of Sethe's maternal heroism is developed in Jean Wyatt's psychoanalytically based article, "Giving Body to the Word: The Maternal Symbolic in Toni Morrison's *Beloved*" (1993). Wyatt argues that the heroism is tied to the contradictory positioning of Sethe's maternal body. "On the one hand," Wyatt writes, "Sethe's self-definition as maternal body enables Morrison to construct a new narrative form—a specifically female quest powered by the desire to get one's milk to one's baby—that features childbirth as high adventure. On the other hand, this same self-definition forecloses Sethe's full participation in language" (475).[12] Of particular interest to us here is Wyatt's emphasis on "a new narrative form." I would suggest that Sethe's flight to freedom is structured specifically as a heroic quest. The ambition of Sethe's quest is not to discover new lands or to find a Holy Grail but to "get milk to [her] baby girl" (16). And the central triumphant achievement of Sethe's quest is not the slaying of a dragon but the birth of a child. The very meaning of a hero and heroism is redefined, making it possible for Sethe to inscribe herself as subject and celebrate the reproductive feats of nursing and birth as heroic labor.[13] Indeed, in deconstructing the conventions of the traditional male quest genre, Sethe's narrative gives voice to a gynocentric model of achieving and expressing selfhood: what Kathryn Allen Rabuzzi calls "the way of the mother" (1988).[14] Through her love for the children, Sethe finds the confidence and courage to resist slavery and she becomes a hero of epic proportions.

However, this same motherlove caused Sethe to place a handsaw at the throat of her already-crawling girl. When Sethe recognizes schoolteacher's hat, as she tells Paul D.:

> She just flew. Collected every bit of life she had made, all the parts of her that were precious and fine and beautiful, and carried, pushed, dragged them through the veil, out, away, over there where no one could hurt them. Over there. Outside this place, where they would be safe. (163)

> "Your love is too thick," [Paul D. replied]. . . .
> "Too thick?" she said. . . . "Love is or it ain't. Thin love ain't love at all." (164)

Many readers of *Beloved* agree with Paul's accusation that Sethe's motherlove is indeed too thick. Stephanie Demetrakopoulos argues, in "Maternal Bonds as Devourers of Individuation," that *Beloved* exposes "the dangers of mothering to the individuation of the mother herself" (52). The text, Demetrakopoulos concludes, is "[u]ltimately . . . [about] the death of the maternal in a woman so that her Self might live" (58). Sethe's mothering is described in this article as "pathological" (54) and the mother-daughter relationship of Sethe and Beloved is termed "psychic incest" (58).[15]

Paul D., who accuses Sethe of a too-thick love, is portrayed as a sympathetic character. "Not even trying, he had become the kind of a man who could walk into a house and make the women cry. Because with him, in his presence, they could. There was something blessed in his manner" (17). In an interview with Marsha Darling, Morrison describes Paul D. as a healer (Taylor-Guthrie 1994: 246–54).[16] Paul D., the last of the Sweet Home men, is presented as a kind, tender, and decent man who frees Sethe from her past and promises her a future: "[M]e and you, we go more yesterday than anybody. We need some kind of tomorrow" (273).[17] However, the "blessed[ness] of his manner" did not keep Paul D. from wounding Sethe with his unbelievably cruel insult, "You got two feet, Sethe, not four" (165)—cruel because it is a direct allusion to schoolteacher's beliefs—or keep him from walking out on her. Paul D.'s insult is particularly offensive when we perceive the hypocrisy of it: the man who mated with calves dares to call Sethe an animal in her love for her children. And while Paul D. faults Sethe for her excessive loving, he does not regard his own belief "to love just a little bit" (45) as at all problematic. If Sethe loves too much, Paul D. does not love enough.

The development of Sethe and Paul D.'s romantic relationship, in particular the presentation of Paul D. as Sethe's rescuing hero, warrants further consideration. In her article on *Beloved,* Carole Boyce Davies discusses a friend's response to the book. Davies writes:

> My Prototypical black woman reader (a friend, nonacademic but aware, struggling alone with a difficult child after leaving an abusive marriage) was not empowered by reading *Beloved* at this juncture in her life. Contemplating it and her life, she felt herself going into a spiral of depression, wondering if she should go back and offer her breasts to her man, allowing "the responsibility for her breasts, at last [to be] in somebody else's hands" (18), or find another man to affirm for her that she was her own "best thing." (273)[18]

No critic, to my knowledge, has analyzed Sethe's relationship with Paul D. in the way her relationship with her children has been examined.[19] Nor have critics asked if Sethe's love for Paul D. is, indeed, "too thick."[20]

Sethe's love is judged as too thick by Paul D. because of the infanticide. The infanticide is not, however, an isolated event and thus must be read in the context of Sethe's earlier mothering at Sweet Home and the time she spends with her children at 124. In other words, we must distinguish between Sethe's mothering before and after "the white men came into her yard." Prior to the sight of schoolteacher's hat, Sethe behaves in the way expected of mothers: she loves her children and strives to ensure their well-being and safety.[21] As well, it is Sethe's determination and courage that bring her children to freedom. Had it not been for Sethe's breathtaking resolve the children would have, in all likelihood, been sold off and the youngest, Denver, would not have been born. Sethe tries to kill her children because, for her, death is preferable to slavery. When Paul D. says, "[T]here could have been a way. Some other way," Sethe is right to ask, "What way?," and he has no response. In the split second it took to make the decision, there was no other way: as Sethe says, "[L]ove is or it ain't. Thin love ain't love at all" (164). Later in the narrative Sethe defends her so called "too thick" motherlove:

> Too thick, he said. My love was too thick. What he know about it? Who in the world is he willing to die for? Would he give his privates to a stranger in return for a carving? Some other way, he said. There must have been some other way. Let schoolteacher haul us away. I guess, to measure your behind before he tore it up? . . . I wouldn't draw breath without my children. (203)

For Sethe, "what she had done was right because it came from true love" (252).

Sethe claims, through her act of infanticide, the right to decide what is best for her children. The nineteenth-century cult of moral motherhood said that women were born with a maternal instinct, which rendered motherhood natural to them.[22] The racial specialization of gender ideology in the nineteenth century precluded black women from this so-called natural law by defining them as breeders and not-mothers. In *Beloved,* Sethe claims the rights and responsibilities accorded to white women under the cult of moral motherhood. She demands that she, and not schoolteacher, will determine the fate of her children. Her decision to protect her children through death is, for Sethe, hers to make because, as a mother, she is responsible for assessing and providing for the well-being of her children. As Morrison explained in her 1988 interview with Marsha Darling: "Under the theatrical circumstances of slavery, if you made that claim . . . that you are the mother of these children . . . [you] claim[ed] responsibility for [the] children." Morrison goes on to emphasize that Sethe's claim is "an unheard-of . . . outrageous claim for a slave woman to make"; for what Sethe is claiming is the right and responsibility to "say something about what happens to [her children]" (Taylor-Guthrie 1994: 252).

This is not to suggest that the nineteenth-century gender ideology accorded white women control over their children nor is it to imply that children should be owned. Rather it is to emphasize—and remind—that under slavery black children were property, and white men—not black mothers—held life-and-death powers over them. Moral questions of rights and responsibilities must be framed in terms of the larger historical reality represented in the text: under slavery people owned other people. Sethe does claim ownership of her children but such is made *against* the master's legal claim on them. Repeatedly, throughout the text, Sethe says to her children, "You are mine," and she calls her children, "my best thing"—"the parts of her that were precious and fine and beautiful" (272, 163). Belonging or owning is reciprocal between mother and child. As Sethe says to Beloved: "When I tell you you mine, I also mean I'm yours" (203). The belonging of mother and child is constructed and interpreted as ownership because such is the economic, legal, and linguistic currency of the text and the slave system it represents. What Sethe claims is not necessarily ownership but a biological, emotional mother-child bond, which for her has primacy and authority over the law of the Father.

Mothers are expected to protect their children. Infanticide for Sethe, I would suggest, is an act of preservative love. As Sethe says about the killing of Beloved: "She had to be safe and I put her where she would be" (200).[23] Acting as a mother, Sethe must make sure her children are kept safe and away from harm; "It ain't my job to know what's worse. It's my job to know what is and to keep them away from what I know is terrible. I did that." Indeed, Sethe's plan to keep her "babies safe" is successful: "Schoolteacher ain't got em" (165). When schoolteacher saw the murdered child he recognized "right off . . . there was nothing there to claim" (149).[24] Three of the children are raised as a family in freedom. Had they been returned South, the children, in all likelihood, would have been sold off and separated from their mother.

In the sociohistorical context of slavery, a black woman who defines her self-hood through and in her mothering is resisting the ideological construction of the slave mother as breeder. In calling herself "her children's mother" (30), Sethe claims a maternal subjectivity and responsibility over her own children. As Paul D. reflects: "More important than what Sethe had done was what she claimed. It scared him" (164).

Contemporary feminist readers often fault Sethe for defining her identity through her maternal role. The critic Jean Wyatt writes: "While celebrating the courage and determination Sethe draws from this attachment [with her children], Morrison's narrative also dramatizes the problems of Sethe's maternal subjectivity, which is so embedded in her children that it both allows her to take the life of one of them and precludes putting that act into words" (476). Stephanie Demetrakopoulos argues "[that] Sethe carries mother instinct to an absurd and grotesque length" (58). And while Carole Boyce Davies reads Sethe's motherlove as a political gesture of defiance she, nonetheless, concludes that this same motherlove is

> definitely "too-thick," as Paul D. says, because it too fully accepts the given paradigm of motherhood as exclusive responsibility of the biological mother. . . . A slave mother is not supposed to demonstrate deep love for her children. Sethe defies that. Yet her heroic response to enslavement paradoxically becomes the kind of motherlove which society enforces for women. Sethe shuttles back and forth between enslavements, exchanging one for the other, unable to be freed from both at once. (54)

Sethe defies the ideological prohibition against slave mothering, Carole Boyce Davies reasons, only to embrace the gender ideological prescription that defines women through their motherhood role. These critics, I suggest, interpret Sethe's motherlove from the dominant ideology of motherhood, which defines home as a politically neutral space and views nurturance as nothing more than the natural calling of mothers. Thus, they have misread Sethe's maternal narrative. In African American culture the practice of nurturance is a political act, and homeplace, in bell hooks's words, is "a site of resistance." In her motherlove, Sethe seeks to foster in her children a loved sense of self, and through the infanticide protect them from harm and deliver them to safety.

In all of Morrison's novels, mothers put the nurturance and protection of the children at the center of their lives.[25] In *Sula*, Eva "takes the last bit of food she had in the world (besides three beets)" and inserts it up Plum's bottom to relieve his constipation, and is rumored to have deliberately placed her leg in front of a train to collect insurance money so she could return and support her young family. Later, Eva risks her own life, jumping out of the window, to save the life of her adult daughter Hannah.[26] In *Song of Solomon,* Pilate puts a knife to the throat of the man who has abused her daughter, Reba; and Ruth tells Hagar, "You are trying to kill him. . . . If you so much as bend a hair on his head, so help me Jesus, I will tear your throat out" (137).

Morrison does not present these mothers as "too embedded in, or enslaved by" their maternal identity. Morrison's maternal standpoint and theory of motherwork defines nurturance as a political and social act because it instills in children a loved sense of self which enables them to be subjects in a culture that denies their subjectivity. Sethe differs from these mothers only in the way she interprets nurturance. As Paul D. comments: "This here Sethe talked about love like any other woman; talked about baby clothes like any other woman, but what she meant could cleave the bone. This here Sethe talked about safety with a handsaw" (164). However, extreme circumstances call for extreme measures.

Readers who fault Sethe for excessive motherlove, emphasize that she must come to see her own Self as her "best thing." This argument points to a misreading of Morrison's maternal stance. First, it assumes that female subjectivity is divisible into a mother self and a non-mother self; further, it positions motherlove in opposition to self-love. According to Morrison's maternal standpoint, black women of the ancient properties are both "builders" and "nurturers": they are both ship and harbor, and inn and trail. As Sethe claims an identity as a mother, she is also a worker, first as a slave and later as a cook; she is never only a mother. Furthermore, as discussed in chapter 1, motherlove and self-love are equally important, particularly because through motherlove one obtains self-love. What interests Morrison is not the importance of one over the other but how the two are held in balance. Discussing *Beloved*, Toni Morrison comments:

> The story seemed to me to yield up a persistent struggle by women, Black women, in negotiating something very difficult. The whole problem was trying to do two things: to love something bigger than yourself, to nurture something; and also not to sabotage yourself, not to murder yourself. . . . This story is about, among other things, the tension between being yourself, one's own Beloved, and being a mother. (6)

Moreover, Sethe comes to love her self in loving her children and the strong selfhood she eventually creates for herself is formed from her maternal heroism. Sethe must learn to love herself as she loves her children, and love her children as they need to be loved. Both acts are possible because Sethe has been blessed with a generous "thick love."

I agree with Carole Boyce Davies when she asserts: "*Beloved* . . . simultaneously critiques exclusive motherlove and asserts the necessity for black women to claim something as theirs." "The work demands," Davies continues, "that the reader hold open a range of possibilities. An unquestioning endorsement of Sethe's action cannot reveal the text's complexity" (45–46). She goes on to caution: "The attempt to construct Sethe as resisting mother is highly charged but also problematic" (53). Sethe's act of infanticide was, in the words of Toni Morrison, "absolutely the right thing to do . . . but also the thing you have no right to do."[27] Of the infanticide, Stamp Paid says: "She love those children. She was trying to outhurt the hurter" (234). In *Beloved*, unspeakable thoughts *are* spoken: a slave woman speaks as a mother and expresses her motherlove for her children. Although Sethe bites off a piece of her tongue when she is assaulted, her tongue is not severed as in the Greek myth of Philomela's rape. Sethe is not silenced, and her story becomes a story to pass on.

In *Beloved,* nurturance emerges as a site of resistance against the commodification of African Americans under slavery and the resulting disruption of the African American motherline. Sethe understands that only through nurturance do her children stand a chance of surviving slavery. The narrative is propelled by Sethe's often desperate desire to be a mother to her children when such was forbidden. Sethe's inability to fully protect her children—"Your boys gone you don't know where. One girl dead, the other won't leave the yard" (165)—however, does not signify an individual woman's failed maternal nurturance, as with Pauline in *The Bluest Eye*. Rather, Sethe's "failure" symbolizes the larger cultural trauma that results from the absence of maternal nurturance, just as the character Beloved, as discussed in chapter 4, represents the historical trauma of severed motherlines. In this, the novel *Beloved* anticipates Morrison's most recent novel *Paradise* in which failed maternal nurturance signifies a loss of community.

RESISTANCE AGAINST PATRIARCHY

RESISTANCE AGAINST PATRIARCHAL ERASURE OF THE FUNK

In the previous discussion, nurturance was represented as an act of resistance in so far as it gave to children a loved sense of self to empower them to survive and resist the psychological wounding of racism. But nurturance in Morrison is also used to signify resistance against patriarchal culture, in particular the institution of motherhood. In Morrison's first six novels, maternal failure of nurturance and abandoned/abused children signified an individual woman's inability to mother. In *Jazz,* for example, Rose Dear's despair and death prevented her from being a mother to and for her daughter. Pauline Breedlove in *The Bluest Eye* is unable to nurture her daughter because of her identification with the normative discourses of the family and female beauty. In *Beloved,* under the institution of slavery, Sethe, as she explains to Paul D., "could not lov'em proper because they wasn't mine to love."[28] In each instance, the mother is unable to nurture her daughter or practise cultural bearing and this "failure" is caused by a disconnection or disruption of the motherline. Whether it was occasioned by assimilation, as with Pauline, or slavery and its aftermath, as with Rose Dear and Sethe, the mother is disconnected from her motherline and is not able to nurture her daughter or bequeath to her the ancient properties or the sustaining values of the funk.

In *Paradise* (1998) fractures or failures in maternal roles and relationships mark a much larger communal failure of care and nurturance. In *Paradise,* maternal failure signifies not so much an individual woman's inability to mother because of her disconnection from her motherline; but a *community's* failure to nurture its own because of its denial, disparagement, and displacement of the funk and the ancient properties. The well-being of a community may be measured, it is often argued, by the well-being of its children. The barenness, abortions, miscarriages, sickly children, and dead babies, as well as the maternal abandonment and neglect, motherlessness, mother loss, mother-daughter estrangement described in *Paradise* represent Haven's and later Ruby's

inability to sustain community. And this is precisely because it is *not* a community—modeled as it is on patriarchal values of power, status, ownership, and control. These patriarchal values are signified by the Oven's words and enacted
through the town's philosophy of racial seclusion and selection. In so doing, the
town fathers have exorcized the ancient properties and the funk that Morrison
positions at the center of black resistance and empowerment. In Haven and later
Ruby, the sustaining values of the funk are lost through the valorization of masculine values and the subsequent marginalization of women and the feminine.

The erasure of the funk in Haven and Ruby is represented by reproductive
loss and failure because the maternal in Morrison both engenders and signifies
the continuation of the African American motherline and the values of the funk
and ancient properties it conveys. None of the town women experience fulfillment or connection through their maternal function. This absence of connection and fulfillment is symbolically marked by the absence of baby's breath flowers in Arnette's bridal bouquet. Billie Delia, as the text tells us, "had suggested
baby's breath to flatter the yellow buds but was astonished to find that no one
garden had any. No baby's breath anywhere" (149). For each of the town
women, motherhood is associated with loss and harm, pain and suffering. Both
Arnette and Soanne seek an abortion at the convent (102). Denied an abortion
by Connie, Soanne has a miscarriage; brought on, Soanne believes, by "the evil
in her heart" (240). Arnette also, "advised to wait her time," brought on a pre-
mature delivery by "bash[ing]the life out of [her baby]; "inserted [a mop han-
dle] with a rapist's skill—mercilessly, repeatedly—between her legs" (249, 250).
The unborn baby, "[f]eisty, outraged, rigid with fright . . . tried to escape the
battering and battered ship that carried it. . . . Had it not tried to rescue itself ,
it would break into pieces or drown in its mothers' food. So he was born, in a
manner of speaking, too soon and fatigued by the flight" (250). Close to twenty
years later, Soanne's "sweet colored boys, unshot, unlynched, unmolested, unim-
prisoned," Scout and Easter are killed in Vietnam within two weeks of each
other (101). Dovey Morgan is unable to bear children. Of Sweetie and her sickly
children we are told that "[f]or six years she slept on the pallet near the cribs, or
in bed with Jeff, her breath threaded, her ear tunnel ready, every muscle braced
to spring . . . it was getting harder and harder to watch and sleep at the same
time" (125). Billie Delia took refuge in the convent after "a quarrel with her
mother turned ugly" (152). Pat Best, Billie Delia's mother, reflecting upon the
fight with her daughter discerned that "[s]he, the gentlest of souls, missed
killing her own daughter by inches . . . [t]rying to understand how she could
have picked up that pressing iron, Pat realized that ever since Billie Delia was an
infant, she thought of her as a liability somehow" (203). Pat Best's mother Delia,
the woman "with no last name [and] of sunlight skin," was the only person
other than Ruby to die in either Haven or Ruby. Delia and her daughter Faus-
tine both died in childbirth (197, 198).

Maternal loss, whether it is the loss of the mother or loss of children, is what
brings Mavis, Seneca, and Pallas to the convent. Mavis, fleeing after the death of

her twins, arrives at the convent when her car runs out of gas. Seneca is abandoned at the age of five by Jean, her mother, who she believed was her sister. After
waiting a week for Jean's return, Seneca, "demoralized by unanswered prayers,
bleeding gums, and hunger she gave up goodness, climbed up on a chair and
opened the bread box. Leaning against the box of Lorna Doones was an envelope
with a word she recognized instantly: her own name printed in lipstick . . . carried it [the letter] for the rest of her life" (128). When Seneca comes to realize
that she is not able to help Eddie, there is "no danger of tears. She had not shed
one even when she found Jean's letter next to the Lorna Doones. Well cared for,
loved, perhaps, by the mothers in both of the foster homes, she knew it was not
her self that the mothers had approved but the fact that she took reprimand qui-
etly, ate what she was given, shared what she had and never ever cried" (135).
With five hundred dollars in her pocket after her three weeks with Norma Fox,
Seneca catches car rides as a stowaway, "travelling resolutely nowhere, closed off
from society, hidden among quiet cargo—no one knowing she was there" (138).
The sight of Sweetie, "a black woman weeping on a country road broke her heart
all over again" (126), and causes Seneca to jump from the truck and follow her
to the convent.

Seneca's travels are prompted by another woman's maternal loss. Seneca
arrives in Wichita to ask Mrs. Turtle for money to help get her son Eddie,
Seneca's boyfriend, out of prison, who significantly, in terms of the theme of
reproductive loss, is serving time for the murder of a child. Mrs. Turtle, as she
explains to Seneca, "wasn't about to cash in the savings bonds her husband left
her for anybody, let alone somebody who drove a car over a child and left it
there, even if that somebody was her only son" (133). However, later, when
Seneca returns to use the phone, we are told that she heard a "flat-out helpless
mothercry—a sound like no other in the world. . . . Alone, without witness,
Mrs. Turtle had let go her reason, her personality, and shrieked for all the
world . . ." (134).

The final woman to arrive at the convent, Pallas, comes as a consequence
of her estrangement from her mother. At the age of sixteen Pallas with her
new, and much older boyfriend Carlos, "the movie-star looking maintenance
man at her high school" (166) "elope" in a car "crammed with Christmas presents" to visit her mother who lives seven hundred miles away and whom Pallas has not seen in thirteen years. Unknown to Pallas, Dee Dee, her mother,
and Carlos develop a relationship: "Carlos was closer in age to Dee Dee than
to her. Had she noticed," the text tells us, "she could have prevented the grap-
pling bodies exchanging moans in the grass, unmindful of any watcher. Then
there would have been no stupefied run to the Toyota, no blind drive on roads
without destinations, no bumping, sideswiping trucks. No water with soft
things touching beneath" (169). On the run, Pallas hides in a swamp. The
memory of the cold water with fearful "touching things" below haunts her and
she later dreams of black water seeping into her mouth (163, 173). Water, suggestive as it is of the amniotic fluids of the womb, frequently signifies healing

and cleansing, particularly in its association with rebirth. In this instance the water is cold and terrifying, signifying not maternal trust or love but its opposite: maternal deceit and abandonment.

Pallas's wounding, like that of Mavis and Seneca, is caused by reproductive harm or absence of a maternal relationship and signifies the suffering of women in a patriarchal culture. As well, it underscores the maternal loss of the town women and thus symbolizes the denial and repression of the funk in the town of Haven and later Ruby. A town that, as Mavis observed, looked "as though no one lived there" (45). However, through the love of Consolata, the convent women do eventually join together and create from their own individual losses a maternal community that heals the individual women and affirms the communal values of the funk that the town has outlawed. This theme will be examined in the following chapter.

MOTHERING AGAINST MOTHERHOOD

Mothers, in Morrison, as they confront racism on behalf of their children, also challenge their own oppression in the patriarchal institution of motherhood. Opposition to patriarchal motherhood is represented either as "deviant" maternal nurturance, as with Ruth's late nursing of her son, or as failed maternal nurturance, as with Margaret's child abuse.

It has been argued that it was Ruth's late nursing of Milkman that prepared him for the teachings of Pilate. Holloway writes: "Suckled so long by his mother, he has so much womaness in him that he alone gains the power to return to the feminine myth of the song" (112). Ruth's "late" nursing of her son signifies that Milkman, as his name suggests, remains, at least viscerally, connected to the motherline. In nursing her son, Ruth also, I would argue, resists the white patriarchal encoding of her self as "Mother-Wife" and seeks to reclaim the funk of her motherline. In nursing her son, Ruth keeps alive her sensual self, in defiance of a culture that demands clear division between women's reproductive and sexual selves. Breastfeeding also signifies a mother-son bond that stands in opposition to the patriarchal culture and the mother-son separation it demands. Morrison's texts emphasize the importance of mother-child connectedness for psychological well-being.

Many readers of *Song* interpret Ruth's late nursing of her son as evidence of her psychological malaise. Critic Rigney calls "nursing her half-grown son" a "perversion" (102). I would suggest that such a reading assumes a too literal representation of the act of breastfeeding. Demetrakopoulos, as noted above, argues "milk is the symbol for the essence of mother love" (439). This is particularly so with Morrison, where nursing is a powerful symbol of mother-child attachment, particularly as it is threatened under the institution of slavery. What also must be emphasized is that it is the age of the child being nursed and not the act of nursing itself that so troubles the readership of *Song*. But this is itself problematic because it assumes a Western understanding of the proper age for nursing and weaning. Even Freddie acknowledges that nursing and weaning are culturally mediated events: "When the last time I seen that? . . . I mean, ain't nothing wrong with it. I mean, old folks swear by it. It's just, you know, you don't see it up here much . . ." (14). Western practices of early weaning, coupled with discomfort with close mother-son attachment, particularly if expressed physically, is what renders the scene so unsettling for readers.

In nursing her son, Ruth breaks the taboo of maternal sexuality and that of mother-son intimacy. Breastfeeding is thus, at least metaphorically, and from Ruth's perspective, an act of defiance against the repression of the values of the funk. This sense of breaking the rules is underscored by the reference to the story of Rumpelstiltskin. Ruth tells us that nursing her son "[s]he had the distinct impression that his lips were pulling from her a thread of light. It was as though she were a cauldron issuing spinning gold. Like the miller's daughter— the one who sat at night in a straw filled room, thrilled with the secret power Rumpelstiltskin had given her: to see golden thread stream from her very own shuttle" (13).

Ruth's identity is marked in the text by the water mark on her dining room table:

> She never set the table or passed through the dining room without look-
> ing at it. Like a lighthouse keeper drawn to his window to gaze once again
> at the sea, or a prisoner automatically searching out the sun as he steps into
> the yard for his hour of exercise, Ruth looked for the water mark several
> times during the day. She knew it was there, would always be there, but
> she needed to confirm its presence. Like the keeper of the lighthouse and
> the prisoner, she regarded it as mooring, a checkpoint, some stable visual
> object that assured her that the world was still there; that this was life and
> not a dream. That she was alive somewhere, inside, which she acknowl-
> edged to be true only because a thing she knew intimately was out there,
> outside herself. (11)

Hudson-Weems and Samuels read the water mark as symbolizing Ruth's "flawed existence" (56). The water stain may, however, also be read as a signifier of Ruth's subjectivity. Ruth, we are told, "talked about getting rid of it. . . . But her glance was nutritious; the spot became if anything, more pronounced as the years passed" (11). Although situated outside of herself, the water mark anchors her subjectivity—"the stable visual object . . . assured her . . . that she was alive . . ."—and thus is a sign of resistance against her husband and the dominant culture that would seek to erase her. Ruth's lack of culinary ability may be also read from this perspective. Ruth, we are told, "prepar[ed] . . . food her husband found impossible to eat. She did not try to make her meals nauseating; she simply didn't know how not to" (11). Because culinary talent is so integral to the domesticity that defines women's role as both mother and wife, Ruth's "red at the bone chicken and lumpy potatoes" could be read as a gesture of resistance, intentional or not, against patriarchal wifedom and motherhood. Ruth's lack of culinary ability, the water stain, and her nursing of her son signify a deviation from the script of the good and proper wife/mother that, in turn, implies that Ruth is not wholly a submissive woman and that, in some way, she struggles to articulate the funk she has been forced to repress.

Failed Maternal Nurturance: "The Heart of Maternal Darkness"

Morrison's fourth novel *Tar Baby* exposes what Erickson calls, "failed [maternal] nurturance" (Gates and Appiah 1993: 294). "In Margaret," as Demetrakopoulos observes, "we have the first full-fledged portrait of a child abuser in all of literature" (138). The secret, repeatedly hinted at throughout the narrative, is finally told by Ondine at the Christmas dinner, symbolically the celebration of the son, Christ's, birth: "You white freak! You baby killer! I saw you! . . . You cut him up. You cut your baby up. Made him bleed for you. For fun you did it. Made him scream, you, you freak. You crazy white freak. . . . She stuck pins in his behind. Burned him with cigarettes. Yes, she did. I saw her; I saw his little behind. She burned him!" (208). In her chapter on maternal violence, appropriately entitled "Violence: The Heart of Maternal Darkness" (1986), Adrienne Rich examines how child abuse, such as that performed by Margaret, is created by the institution of motherhood itself. Patriarchal motherhood gives to mothers all of the responsibility, but none of the power. Women who mother in the institution of motherhood do so under the rule of men with no or little control over the material conditions of their mothering. The "expectations laid on [mothers]," Rich writes, "are insane expectations." Instead of recognizing, in Rich's words, "the institutional violence of patriarchal motherhood, society labels those women who finally erupt in violence as psychopathological" (263). Margaret is, I suggest, as much a victim of the institution of motherhood as is her son Michael.

Margaret is a child bride; she is married eight months out of high school and becomes a mother nine months after that. What attracts Valerian to Margaret is her beauty: "A rosy-cheeked girl was holding on to one of the bear's forefeet like a bird. The plastic igloo behind them threw into dazzling relief her red velvet coat and the ermine muff she waved to the crowd. The moment he saw her something inside him knelt down" (16). More specifically, Margaret, in red and white, reminds Valerian of the candies named after him (51). As the candies did, she would take his name and be one of his confections. Upon marriage he keeps her sequestered as a princess in a castle and puts an end to the only friendship she has because it was, in his eyes, inappropriate: "Valerian put a stop to it saying she should guide the servants, not consort with them" (59). When Valerian retires to the Isle des Chevaliers, the narrator tells us that the "rest of what he loved he brought with him: some records, garden shears, a sixty-four bulb chandelier, a light blue tennis shirt and the Principle Beauty of Maine" (11). Margaret is listed here as one of his valued possessions, of less importance, it would seem, than his records, shears, chandelier, and shirt. We are introduced to Margaret only after Valerian's personal history has been narrated and her story is then told only in the context of his. Margaret enters the text only after Valerian, Sydney, and Ondine have been introduced. In this scene, we learn of Valerian's control of the food Margaret eats: "[T]here's your mango. Four hundred and twenty five calories. . . . Slurp away. But you had three helpings of mousse last night" (23). Food, both literally and metaphorically, represents nurturance; Valerian's monitoring of Margaret's suggest that she is not nurtured.

In *Tar Baby,* eating symbolically represents Margaret's self-fragmentation: "She was usually safe with soup, anything soft or liquid that required a spoon, but she was never sure when the confusion would return: when she would scrape her fork lines along china trying to pick up the painted blossoms at its centre, or forget to unwrap the Amaretti cookie at the side of her plate and pop the whole thing into her mouth. . . . [S]he was careful at the table, watching other people handle their food—just to make sure that never again would she pick up the knife instead of the celery stalk or pour water from her glass over the prime ribs instead of the meat's own juices" (63). Earlier, in a discussion about what bird should be ordered for Christmas dinner, the narrator tells us that Valerian says geese, and Margaret responds: "Geese? . . . Like a blank frame in a roll of film, she lost the picture that should have accompanied the word. Turkey she saw, but geese . . ." (32). Margaret often experiences, in her words, "a blank frame where the picture or concept should be"; in the face of material objects she loses the ability to name.

This disassociation stems from her own objectification as the Principle Beauty of Maine. No one in Margaret's life has seen her as real. Margaret's "blue-if-it's-boy blue eyes" and her "flaming hair" caused her parents to stand back in awe and wonder: "Joe and Leonora left her alone. . . . Maybe her beauty scared them a little, maybe they just felt well, at least she has that. She won't have to worry. And they stepped back and let her be. They gave her care, but withdrew attention" (56–57). Margaret is not a nurtured child. She lacked an attentive mother who would foster her developing female self. Thus, she becomes a woman whose sense of self comes not from within but from outside, formed through the gaze of others. Not until the end of the novel, after the secret has been disclosed, does Valerian finally see her as a "flesh and blood" person: "She looked real. Not like a piece of Valerian candy, but like a person on a bus, already formed, fleshed, thick with a life which is not yours and not accessible to you" (239).

The child abuse itself grows out of Margaret's own selflessness. Margaret speaks of "an outrage [at] that infant's needfulness":

> There were times when she absolutely had to limit its *being there;* stop its implicit and explicit demand for her best and constant self. She could not describe her loathing of its prodigious appetite for security—the criminal arrogance of an infant's conviction that while he slept, someone is there; that when he wakes, someone is there; that when he is hungry, food will somehow magically be provided. . . . [S]he felt hostage to that massive insolence, that stupid trust, she could not help piercing it. (236)

Margaret also tells us of a profound emptiness: "[T]here was no way or reason to describe those long quiet days when the sun was drained and nobody was ever on the street. There were magazines, of course, to look forward to but neither *Life* nor *Time* could fill a morning. It started on a day like that. Just once she did it, a slip, and then once more, and it become the thing to look forward to, to resist, to succumb to, to plan, to be horrified by, to forget, because out of the doing of it came the reason" (236). All mothers who have mothered in the patriarchal institution of motherhood can understand the loneliness, aloneness, isolation, emptiness, boredom, of early motherhood that Margaret describes in this passage. Without companionship or work other than that of motherhood, Margaret abuses her son to fill up the emptiness and give some meaning to her life. The abuse makes her somehow more real.

The self-erasure required of Margaret and all new mothers in the institution of motherhood collides against the very real and persistent affirmation of selfhood expressed by the infant in his constant need of attention. His affirmation of selfhood emphasizes the mother's own selflessness. "[With the] torture of her son," Denise Heinze writes in *The Dilemma of Double Consciousness* (1993), "[Margaret] finally creates a self" (49). *Tar Baby* suggests that, as a daughter, Margaret did not receive motherlove and hence she did not develop self-love.

Margaret may also be read as a Medea figure; the abuse of her son is an act of retaliation against her husband. It is Valerian's child that she hurts. As Ondine says: "She didn't stick pins in her baby. She stuck em in his baby. Her baby she loved" (279). Perhaps, like Sethe, Margaret was trying to outhurt the hurter. Valerian's part in both causing and concealing the child abuse is made evident in the novel. As Ondine explains to Jadine: "He kept her stupid; kept her idle. That always spells danger" (279). Valerian finally acknowledges his own complicity: "[He] had chosen not to know the real message that his son had mailed to him from underneath the sink. All he could say was that he did not know. He was guilty, therefore, of innocence. Was there anything so loathsome as a wilfully innocent man?" (243).

Margaret's child abuse and the similar act of Sethe's infanticide are acts of resistance against slavery in the instance of Sethe and patriarchal motherhood in the case of Margaret. Rage and revenge are represented through harm to children. This theme is elaborated in *Paradise* in the character of Mavis. The deaths of her twins may be read as Mavis's resistance, albeit conveyed unconsciously, against her oppression as a battered wife and disempowered mother. Significantly, the suffocation of her twins occurs when is she is buying wieners, symbols of patriarchal power, for her husband because, as she explains during the interview, "he was fit to be tied; Spam ain't nothing for [a] working man to eat" (240).

MATERNAL POWER

Morrison's representation of maternal power, as with her themes of preservative love and maternal nurturance as resistance, have more often than not been misread as problematic if not pathological by the critical community. Just as Mrs. MacTeer was chastised for her harsh preservative love and Sethe criticized for her "too-thick" nurturance, Eva in *Sula* is condemned for exercising maternal power and deciding to end her son's life. In all three incidents, the maternal acts conveyed do not conform to the received view of what a mother should be, and hence the mothers in question—Mrs. MacTeer, Sethe, and Eva—are judged to be "bad" mothers. Eva in particular distresses readers because the maternal power she claims upsets the comfortable notions of maternal powerlessness. While such power may disturb readers, maternal power is central to Morrison's maternal standpoint and recognized as necessary for a black mother's essential motherwork. This final section will argue that Eva claimed maternal power to protect and nurture her son the only way she could and that this distresses readers because maternal power, while central to Morrison's maternal standpoint, is not something with which most readers are comfortable.

As with Hannah's comment and Eva's preservative motherlove, Eva's murder of Plum has received much condemnation and little compassion from the scholarly community. Patrick Bjork argues that "[Eva] had no sympathy for [Plum's] weakness" (66). Eva, he concludes, "lack[ed] a loving center" (67). In *Fiction and Folklore*, Trudier Harris writes:

> Eva is a slap in the face to all traditional matriarchs, for there is no God-centred morality informing her actions. . . . In deciding that her son Plum would be better off dead, Eva recognizes no authority, no morality except herself. Plum's drug addiction offends her sense of what a man should be, especially someone she had forced to keep on living when he was a baby and for whom she probably sacrificed her leg. To see such sacrifices thrown back into her face negates the very existence Eva has carved out for herself. . . . Eva becomes the vengeful goddess in destroying a creature who has failed to worship in an appropriate manner at her altar. (71, 74)[29]

We are told of Plum's death on two separate occasions: in the first instance (45–48) the omniscient narrator describes the event; later (70–72), Eva in a conversation with Hannah attempts to explain why she took the life of her son. The first telling describes; the second explains. We learn what happened before we learn why it happened.

The scene of Plum's murder is symbolically linked to the earlier outhouse scene where Eva saves baby Plum from life-threatening constipation by "shoving the last bit of food she had in the world up his ass" (33–34). The critic Stephanie Demetrakopoulos calls this scene "the most poignant and harrowing passage in all literature by women (and it could only be written by a woman)" (55). Through imagery, tone, and style Morrison connects the scene in which Eva saves Plum's life to the later scene in which she ends his life. In the first scene we are told that Eva "wrapped [Plum] in blankets"; later Plum is described as being "engulfed [in] flames" (48). Eva saves Plum's life with lard and later takes his life with kerosene. Both lard and kerosene are household staples; the first provides nurturance, the latter gives us light. Both times Plum is held by his mother; as an infant "she squatted down, turned [him] over on her knees" (34); and later she "gathered [him] into her arms . . . held him closer and began to rock. Back and forth she rocked him" (46). As an infant, "food is shoved . . . up his ass" (34) and later the kerosene covered his "legs and stomach . . . wound itself all about him . . . running into his skin" (47). As Eva describes a "freezing darkness," Plum tells us of "felt twilight . . . a wet light" (47). We move from the cold darkness of the outhouse to the bright heat of the flames (34). When the adult Plum "s[inks] back into the bright hole of sleep" (47) we are reminded of the "grateful" sleep of baby Plum (34). Eva's resolve "to end his misery once and for all" (134) echoes Plum's thought that "everything is going to be all right" (47).

The striking similarity of these two passages, in both tone and language, invite a comparative reading. We are encouraged to interpret Eva's murder of Plum as we did her earlier "saving" of him. Both are acts of preservative love. Just as Sethe "killed her baby girl so she should would not have to die," Eva, as DeLancey observes, "must deliver the adult Plum to death in order to save him from the drug addiction that is worse than death itself" (16).

Bjork argues that Eva "lacks a loving center" and "has no sympathy for Plum's weakness." The latter is her motivation for the murder: the former is what enabled her to carry it out. Trudier Harris interprets the murder of Plum as an act of vengeance: in her words, "Eva destroys a creature who has failed to worship her in an appropriate manner" (1991: 74).[30] Leaving aside for the moment the larger question of whether Eva had the right to kill her son, I argue that Eva sees the killing as a gesture of motherlove. The narrator tells us that Eva "gathered Plum into her arms . . . and rocked him back and forth." Holding him she remembers Plum as an infant: "Eva let her memory spin, loop and fall. Plum in the tub that time as she leaned over him. He reached up and dripped water into her bosom and laughed. She was angry, but not too, and laughed with him" (46–47). And, "Eva lifted her tongue to the edge of her lip to stop the tears from running into her mouth. Rocking, rocking. Later she laid him down and looked at him a long time" (47).

This scene, a mother killing her beloved child, is, at least for me, "the most poignant and harrowing passage" of the text. What I see in this passage is not callousness or vengeance, as the critics suggest, but a maternal anguish so deep that it is ultimately unrepresentable in language. Eva's pain can only be glimpsed and signified by the prediscursive language of her maternal body. Eva expresses her love for her son physically; she gathers him up and rocks him in her arms. Pain is, also, ultimately unrepresentable in language. In her book *The Body in Pain: The Making and Unmaking of the World* (1985), Elaine Scarry argues that pain exists at the edges of language, resisting articulation. Eva's grief and love can not be enunciated and this, I think, is the reason why so many critics have misread Eva's maternal pain as coldhearted vengeance. Unspoken, Eva's maternal love and grief are unheard.

The second part of this passage conveys a symbolic narrative of ritual and rebirth. The numerous references to the wet light in the passage suggest, as Samuels and Hudson-Weems observe, "a rite of purification." The water refers to the amniotic fluid of the womb; while the twilight, as Samuels and Hudson-Weems note, "signifies rebirth, the dawning of a new day" (40). Plum himself believes that the "wet lightness" is "some kind of baptism, some kind of blessing" (47). The narrator's description of Eva as "swinging and swooping like a giant heron" (46), and Plum's perception of her as an "eagle" (47) give majesty to Eva's act of murder and mythologizes it as a ritual ceremony, a type of blood sacrifice. The images of ritual and renewal promise a rebirth from death. Eva kills Plum so that he may be reborn.

What is also important about this passage, and not observed by the critics, is that it is told from Plum's perspective, the first and only time we have the son's point-of-view is when he is about to be murdered. While we could interpret this as yet another example of Eva's so-called matriarchal, man-hating consciousness—male subjectivity expressed only in its silencing—I suggest that the son's perspective allows us to see the murder as both a personal gesture of preservative love and a ritualized ceremony of rebirth. What matters is that Plum feels loved and cared for at the moment of his death. Like Lennie Small in Steinbeck's *Of Mice and Men,* Plum dies believing that "everything is going to be all right" (47). The son, the one who is about to die, tells this to the reader. I see this murder as an act of euthanasia, a mercy killing: Eva only hastens death and provides for her son "snug delight" at the time of his passing.

In an interview with Robert Stepto (1976), Morrison remarked: "[Eva] decided that her son was living a life that was not worth his time. She meant it was too painful to her; you know the way you kill a dog when he breaks his leg because he can't stand the pain. He may very well be able to stand it, but you can't, so that's why you get rid of him" (Taylor-Guthrie 1994: 15). More specifically, Eva is a mother who "can't stand to see her child in pain." When a child is in pain, the first desire and duty of the mother is to put an end to that child's suffering. The only way Eva can see to stop the suffering of her child is to kill him.

Eva explains to Hannah that she wanted Plum "[to] die like a man not all scrunched up inside my womb" (72). Eva recognizes that Plum's drug addiction has reduced him to an infantile state. She tells Hannah:

> After all that carryin' on, just gettin' him out and keepin' him alive, he wanted to crawl back in my womb and . . . I ain't got the room no more even if he could do it. There wasn't space for him in my womb. And he was crawlin' back. Being helpless and thinking baby thoughts and dreaming baby dreams and messing up his pants again and smiling all the time. I had room enough in my heart, but not in my womb, not no more. I birthed him once. I couldn't do it again. (71)

When Plum returns home from the war, his family, the narrator tells us, "waited for him to tell them whatever it was he wanted them to know." However, Plum does not voice his pain in words: instead it is "spoken" from his body. Plum's "sweet, sweet smile," "pointless clothes," "thinner" body, and "for days" sleep express the pain that is ultimately unrepresentable in language. As the narrator tells us, "They waited in vain for his telling but not long for the knowing" (45). The night he is killed, Plum speaks "drowsy and amused" mutterings and "chuckles [at] some private joke" (46). He speaks as a child would—"Hey, You holdin' me, Mamma?"—and expresses the adoration very young children feel for their mothers—"Mamma, you so purty. You so purty, Mamma" (47). When Hannah tells Eva that Plum is burning she responds: "My baby? Burning?" Years later when Eva speaks to Hannah about the death of Plum, she calls him "Sweet Plum. My baby boy" (72).

Plum is Eva's last child; the narrator tells us that he "floated in a constant swaddle of love and affection, until 1917 when he went to war." The phrase "constant swaddle of love and affection" signifies a mother-child bond and the word "floated" suggests the amniotic waters of the womb. Plum's going to war marks his entry into patriarchal culture. Plum, like Shadrack before him, is psychologically wounded by his participation in World War I: "[H]e arrived [home] with just the shadow of his old dipdown walk" (45). It is Plum's entry into the male world that destroys him and causes his drug addiction. Plum longs to return to the maternal space and reclaim the wholeness and unity of self he once knew. Eva tells Hannah that she dreamed "[Plum] [was] creepin' to the bed trying to spread my legs trying to get back up in my womb" (72–73). Plum desires the now forbidden maternal body and longs to reexperience maternal-child closeness—"[a] smiling all the time." With drugs, Plum both longs to forget the loss of the maternal world and seeks to recreate it.

"[A]ll of Morrison's male characters," Barbara Rigney writes, "are helpless with desire for the Great Mother—terrifying though she always is, representing as she always does the violation of the law of the father" (99). Plum is literally killed for his desire of the mother. The dream of her son "crawling back into her womb" is what brings Eva to finally decide upon murder. Readers of *Sula* tend to agree with Eva and regard Plum's desire as both perverse and pathological. Barbara Lounsberry and Grace Ann Hovat argue that Eva recognizes, in their words, that "the diminishment of the Black male may be caused by excessive mothering by both Black wives and mothers, as well as by social discrimination" (218). Eva kills her beloved son because, in her words, "[a] big man can't be a baby all wrapped up inside his mamma no more; he suffocate" (72). Ogunyemi argues that "[r]ather than sustain him in a hideous relationship similar to that of Oedipus and Jocasta, Eva sets him on fire to get rid of him. . . . The Peace women love men naturally, not unnaturally as Jocasta did Oedipus" (132). Plum's desire is interpreted by Eva and these critics as an unnatural love that threatens to "diminish" Plum's identity as a black man.[31]

However, Eva later admits to Hannah that "she would have let him [return] if [she'd] have the room" (72). This sentence, though, is followed by, "I done everything I could to make him leave me and go on and live and be a man . . .

but he wouldn't and I had to keep him out" (72). Hannah observes that "when Eva spoke . . . it was with two voices. Like two people were talking at the same time, saying the same thing, one a fraction of a second behind the other" (71). The two voices Hannah hears both belong to Eva; but one is the voice of Eva the maternal mother and the other is Eva the woman. As mother, Eva would gladly take her son back and welcome his return to the maternal. Eva mourns the loss of her son and longs to heal his scars by returning him to her maternal world. But the other Eva, the woman who lives in the patriarchal world, knows that there can never be a going back. However, at the time of his death Plum returns to the womb, to be, one last time, Eva's son. Covered in "a wet lightness" "he sank back into the bright hole of sleep." Killed by fire, Plum's end is his beginning.

Thus, *Sula* affirms mother-son connection at the same time as it problematizes it. Critics of mother and son attachment could interpret Plum's mental illness and drug addiction as evidence that his mother's closeness emasculated him, rendering him unfit for the manly duty of war. A real man would return from war a hero, made more manly because of his war involvement. This interpretation is undercut by the character Shadrack, who also returns from the war "mad" though there is no indication that he was "unmanned" by a mother. Plum is born to the Peace motherline and is destroyed by war. In giving the name Peace to Plum and having him engage in war, Morrison underscores the problematic of mother-son connection in a patriarchal society. For daughters, as well as sons, in Morrison, loved and proud African American selfhood depends upon connecting to the motherline, keeping the values of the funk and ancient properties intact, and receiving the motherlove that fosters self-love. Sons, however, more so than daughters, are required to separate from their mothers and the motherline to assume their normal masculine identity. Plum's death is a critique of this patriarchal imperative. Likewise, the murder of this son represents one mother's refusal to give up her son to patriarchy. Eva, recognizing that neither her nurturance nor the motherline can save Plum, kills him in order to save him.

CONCLUSION

The mothers' struggles to provide preservation, nurturance, and cultural bearing described in *The Bluest Eye, Sula,* and *Beloved* as well as black mothers' resistance against patriarchy portrayed in *Song of Solomon, Tar Baby,* and *Paradise* reveal that most mothers in Morrison understand the importance of motherwork for the well-being of their children and battle racism and patriarchy in order to provide it. However, even as these representations demonstrate how crucial preservation, cultural bearing, and nurturance are for the psychological health of African Americans and the larger cultural well-being of the black community, the critical commentary on the novels reveals that motherwork and the maternal power that mothers must claim in order to do this motherwork are frequently misunderstood or, worse, criticized. Mrs. MacTeer's and Eva's preservative love were dismissed by many as "deficient" while Sethe was chastised for her so-called "too thick" love and Eva censured for her "immoral" maternal power. These critical miseadings are genuinely worrisome; for not only do they fault black mother-work and maternal power, they also, in so doing, condemn the very thing that, for Morrison, makes possible the salvation of African American people. Readers must come to realize with Morrison that the preservation, nurturance, and cultural bearing of motherwork and the maternal power needed to do it, do indeed, to use Eva's own word, "count."

chapter six

Maternal Healing

Reconciliation and Redemption: *Jazz, Paradise*

MORRISON'S RENDITIONS OF MOTHERHOOD are truly horrifying: a son burnt to death; a baby whose throat is slit; children who are abused, abandoned, beaten, and neglected by their mothers—these harrowing events permeate all seven of her novels. The last chapter considered how these violations may be read as gestures of nurturance and preservation and, in particular, as maternal acts of resistance against a white supremacist and patriarchal culture. Motherwork, in Morrison's first five novels, is represented as an act of prevention insofar as mothers, through preservation, nurturance, and cultural bearing, seek to empower children to survive and resist. With her last two novels, *Jazz* and *Paradise*, Morrison's concern becomes how to heal these wounds once inflicted.

Song of Solomon and *Tar Baby* narrate an individual's quest to reclaim the ancient properties and ancestral memory of the African American motherline; with Morrison's last two novels the emphasis is upon the reclamation of the lost selfhood of the unmothered child. This chapter will explore how Violet and Joe in *Jazz* and the convent women in *Paradise* are healed when they remember the mother, mourn her loss, reconnect with her, and recreate for themselves an identity as a mothered child. This psychic journey of return, reconnection, and reclamation, while directed to a spirit of a lost mother, is initiated and overseen by an actual mother figure. For Violet this othermother is Alice, while in *Paradise*, Consolata heals the convent women by prompting them, as did Alice with Violet, to take this journey of rememory and assisting, comforting, and sustaining them as they do so. Healing, in the form of acceptance and forgiveness becomes possible when the women, under the care of Consolata, reclaim their identities as mothers and/or daughter that maternal failures had caused them to deny. As Joe and Violet must go in search of their lost mother to find their lost selves, the convent women must remember the daughters and mothers they once were to become the women they wish to become.

153

"IN SEARCH OF MY MOTHER'S GARDEN:
I FOUND MY OWN": REMEMBERING MOTHER,
RECLAIMING SELF IN *JAZZ*

Morrison's sixth novel *Jazz,* the second book in a trilogy, tells the story of unmothered children who never take the journey from motherlove to self-love, and thus never come to know their own selves. Morrison argues that before a child can love herself, she must experience herself being loved and learn that she is indeed valuable and deserving of affection. This novel, more than Morrison's earlier writings, emphasizes how essential mothering is for the emotional well-being of children. This section on *Jazz* will examine the mother-child relationship of Violet and Rose, Joe and Wild, and explore how the loss of the mother fractures and displaces the child's developing self. As Violet and Joe grow into adulthood, they simultaneously seek to forget and to find the mother they lost through coping strategies of denial and substitution. However, in repressing the pain of their loss and in attempting to replace the mother in adult relationships, Violet and Joe move farther from their own original selves. Only when they mourn the loss of their mothers is recovery of adult selfhood made possible. *Jazz* is thus a story about the wounding and healing of the unmothered children.

ROSE VIOLET: "THE GIRL HER MOTHER WOULD HAVE LIKED"

Near the beginning of the novel the narrator describes what she calls Violet's "private cracks":

> I call them cracks because that is what they were. Not openings or breaks, but dark fissures in the globe light of the day. She wakes up in the morning and sees with perfect clarity a string of small, well-lit scenes. In each one something specific is being done. . . . But she does not see herself doing these things. She sees them being done. The globe light holds and bathes each scene, and it can be assumed that at the curve where the light stops is a solid foundation. In truth, there is no foundation at all, but alleyways, crevices one steps across all the time. But the globe light is imperfect too. Closely examined it shows seams, ill-glued cracks and weak places beyond which is anything. . . . Sometimes when Violet isn't paying attention she stumbles onto these cracks. (22–23)

This passage describes radical dislocation of self, a fragmented subjectivity. Violet's observation that "[s]he sees them being done," not herself doing them, suggests a mind-body split or splintering of schizophrenia. The absence of foundation marks a selfhood without core or center. The metaphorical references to "crevices," "dark fissures," "ill-glued cracks" also position Violet's subjectivity as alienated and fragmented.

In the second part of Violet's story (89–114), this split in subjectivity becomes actualized; two "persons" inhabit Violet's body. There are two Violets, textually differentiated as Violet and *that* Violet. *That* Violet is the young Violet, supposedly the real, authentic, or original Violet. *That* Violet is the younger version of her self; the woman, Violet tells us later, "my mother didn't stay around long enough to see . . . the one she would have liked and the one I used to like before. . . . My grandmother fed me stories about a little blond child" (208). The little blond child referred to is Golden Gray, the son of Miss Vera Louise and "a Negro boy from out Vienna way." The text suggests that Violet's "fatal attraction" for Golden Gray is responsible for her emotional scarring, that the pain of unrequited love damages Violet's developing selfhood. However, not only is Violet's love for him not reciprocated, but in loving him, a white male, Violet locates that which is beautiful and desired outside of her self. From her grandmother's tales of the pampered and worshipped Golden Boy, Violet learns that whiteness and maleness ensure love and happiness. She also learns from these stories that True Belle's daughters, one of whom was Rose Dear, were left behind when True Belle accompanied Miss Louise to Baltimore. The motherlove that rightfully belonged to the daughters was lavished on a white boy with "the yellow curls."[1] Rather than hating this boy who took her from her children, True Belle feels only love for this "beautiful young man" (139). The man who so dazzled True Belle that he made her forget the daughters she left behind simultaneously captivates Violet's heart and damages her self-worth. Her desire becomes not only to love Golden Boy, but to become him.

It is not until the end of *Jazz* that Violet sees, in Felice's words, that a "tricky blond boy [had been] living inside [her head]" (211). In a conversation with Felice, Violet explains how she "messed up [her] life" by forgetting who that life belonged to:

> "'Forgot it was mine. My life. I just ran up and down the street wishing I was somebody else.'
> "'Who? Who'd you want to be?'
> "'Not who so much as what. White. Light. Young again.'
> "'Now you don't?'
> "'Now I want to be the woman my mother didn't stay around long enough to see. That one. The one she would have liked and the I one I used to like before. . . . My Grandmother fed me stories about a little blond child. He was a boy, but I thought of him as a girl sometimes, as a brother, sometimes as a boyfriend. He lived inside my mind. Quiet as a mole. But I didn't know it till I got here. The two of us. Had to get rid of it.' . . .
> "'How did you get rid of her?'
> "'Killed her. Then I killed the me that killed her.'" (208–209)

Violet's realization is complex and requires some fleshing out. Violet recognizes that the stories of the adored blond child produced in her a longing to be white, bright, and young. This desire demanded from her a denial of her real, original black female self. The headstrong Violet of Virginia is further displaced by the citified Mrs. Trace. The recovery of her original self occurs when both the "tricky little blond child" and the Mrs Trace "who wanted to be something else" are exorcised from Violet's consciousness. Violet's assertion of "me" recalls Sethe's tentative questioning "me? me?" at the end of *Beloved*. Here, at the conclusion of *Jazz*, Violet finds her original self and learns that she is indeed her "best thing."

From this interpretation it would seem that the "tricky blond kid" living inside Mrs. Trace's head (211) was the cause of Violet's psychological wounding and the subsequent displacement of her original self. However, Golden Gray is, I think, a substitute for the lost mother. Deborah McDowell argues in her review of *Jazz*: "[T]he memory of the lost mother is the motor force of *Jazz*" (3). More specifically, the motor force of the text is, I would suggest, the *search* for a surrogate mother. What propels Violet's narrative is a series of replacements, a chain of substitutions. From her infatuation with Golden Boy to her love for Joe Trace, and "mother hunger [that] hit her like a hammer," and her obsession with the dead girl, Violet seeks to fill up the space in her self that the death of her mother created.

Violet's rejection of motherhood is also tied to her mother's death. "The important thing, the biggest thing Violet got out of that," the text tells us, "was to never never have children. Whatever happened, no small dark foot would rest on another while a hungry mouth said, Mama?" (102). The many miscarriages Violet later suffers are thus "more inconvenience than loss" (107). Later Violet imagines Dorcas as one of her own long-lost daughters. Significantly, when Violet speaks of the loss of this daughter she describes it as an abortion:

> Was she the woman who took the man, or the daughter who fled her womb? Washed away on a tide of soap, salt and castor oil. Terrified, perhaps, of so violent a home. Unaware that, had it failed, had she braved mammymade poisons and mammy's urgent fists, she could have had the best-dressed hair in the City. (109)

It would seem then that these miscarriages were in fact self-induced abortions, signifying Violet's rejection of motherhood, or more accurately her refusal to become her mother. When Violet says "[s]he didn't want to be like that [her mother]. Oh never like that" (97), she expresses what Adrienne Rich has termed matrophobia: "the fear not of one's mother or of motherhood but of *becoming one's mother*" (1986: 235, italics in original).

In *Beloved*, Sethe explains to Paul D. how difficult it was to mother her children at Sweet Home without a community of elder women to turn to for guidance and support. Sethe recognizes that daughters learn "how to mother" from the knowledge and example of their foremothers. From *Beloved*, we also learn that a mother bequeaths more than practical advice to her daughter. In loving her daughter, the mother enables the daughter to love when she herself becomes a mother. Rose Dear's despair and death prevent her from giving maternal love and being a mother to and for her daughter. Violet is not mothered; and so she is not able to fulfill that role of daughter described in Morrison's *Tar Baby*: "I'm just saying what a daughter is. A daughter is a woman that cares about where she come from and takes care of them that took care of her" (281). Not having been a daughter, Violet is unable to become a mother.

However, while Violet refuses to become like her mother and realizes that she is psychologically unprepared for mothering, having not been mothered herself, she continually claims a maternal identity. We are told how Violet catches herself "staring at infants and hesitating in front of toys displayed at Christmas" (107). "By and by longing became heavier than sex: a panting" (108). Violet comforts herself with a doll that she hides beneath the bed and thinks about the babies she has lost. On one occasion she finds herself holding somebody else's baby and planning the bed and bath she will prepare the moment she has him home. Holding the baby, Violet speaks of a "brightness that could be carried in her arms. Distributed, if need be, into places dark *as the bottom of a well*" (22, emphasis added). She also takes on a maternal identity by mothering other women. Violet's hairdressing represents a type of mothering activity; her customers are her surrogate children, the daughters she never had. In grooming and advising these women Violet assumes a maternal role and offers nurturance and counsel to her "daughters." Upon seeing the picture of Dorcas, Violet reflects: "She needed her ends cut . . ." (15). As her customers are her children, so too are the birds. As Joe explains to Malvonne: "Violet takes better care of her parrot than she does me" (49).

Thus, while Violet rejects motherhood she attempts to find her lost self through mothering. With Dorcas, the doll, the stolen baby, her hairdressing customers, and the parrot, Violet seeks to actually become the mother she lost. By maternally caring for others, Violet also desires to find her old self as daughter. She projects herself onto the person or animal that is being cared for. Through such projections, the adult Violet mothers the child Violet. She mothers herself. Through her mothering, Violet can both be the mother she lost and the daughter she once was.

In a conversation with Alice, Violet speaks of an absence, a void in her life: "I thought it would be bigger than this. I knew it wouldn't last, but I did think it'd be bigger" (112) and expresses a longing for something more, "something real . . . some fat in my life" (110). During this discussion Alice utters from out of nowhere, "'Oh Mama': . . . blurted it out and then covered her mouth." This Freudian slip triggers Violet's realization:

> Violet had the same thought: Mama. Mama? Is this where you got to and couldn't do it no more? The place of shade without trees where you know you are not and never again will be loved by anybody who can choose to do it? Where everything is over but the talking? (110)

At this critical moment Violet identifies with her mother and is at last able to understand her mother's life. Violet's later statement on what she would do if she threw Joe out—"Watch the floor boards, I guess" (112)—is also a direct reference to Rose Dear, for that is what Rose, as the narrator tells us, watched after she was tipped from her chair. This reference and the earlier epiphany reveal that Violet now realizes why her mother committed suicide. Violet is able, at last, to understand, know, and name her mother's pain because she herself has lived it. This realization marks a vital mother-daughter connection; identifying with her mother's pain she comes to understand and then forgive her mother.

As Violet gains insight into her mother's life as a woman, she also comes to understand the life her mother lived as a daughter. Rose Dear is eight when her mother, True Belle, is taken to Baltimore. Years later, when True Belle eventually returns home to Rose, she entertains her now grown daughter with tales of Golden Gray. What Rose learns from these stories is that her mother does not hate this boy who took her from her own daughters years ago. The stories tell her, as they did with Violet, that this boy has claimed her mother's heart; he, not she, is the beloved child. The narrator remarks:

> I don't know how hard it was for a slave woman to leave a husband that work and distance kept her from seeing much of anyhow, and to leave two daughters behind with an old aunt to take care of them. . . . Maybe, she felt bad. Anyway, choiceless, she went, leaving husband, sister, Rose Dear and May behind, and if she worried, the blond baby helped soothe her, and kept her entertained for eighteen years, until he left home. (141–42)

Years later, Violet understands why her mother failed at mothering. Rose could not be a mother to her daughter because she herself was not mothered as a daughter. Violet experiences firsthand what may be called, to paraphrase the title of Nancy Chodorow's book, the reproduction of motherlessness. Violet's recognition of her own mother's missed mothering allows for a daughter-to-daughter identification that, in turn, strengthens the mother-daughter bond.

Violet's life moves along a chain of substitutions. With each link on the chain—forgetting, replacing, becoming the lost mother—Violet is further alienated from her original self. Each attempt to recover her lost self through a replacement of her mother deepens the cracks of her splintered subjectivity and distances her from her real original mother, Rose Dear. When Violet finally identifies with her mother as a woman she is able to understand and appreciate Rose Dear's life. This recognition makes understanding and forgiveness possible. Violet no longer blames her mother for her desertion and she no longer blames herself for her mother's suicide. Freed from denial and blame, Violet can remember her mother and recover her lost maternal identification. She can now be "the girl her mother would have liked."

Toni Morrison's *Jazz* narrates the recovery of a matrilineal heritage and returns the daughter to the lost mother. In remembering her mother as mother, woman, daughter, Violet recovers her own self. The dead girl inside her is brought back to life. In Morrison's words: "She is here now, alive. I have seen, named and claimed her—and oh what company she keeps."[2] Violet has claimed her original self, "that headstrong Virginia Violet," and found "the lost lady she put down someplace." The "so narrow, so dark" space inside is closed, and the "ill-glued" cracks are mended. Violet's selfhood is made whole and complete. The final paragraph of this section on Violet reads:

Committed as Violet was to hip development, even she couldn't drink the remaining malt—watery, warm and flat tasting. She buttoned her coat and left the drugstore and noticed, at the same moment as *that* Violet did, that it was spring. In the City. (114)

Carole Boyce Davies argues, as noted in chapter 1, that "[m]othering and healing are intricately connected and of central thematic importance in recent novels by Black women. . . . These writers reveal that Black women, at certain junctures in their lives, require healing and renewal and that Black women themselves have to become the healers/mothers for each other when there is such need" (1991: 41). In *Jazz,* Violet is "daughter" to Alice who takes Violet on a healing journey back to her original self and the mother she lost.³ Alice is a seamstress: as she repairs the "loose running threads" and the "ripped lining" of Violet's clothing, she mends the "so dark, so narrow" tear in Violet's selfhood and stitches together the frayed pieces of her splintered subjectivity. The second time Violet shows up at Alice's door "she looked so bad Alice wanted to slap her" (82). Instead, Alice asked Violet to remove her dress so that she could repair the torn cuff. As Violet sat in her slip, "Alice mended the sleeve with the tiniest stitches" (82). Later, when the long and deep silence that followed Alice's cry "Mama" and Violet's disturbing realization is broken, Alice demands: "Give me that coat. I can't look at that lining another minute" (110). The maternal affections and admonitions that do not find expression in words are "spoken" in the stitches Alice sews. In *Jazz,* one woman mothers another woman and returns her to her lost mother. Violet finds her mother's garden because Alice, her friend, has shown her the way.

WILD'S TRACE: A MOTHER'S SON

The other lost mother in *Jazz* is Wild: "[A woman] too brain-blasted to do what the meanest sow managed: nurse what she birthed" (179). In her review of *Jazz,* Deborah McDowell speculates that Wild may be Beloved: "Could she even be that 'devil child' who take[s] the shape of a pregnant woman before vanishing at *Beloved's* end?" (1). Joe is born in 1873 in Vesper County, Virginia (123), the same year Beloved disappeared from 124. Beloved is last seen "down by the stream, and saw, cutting through the woods, a naked woman with fish for hair" (267); Wild is first seen by Golden Gray "among the trees." Golden Gray's characterization of Wild as "a naked berry-black woman . . . covered with mud and leaves are in her hair" (144) recalls the neighborhood women's description of Beloved: "Thunderblack and glistening, she stood on long straight legs, her belly big and tight. Vines of hair twisted all over her head" (261). Golden Gray is startled by Wild's stomach, which is also described as "big and tight" (144). He too wonders whether she is a "vision." As Beloved "walked out of the water" in the stream (50), Wild is found "in the woods. Where wild women grow" (171). As devil-child and wild-woman, neither are "of woman born." They exist in an almost timeless natural and supernatural place. Both seem to be fairies or witches with a magical "shining" and supernatural power. The narrator says of Wild:

Cutting cane could get frenzied sometimes when young men got the feeling she was just yonder. . . . Just thinking about her . . . could mess up a
whole morning's work. . . . [The old men] weren't prepared for the way
their blood felt when they caught a glimpse of her, or for how trembly their
legs got hearing that babygirl laugh. . . . [T]he grandfathers . . . went soft
in the head, walked out of the syrup house, left their beds in the shank of
the night, wet themselves, forgot the names of their grown children and
where they'd put their razor strops. (166–67)

Paul D. is charmed by Beloved and under her "spell": "[S]omething is hap-
pening to me, that girl is doing it . . . she is doing it to me. Fixing me . . . she's
fixed me and I can't break it" (127).

The interfacing of the words "Trace" and "disappear" also suggest that Wild
may be Beloved. At the conclusion of the novel *Beloved,* Beloved and her memory "disappear": "By and by all trace is gone" (275). Significantly, Joe, the son
of Wild, takes on the surname Trace after his adoptive mother explains to him
that his real parents "disappeared without a trace." "The way I heard it I understood her to mean the 'trace' they disappeared without was me" (124). At the
end of *Beloved,* we are told that "her footprints come and go. . . . By and by all
trace is gone, and what is forgotten is not only the footprints but the water too
and what is down there" (275). Wild in *Jazz* leaves little trail for Joe, her son, to
"track" her by (130).

Wild is the archetypal wild woman.[4] She exists outside and beyond the masculine realm of law, order, and reason. Within nature and inside her womb-like
burrow, Wild inhabits a specifically feminine space or what has been called a
female "wild zone" (Showalter 1985). Wild emits howls, laughs, bites, and sings,
but she does not speak. When Joe first hears Wild singing he mistakenly thinks
that her song is only "a combination of running water and wind in high trees . . .
the music the world makes" (176–77). Like the three whores from *The Bluest Eye*
and Pilate in *Song of Solomon,* Wild voices a specifically feminine language
through song. Significantly, when Joe seeks out Wild among the bushes "to confirm, for once and for all, that she was indeed his mother," what he wants from
her is "[j]ust a sign": "[H]e didn't need words or even want them because he knew
how they could lie. . . . All she had to do was give him a sign, her hand thrust
through the leaves . . ." (37). Wild's mode of communication is touch: the primal "language" of the body, that which circulates outside of words. When she
does speak, she does so only in song and laughter. Wild speaks the prediscursive
"language" of the pre-Oedipal maternal space.

Julia Kristeva calls this prediscursive language the Semiotic. The Semiotic is
the language before language, that which was spoken in the preverbal, pre-Oedipal space of the mother and child. I contend that Wild represents that uncon-
trollable excess that Kristeva calls the Semiotic. Her laughter, song, and touch
are the language of semiotic discourse. In *Revolution in Poetic Language* (1984),
Kristeva discusses how the Semiotic interrupts the symbolic and "returns" in the

form of rhythm, wordplay, melody, and laughter. Wild also exists outside of the Symbolic, and disrupts the symbolic male wor(l)d through her "babygirl laugh" and the "tap of her fingertips." Kristeva defines the Semiotic as a trace: significantly, the son of Wild takes on the surname Trace. Wild's home is also presented as a pre-Oedipal maternal space. She lives within the earth in a cave or burrow, described as a womb. The first time Joe looks for his mother he finds an "opening in the rock formation but could not enter it from that angle. He would have to climb above it and slide down into its mouth" (177). Years later Joe again tries to enter the cave: "squirming through a space low enough to graze his hair . . . [u]nable to turn around inside, he pulled himself all the way out to reenter head first. . . . Then he saw the crevice. He went into it on his behind until a floor stopped his slide. It was like falling into the sun" (183). What is described here is a return to the maternal body. Joe journeys down the birth canal, through the cervix, and into the womb. The baby's passage of birth is reversed; an adult male seeks to reenter the womb of the mother. Milkman in *Song of Solomon* entered the maternal space of the cave in search of gold and found instead his ancestral Self. Joe goes into the maternal space of "Wild's chamber of gold" (221) so that he may be returned to the place of his beginnings. Joe longs to discover where he came from so that he may, at last, know who he is. The reference to the light—"it was like falling into the sun"—inverts the darkness of Plato's Cave. This passage suggests that darkness is light and that the cave, the womb, is the "anchor of origin."[5]

Joe, the son of Wild, does not speak in his mother tongue. The essential "me" that Morrison refers to in her interviews is lacking in Joe. Violet's original self is first displaced through the "tricky blond boy living inside her head" and later on by the citified want-to-be-white Mrs. Trace. In contrast, Joe does not seem to have ever had an original self because at birth he was abandoned by his mother. We are told that "he travelled with an inside nothing" (37). Later, Joe says: "Before I met her [Dorcas] I'd changed into new seven times" (123). With no familial identity to call his own, and severed from his motherline, Joe makes up his own identity and literally names himself. In 1925 Joe recognizes that he "changed once too often" (129). Joe's shifting selfhood is experienced in a diachronic mode; he continuously shifts from one self-identity to another. In contrast, Violet's splintered subjectivity is experienced synchronically; several selves inhabit Violet simultaneously. Despite these differences, both Violet and Joe lost their selves when they lost their mothers and both carry the wounds of unmothered children.

Contemporary writing from the so-called men's movement has much to say on the wounds of the modern American male. Robert Bly, for example and as noted in chapter 1, argues that the modern man has left unexplored his true essential masculine identity (234). Healing occurs only when the man "gets in touch with" his own masculinity—frees the wild man inside. The son must "move from the mother's realm to the father's realm" (ix). The journey to manhood requires "a clean break from the mother" (19) because the American male grows up with too much mothering and not enough fathering; he suffers from what Bly calls "father hunger."[6] Morrison's *Jazz* tells quite a different story of the wounding and healing of men and thus may be read as a critique of Bly's misogynist and mother-blaming narrative of manhood. What Joe suffers from is not father hunger, as Bly would theorize, but grief as an unmothered child. Joe is psychologically wounded by the loss of his mother. At no time does Joe mourn the absence of his biological father. Interestingly, Joe does not wonder who his biological father may be, nor does the text speculate on the identity of the father.

The one son in *Jazz* who suffers from father hunger and goes in search of the father he never knew is the pretty Whiteboy Golden Gray. This son is characterized as a selfish, spoiled child more interested in finding out the color of his father's skin than in being a son to the father he never knew. What motivates this son's quest is not reconciliation but revenge and thoughts of patricide: "to blow the man's head off" (173). In contrast, Joe's search for his mother begins with the promise of healing and moves toward understanding and forgiveness.

Joe "made three solitary journeys to find [Wild]. In Vienna he had lived first with the fear of her, then the joke of her, finally the obsession, followed by rejection of her" (175). What Joe wants from Wild is confirmation that "she was indeed his mother. And even though the confirmation would shame him, it would make him the happiest boy in Virginia" (36). When his pleas for confirmation, "Yes. No. Either. But not this nothing," go unanswered he turns away from Wild in anger and shame:

> [A] simple-minded woman too silly to beg for a living. Too brain blasted to do what the meanest sow managed: nurse what she birthed. . . . There are boys who have whores for mothers and don't get over it. There are boys whose mothers stagger through town roads when the juke joint slams its door. Mothers who throw their children away or trade them for folding money. He would have chosen any of them over this indecent speechless lurking insanity. (179)

Joe attempts to forget his Wild, first in "maniacal work" and later through his marriage to Violet: "[She] help[ed] him escape all the redwings in the country and the ripe silenced that accompanied them" (30). However, Wild remains "always on his mind" (176).

Years later, Dorcas fills up Joe's "inside nothing." Joe finds in Dorcas the mother he never knew and wants from her the love he never had. What attracts him to Dorcas are the hoof marks on her cheeks: "I bought the stuff she told me to, but glad none of it ever worked. Take my little hoof marks away? Leave me with no tracks at all? In this world the best thing, the only thing, is to find the trail and stick to it. I tracked my mother in Virginia and it led me right to her . . ." (130). These tracks signify the motherline with which Joe seeks reconnection. Wild and Dorcas eventually merge to become one person. Joe's search for Dorcas becomes confused with his earlier search for his mother. Just as he sets out to "stalk" the City and "hunt" Dorcas, he remembers Hunter's cautionary words concerning his mother: "She is female. And she is not prey" (180). Joe's search for Dorcas on that January day becomes more and more blurred with his memory of the earlier search for his mother in Virginia; by the end of the section the two searches have merged into one.[7] Joe's words to Dorcas, "She don't have to explain. She don't need have to say a word" (183), recall the words spoken by a younger Joe to his mother: "She wouldn't have to say anything" (37). Later, he describes Dorcas as "Hardheaded. Wild, even" (182). And when Joe shoots Dorcas he describes the crowd as a "flock of redwings" (30). Later, the narrator admits that she was mistaken in thinking that Joe was tracking only Dorcas: "To this moment I'm not sure what his tears were really for, but I do know they were for more than Dorcas. All the while he was running through the streets in bad weather I thought he was looking for her, not Wild's chamber of gold" (221).

Wild is the woman shot and it is her death that Joe mourns. As a boy Joe never came to terms with the loss of his mother; he spent his life trying to forget his mother and trying to become someone other than his mother's son. When he loses his mother this second time, he relives the pain and loss he denied and repressed as a boy. Only when Joe truly acknowledges and feels the emotional wounds of his motherlessness is healing made possible. With the death of Dorcas, Joe is, at last, able to grieve the loss of his mother and move beyond the grief to forgive and accept his mother. He now can be his mother's son. Both Joe and Violet have learned to live with the past and have found the person they used to be. Their searches make their reconciliation as husband and wife possible. The last image we have of Joe and Violet is the two of them together, both thinking of their mothers:

> Lying next to her, his head turned toward the window, he sees through the glass darkness taking the shape of a shoulder with a thin line of blood. Slowly, slowly it forms itself into a bird with a blade of red on the wing. Meanwhile Violet rests her hand on his chest as though it were the sunlit rim of a well and down there somebody is gathering gifts (lead pencils, Bull Durham, Jap Rose Soap) to distribute to them all. (224–25)

As numbers—124—open the text of *Beloved,* a sound begins the narrative of *Jazz:* "Sth," the noise of a woman's mouth as she wets her thread before directing it through the eye of the needle. Thus, we enter the text, not through language, but through nonverbal, prediscursive sound similar to the chanting of the thirty conjure women in *Beloved* and the "fine cry—loud and long—[with] no bottom . . . or top" that closes the narrative of *Sula.* "Sth" is a sound made from tongue and lips touching; it is a lexicon of the primal, original "language" of the body that circulates outside of words. "In the beginning there were no words. In the beginning was the sound" (259). The narrative of *Jazz* opens with a specifically maternal discourse, the nonverbal language of the maternal, and closes with Joe and Violet remembering the mother they lost.

Jazz affirms the importance of motherwork and celebrates the power of maternal healing. The deep psychological wounds of the Violet and Joe remind us of how essential preservation, cultural bearing, and in particular nurturance are for emotional well-being. The healing that is made possible through other-mothering and by way of a journey of return to the lost mother give us cause for hope. While the hand that rocks the cradle may not rule the world, it does lead us back to our past and point the way to our future. In search of our mothers' gardens, we may find our own.

MATERNAL RECONNECTION AND
REDEMPTION IN PARADISE

As in *Jazz,* the convent women in *Paradise* must, to borrow Sethe's words, remem-ory their own selves as mothers and daughters and reclaim their lost relationships with their mother and/or daughter in order to he healed. In *Paradise,* the healing of the convent women becomes possible when Consolata herself is healed through her encounter with the mysterious walking man and she assumes the role of healer for the other women. This theme of woman to woman healing can be traced in Morrison's fiction from the three whores in *The Bluest Eye* to Alice and Violet's friendship in *Jazz:* women in Morrison frequently function as mothers to each other, providing the care and nurturance that make survival possible. In an inter-view, Morrison commented, "The real healing is often women talking to women . . . Hester Prynne now . . . or Madame Bovary: they needed a good girl friend to come along and say, 'Honey, you did *what* with *him.*' . . . But these women were written by men, so they didn't have girlfriends to confess to, or laugh with. Laughter is a way of taking the reins into your own hands" (Ross 1995: C1).

In the novel, four women—Mavis, Gigi, Seneca, and Pallas—arrive at the convent; each in her own way seeking refuge from the hurts of a patriarchal cul-ture, and in particular, as noted in the previous chapter, from the pain of their reproductive trauma. The convent, Connie's home and the women's refuge, is described as a safe haven; in particular, through the many references to the nour-ishment of cooking and gardening it signifies a place of maternal nurturance. Most, if not all, of the action described in the novel takes place in the large kitchen or in the abundant garden beyond. The kitchen, the center or heart of the convent, is described as "bigger than the house in which either man was born. The ceiling barn-rafter high. More shelving than Ace's Grocery Store" (5). Upon her arrival at the convent, Mavis reflects, "Here in the kitchen she felt safe; the thought of leaving it disturbed her" (41). The kitchen, with "no windows," is also described by the men, as they invade it, as a womb; and, significantly, as Morgan stands in the kitchen he recalls being bathed by his mother as baby and drinks milk in "long measured swallows" (7). Kitchens in Morrison signify care and comfort and in particular the sustaining values of the funk and the ancient prop-erties, as with Pilate's candlelit kitchen with women singing and young Claudia's memory of Big Mama's kitchen with "my lap full of lilacs . . . listen[ing] to Big Papa play his violin for me alone" (21). When the men storm the kitchen, tak-ing the women by surprise, they come upon "stock simmering on the stove"; "a large, yet warm and welcoming stove—signified by the dozen loaves of bread which swell beneath [it]" (5) that stands in sharp contrast to the town Oven introduced on the following page and described as "huge, flawlessly designed," "admir[ed] for its construction and power," and whose "iron lip was recemented into place and its worn letters polished for all to see" each time the town people moved (6). The contrasting values of the convent and the town signified by the two different stoves is further revealed when "Morgan [with] his pistol in his right hand, . . . uses his left to raise the pitcher [of milk] to his mouth" (7). The symbolism here is explicit: milk suggests maternal nourishment; pistols, particularly in their phallic connation, mark patriarchal power.

The convent, as with Pilate's home in *Song of Solomon,* is indeed "a safe haven . . . an inn and harbor" (135). Billie Delia says of the convent, "[Y]ou can collect yourself there, think things through, with nothing or nobody bothering you all the time. They'll take care of you or leave you alone—whichever way you want it" (176). And later, as Pallas climbs the stairs from her visit with Connie in the cellar, she comments upon "images of a grandmother rocking peacefully, of arms, a lap, a singing voice soothed her. The whole house felt permeated with blessed malelessness, like a protected domain, free of hunters, but exciting too. As though she might meet herself here—an unbridled authentic self, but which she thought of as a 'cool' self—in one of this house's many rooms" (177). And Mavis describes the convent as "the most peaceful place on earth" (182). The "peace," "care," and "protection" bestowed by the convent and welcomed by the refugee women, however, are ultimately the gift of Consolata.

Consolata is characterized as a woman of great wisdom and insight; profound love and kindness: "[A] sweet, unthreatening old lady who seemed to love each of them best; who never criticized, who shared everything but needed little or no care; required no emotional investment; who listened; who locked no doors and accepted each as she was" (262). She presides over this female sanctuary from her cellar bedroom, recalling Eva who ruled from the top floor of the house in *Sula.* Connie, described by the narrator as, "a new and revised Reverend mother," is, like Baby Suggs in *Beloved,* a healer to the cast-off and troubled women who arrive at the convent. She is the "ideal parent, friend, companion in whose company they were safe from harm" (262). When Pallas arrives, unable to speak or cry because "the pain was too far down" (172), Seneca brings her to Connie who, as the narrator tells us, "stretched out her hand and Pallas went to her, sat on her lap, talk-crying at first, then just crying." Connie was, as Seneca observes, "magic" (173). Earlier her entrance was described as "like an apparition" (43). Connie is indeed magical and, in this, may be compared to Pilate in *Song of Solomon;* both women possess supernatural otherworldly powers; as Pilate is visited by her dead father, Connie brings dead people back to life. However, as both women are spiritual and magical healers, Connie, more than Pilate, is likened to a priestess or goddess. Connie's home was once a convent; it is called a coven by the Town Fathers. As the men come upon the convent they speculate there may be "witch tracks" hidden beneath the mist (5). The cellar is described by the men as "the devil's bedroom, bath room and nasty playpen" (17).

In the safety of the convent and under the care of Consolata the women do begin to heal, in particular Mavis whose stay at the convent is the longest. Mavis's journey toward healing is marked by her changing relationship with her twins who were "smothered while she was buying Weenies at the Higgledly Piggledly"; "Babies forever unseen now because the mother did not have a snapshot of their trusting faces" (24). Initially Mavis is frightened by the twins who now haunt the convent: "She wished Connie would return lest she start upon imagining babies singing" (42). However, when she traveled back to Maryland to see her other children in 1970 she realized that "she was not safe out there or any place where Merle and Perle were not" (258–59). Later, when Pallas arrives Mavis says, "Hear that? They're happy. . . . I knew it. They love that baby [Arnette's baby who died]. Absolutely love it. They like you too" (182). Reflecting upon what Christmas gifts to buy them, Mavis comments, "It was amazing how they changed and grew. They could not hold their heads up when they departed, but when she first heard them in the mansion, they were toddlers, two years old." "Now they were school-aged" (258). This unfolding of mother-children intimacy both makes possible and marks Mavis own psychological and spiritual maturation. "Pounding, pounding, even biting Gigi was exhilarating, just as cooking was. It was more proof that the old Mavis was dead. The one who couldn't defend herself from an eleven-year-old girl, let alone her husband. The one who couldn't figure out how to manage a simple meal, who relied on delis and drive-throughs, now created crepe-like delicacies without shopping every day" (171). Indeed, as Mavis herself remarks, "[her] pride of place was secure. . . . The twins were happy" (259).

However, while the care of Consolata and the security of the convent does grant protection and foster emotional convalescence, full and complete healing only becomes possible when Consolata herself is healed. The section on Consolata opens with the observation that Consolata "woke to the wrenching disappointment of not having died the night before" (221). However, Connie, in this deep despair, is visited by a mysterious and magical walking man (252); similar to the walking man who visited Dovey. This man, "flirtatious, full of secret fun, . . . [s]uddenly . . . was next to [Connie] without having moved—smiling like he was having (or expecting) such a good time" (252). With "fresh, tea-colored hair [that] tumbled down, cascading over his shoulder and down his back," and with "eyes . . . as round and green as apples," he is described, similar to Son in *Tar Baby*, as a "Green-World" Lover archetype. Immediately after the text introduces this mysterious man, it describes Connie engaged in a sacred food preparation. When she calls the women together for dinner she is described as high priestess: "With the aristocratic gaze of the blind she sweeps the women's faces and says 'I call myself Consolata Sosa. If you want to be here you do what I say. Eat how I say. Sleep when I say. And I will teach you what you are hungry for.'" The women, the text tells us, "look at each other and then at a person they do not recognize" (262).

Consolata now will oversee the rebirth of these sheltered yet still haunted women. In the cellar, Consolata administers, as would a high priestess, a ritual of healing (263–66) wherein the women's pain is exorcised through a collective remembering of their suffering. The women, as Jill Matus has observed, "begin to dream collectively, each entering and experiencing the traumatic re-enactments of the other" (164). Together they return to Mavis's Cadillac: "They enter the heat in the Cadillac. . . . They inhale the perfume of the sleeping infants and feel parent cozy" (264). Eventually their stories merge to become one composite narrative of female affliction under patriarchy: Mavis's narrative leads to that of Pallas, which brings us to Gigi's, which delivers us to Seneca's, first as a child and later as Seneca as a woman, which in turn returns us to Pallas:

> They [twins] kick their legs under water, but not too hard for fear of waking fins or scales down below. The male voices saying saying forever saying push their own down their throats. Saying, saying until there is no breath to scream or contradict. Each one blinks and gags from tear gas, moves her hand slowly to the scraped shin, the torn ligament. Runs up and down the halls by day, sleeps in a ball with the lights on at night. Folds the five hundred dollars in the foot of her sock. Yelps with pain from a stranger's penis and a mother's rivalry—alluring and corrosive as cocaine. (264)

Their "loud dreaming," "[a] monologue . . . no different than a shriek," is choreographed by their bodies' silhouettes, which Connie draws on the floor. Seneca, when overcome with the urge to cut herself, marks the image of her body instead. Anna, when she later sees the templates, recognizes, as the text tells us, "the terribleness K.D. reported, but it wasn't pornography he had seen, nor was it Satan's scrawl. She saw instead the turbulence of females trying to bridle, without being trampled, the monsters that slavered them" (303). "Life, real, and intense, shifted to down there in limited pools of light, in air smoky from kerosene lamps and candle wax" (264). "They had to be reminded of the moving bodies they wore, so seductive were the alive ones below" (265). Having exorcised their suffering, the women are now ready to be reborn.

This rebirth is enacted in the women's dance beneath the "scented rainfall" whose perfume, as the texts tells us, is "stronger north of Ruby, especially at the Convent" (283).

> [The rain] was like lotion on their fingers so they entered it and let it pour like balm on their shaved heads and upturned faces. Consolata started it; the rest were quick to join her. There are great rivers in the world and on their banks and the edges of oceans children thrill to water. In places where rain is light the thrill is almost erotic. But those sensations bow to the rapture of holy women dancing in hot sweet rain. They would have laughed, had enchantment not been so deep. (283)

Cleansed and purified the women are baptized into a new self and world:

> Seneca embraced and finally let go of a dark morning in state housing. Grace witnessed the successful cleaning of a white shirt that should never

have been stained. Mavis moved to the shudder of rose of Sharon tickling her skin. Pallas, delivered of a delicate son, held him close while the rain rinsed away a scary woman on an escalator and all fear of black water. (283)

Healed, these women, as the text tells us, "were no longer haunted" (266). They were, however, "hunted."

The town men fear and eventually hunt down these newly born women because they, as the men remark "don't need men and they don't need God" (276). Described as "bodacious black Eves unredeemed by Mary" (18), these "slack and slovenly" women have become, in their wholeness and unity, a threat to patriarchal culture, particularly as it is enacted in the town of Ruby. As Lone says of the women: "Not women locked safely away from men; but worse, women who chose themselves for company, which is of say not a convent but a coven" (276). "With God on their side," the men storm the convent and "take aim. For Ruby" (18). However, after the killing rampage when the people of town return to the convent for the dead women, "[n]o bodies [were found]. Nothing. Even the Cadillac was gone" (292). While members of the town were "divid[ed] about what really took place," "when they learned there was no dead to report, transport or bury, relief was so great they began to forget what they had done" (298). Anna reports she saw a door when she was there; Richard was sure it was a window (305). Billie Delia, the only person who truly missed "the women she had liked," "was perhaps the only one in town who was not puzzled by where the women were or concerned about how they disappeared. She had another question: When will they return" (308). While Billie Delia awaits their return "with blazing eyes, war paint and huge hands to rip and stomp down this prison calling itself a town," the women have arrived in paradise.

The book concludes with the convent women revisiting the place of their reproductive loss. As the women's shared dreaming exorcised the women's pain and their rain dance cleansed them of their wounded and damaged selves, their journey toward healing is completed when the women individually return to the place of their reproductive loss to accept it, forgive themselves and/or others, and to move beyond it. Gigi visits with her father in prison where she learns that his death sentence has been reprieved. When her father asks whether he will see her again, Gigi promises, "You will, Daddy Man. You will" (310). Pallas returns to her mother's home to reclaim the shoes "she'd left there on her last, and first, visit" (312). Upon returning she comes across her mother, who is trying unsuccessfully to paint her daughter's portrait: "The eyes kept coming up accusatory; the skin tone eluded her; and the hair was invariably a hat" (311). And when her mother tries to say her daughter's name, "it came out different . . . [like] something was wrong with her tongue" (311). Mavis and her firstborn daughter Sally find each other while Mavis is eating breakfast at Jennie's Country Inn. The daughter, whom Mavis once believed wanted to kill her, is truly comforted and restored by her mother's presence: "[T]heir eyes met. Sally felt the nicest thing then. Something long and deep and slow and bright" (314). Hugging at their good-bye, Sally says, "I always loved, always even when" (315). And Jean, Seneca's mother, who has spent years searching for the "chocolate eyes" of her daughter (316), finally meets her daughter again, though neither Jean nor Seneca realize it at the time due to Jean's mistake concerning the street name of the housing project. These returns and reconnections are fragmentary and fleeting; none of the women remain with the daughter or mother (or father as with Gigi) from whom they were estranged, nor do the women reclaim the reproductive—mother and/or daughter—identity they had lost. Moreover, it is highly unlikely and improbable that these encounters actually take place. Nonetheless, these reunions, whether they occur in this life or in another, conclude the recovery of these women because through them the haunted women have come to accept the past, forgive themselves, and in so doing have become the women they wanted to become.

In Haven and later Ruby, as noted in the previous chapter, the sustaining values of the funk are lost through the hegemonic rule of the masculine and the subsequent marginalization of women and the feminine. In contrast, the convent women, as examined in the previous chapter, create a maternal community from their own individual maternal losses and based on the values of the funk. The community of women "endures" while the text suggests that the town, in its present patriarchal configuration, will not. At the conclusion of the novel, after the storming of the convent and the disappearance of the women, Anna discovers five eggs in the convent henhouse. This, I want to suggest, signifies both the "survival" of the five women and the hope that, despite the women's "death," the sustaining values of the funk have prevailed. Eggs have always signified in Morrison female power and the funk. Milkman is captivated by the image of Pilate peeling a hardboiled egg and Jadine is mesmerized by the African woman who carries the eggs cupped beneath her chin. At the conclusion of this novel, Anna stands holding the eggs in the convent garden that is described as:

> Beyond was blossom and death. Shrivelled tomato plants alongside crops of leafy green reseeding themselves with golden flowers; pink hollyhocks so tall the heads leaned all the way over a trail of bright squash blossoms; lacy tops of carrots browned and lifeless next to straight green spikes of onion. Melons split their readiness showing gums of juicy red. Anna sighed at the mix of neglect and unconquerable growth. The five eggs warm umber in her hands. (304–305)

The garden and the brown eggs, I argue, signify the tenacity and ultimate triumph of the women and the values of the funk.

Paradise has been called Morrison's most feminist novel. While I agree that this novel exposes, perhaps more so than her previous books—though this point is debatable—the horror that is patriarchy, I argue that in labeling the book feminist and in reading it as a "woman's novel" we are left with an incomplete and truncated understanding of the novel and Morrison's larger vision. Morrison insists that the well-being of African Americans depends upon their preserving the funk and ancient properties of the African American motherline; of concern to Morrison are the disruption and disconnection of the motherline that prevent mothers bequeathing these values to each successive generation. In her first six novels slavery, migration, and assimilation sever the motherline. In this novel, the motherline is ruptured by the black community itself in its repression of the folk and the feminine, symbolically enacted through the murder of the women. The murder of the women, unspeakably tragic in itself, thus also signifies the death of what Morrison has deemed essential for the survival of African American culture. At a 1999 symposium on Toni Morrison's *Paradise,* the presenters debated whether this book delivers salvation or merely conveys despair.[8] The women are healed. As well, the novel, at least symbolically, ends with the promise of redemption. The women have survived and triumphed over the Town: "The Oven," the text tells us, "shifts just slightly, on one side. The impacted ground on which it rests is undermined" (303). At the novel's end the women, we are told, "rest before shouldering the endless work they were created to do down here in paradise" (318): an image of hope, if not salvation.

CONCLUSION

Morrison's first two novels examined disconnections and disruptions of the motherline, while her middle books—*Song* and *Tar Baby*—looked at how one may be returned to the motherline. Together, Morrison's first five books also explored how mothers seek to prevent motherline loss and empower children through the maternal functions of preservation, nurturance, and cultural bearing. Motherwork in these novels is represented as a powerful site of prevention against all that would harm children in a racist and patriarchal world. With *Paradise* and *Jazz,* Morrison narrates in full and poignant detail the stories of the unmothered children; those children who, because they were orphaned, abandoned, or neglected, were denied the preservation, nurturance, and cultural bearing that would enable them to grow into adulthood whole and complete. However, in *Paradise* and *Jazz* these adults, through othermothering, are healed when they embark on physic journey of rememory that reconnects them with their lost mother and enables them to reclaim an identity as a loved child. *Paradise* and *Jazz,* with their promises of reconciliation and redemption, offer us, more than the first five novels did, a belief in and hope for deliverance. Significantly, the word *deliverance,* the old-fashioned word for being rescued, is etymologically linked to the word delivery, which includes among its many meanings the act of giving birth. Appropriately, then, the oeuvre of Toni Morrison concludes with the promise of birth, or more specifically rebirth, in and through maternal deliverance.

Conclusion

Toni Morrison's theory of motherhood as a site of power and her model of motherwork as concerned with the empowerment of children centers upon a rearticulation of the everyday traditions and practices of black motherhood. More specifically, this rearticulation gives rise to a new consciousness of black motherhood that accords mothers power and enables them to empower children and/or heal adults through the four tasks of motherwork: preservation, nurturance, cultural bearing, and healing. Mothers, by way of these four tasks, seek to empower their children by keeping them alive in a world often hostile to their well-being (preservation), by loving them so that may develop a loved sense of self (nurturance), by teaching children the values and traditions of black culture—in particular the ancient proprieties and funk—so that they may acquire a strong self-defined identity as a black person (cultural bearing), and finally by mending those adults who never received such mothering as children (healing). Motherhood, in Morrison's view, is thus fundamentally and profoundly an act of resistance; essential and integral to black people's, and in particular black women's, fight against racism (and sexism) and their ability to achieve well-being for themselves and their culture. Motherlove and motherwork in the dominant ideology of motherhood are rarely, if at all, regarded in this way; rather, the love and work of mothering is seen simply as a private and more specifically an apolitical enterprise. In contrast, motherhood, according to Morrison's maternal standpoint, has cultural significance and political purpose because motherhood is a site of power for black women and because motherwork is the way by which black people are empowered to survive and resist. In the preface, I suggested that Morrison, in her rendition of mothering as a political enterprise, could be read as a social commentator or political theorist who radically, through her maternal philosophy, reworks, rethinks, and reconfigures the concerns and strategies of African American, and in particular black women's emancipation in America. According to Morrison, the power of motherhood and the empowerment of mothering is what make possible the better world we seek for ourselves and for our children. This is Morrison's maternal theory: a politics of the heart.

Morrison's theory of motherhood as power and motherwork as empowerment, however, as discussed in the previous chapters, is seldom enacted or represented in the novels themselves. Some of the characters, such as Pilate in *Song,*

Consolata in *Paradise,* and Therese in *Tar Baby,* embody the power inherent in Morrison's maternal standpoint of black woman as ship and harbor and inn and trail. As well, the portrayal of Mrs. MacTeer's mothering in *The Bluest Eye* suggests the empowerment of cultural bearing; likewise the descriptions of Eva's and Mrs. MacTeer's preservative love and Sethe's nurturance confirm the importance of motherwork for the child's well-being. However, overall, the promise of motherhood as power and motherwork as empowerment described in her theory (interviews and articles) is not delivered in her fictional writings. The contrast between the idealized, if not romanticized, view of motherhood in Morrison's theory and the depictions of forfeited mothering and fragmented mother-child relations in her fiction suggest, and as some critics have concluded, a contradiction between theory and fiction and, more specifically, a failure of Morrison's maternal vision itself. However, I suggest, and have argued in this book, that the absence of fictional renditions of Morrison's maternal theory, rather than pointing to an error in her theory, actually affirms and confirms the truth and significance of Morrison's maternal theory. Morrison details mothers' desperate struggles to define motherhood as a site of power and their even more desperate struggle to provide the motherwork essential for their children's survival and well-being. Likewise, Morrison demonstrates the importance of this motherwork by describing the devastation, both personal and cultural, that arises when children are not preserved, nurtured, or do not receive cultural bearing. The absences therefore bespeak not a failure of the vision; rather, they signify a narrative strategy; one that seeks to stress the crucial importance of mothering by showing the loss and suffering that occurs in its absence.

The children's suffering—the anguish of Pecola, the loneliness of Sula, the alienation of Jadine and Milkman, and the desolation of Violet and Joe—testify to the necessity of motherwork, in all of its dimensions, for personal well-being and cultural survival. The depth and severity of the children's suffering as a consequence of mother loss and absence compellingly and conclusively confirm the truth of Morrison's maternal vision. While fictional portrayals of successful motherwork, as presented in Morrison's theory, may have made Morrison's maternal vision clearer and more present in her novels—and hence less open to misreadings—I argue that the many and varied descriptions of unmothered children and their suffering demonstrate far more powerfully and convincingly the significance and relevance of Morrison's maternal philosophy. As well, while Morrison may not portray effective motherwork, the novels do describe how to heal those wounded by mother loss or absence: namely, by way of a reconnection to the motherline, as with Milkman, or through a "rememory" of the lost mother, as with Joe and Violet in *Jazz* and the convent women in *Paradise.* Morrison's fiction thus both warns and counsels: in its apocalyptic vision of a world of unmothered children it serves notice of the importance of motherwork, while in its theme of deliverance it gives us cause for hope. Morrison applauds the power of motherhood to achieve the personal and cultural changes so desperately and urgently needed in our world today; as well, she demands that such power be acknowledged and celebrated.

Dorothy Roberts's recent book, *Shattered Bonds: The Color of Child Welfare* (2002) documents the "[staggeringly] disproportionate number of Black children in American's child welfare system" (6), as well as details "the devastating effects of removing a child from [his or her] parents" (18). While Roberts's study is in itself deeply troubling, I want to suggest, as I conclude this book, that the larger and deeper tragedy of child-mother separation documented by Roberts, is its assault on the power of black motherhood and its theft of black motherwork, and the resulting dispossession of black children and black culture.

Love's Unloved

In the fall of 2003, just as this book was going into final production, Toni Morrison's eighth novel *Love* was published. This epilogue will briefly consider how this recently published novel may be read in the context of Morrison's larger maternal vision, what I have called "A Politics of the Heart." From this perspective, what strikes the reader most about *Love* is the absence of mothers and mothering. Unlike her previous seven novels in which mothers are central characters, and in which motherwork and motherlove are integral to both plot and theme, there are few mother characters in this novel and few descriptions of, or reflections upon, the experience and/or meaning of mothering. Little is said of Julia, the first wife of Bill Cosey who dies when their only child, a son, is twelve. No mention is made of May's mother, and the only thing we learn about Heed's mother is that she sold her daughter for a pocketbook. Likewise, Dolly, the mother of Roman, is absent in the story and Junior's mother is mentioned only in passing. Celestial, the enduring love of Bill Cosey, is not a mother. The central characters of the story, Christine and May, are childless; the first had seven abortions as a young woman, the latter a miscarriage in mid-life. May is the only character who is developed and described as a mother and she sends her only child away to a boarding school when that child, Christine, is twelve. No reviewers, to my knowledge, have mentioned motherhood in their reviews except one who, in comparing this novel with *Beloved,* wrote: "Will *Love* receive similar acclaim [as *Beloved*]? Probably not. Even a master like Morrison cannot make the love between friends as compelling as that between mother and daughter" (Rubin).

In *Love,* as the early book reviews have pointed out, the theme of sexual or romantic love is central. The theme of love, as one reviewer noted, "is found throughout Morrison's body of work—from spiritual love in *Beloved* to romantic love in *Jazz.* The new novel is the story of the women bound to Bill Cosey" *(News from Princeton University).* Morrison, explaining the impetus of the story in a recent interview with *Essence* magazine, commented: "I was interested in the ways in which sexual love and other kinds of love lend themselves to betrayal. How do ordinary people end up ruining the thing they most want to protect?" (interview with McKinney-Whetstone). Other reviews have called attention to the feminist perspective of the novel, a theme also emphasized by Morrison in recent interviews on *Love*. "Patriarchy is assumed," explains Morrison, "but women have to agree to the role. You have to say, 'This is the most important person in my life.' It's not that [Cosey] gobbles them up, but they allow themselves to be eaten. When you're able to stop blaming other people—your father, your grandfather, your husband—for your shortcomings or confusion or failure, then language is possible, and so is love" (as quoted in O'Connor). The interplay of race and gender, sexism and racism, has also been noted as a theme: "Since *Paradise* especially," Donna Bailey Nurse writes in her review, "Morrison has been exploring the intersection of race and gender—the point at which racism and sexism meet. The rape of the volunteer [in *Love*] demonstrates the way in which men choose to support one another, rather than the injured woman." Still other reviewers, comparing the novel to *Sula,* have explored the theme of female friendship.

It would seem from these early reviews and a cursory reading of *Love* that indeed the topic of motherhood is no longer integral to Morrison's social or literary imagination. However, I would argue, building upon Morrison's maternal theory examined in this book, that these silences and absences need to be read metaphorically, signifying, as, in Morrison's first seven novels, the importance of motherhood. The absence of fictional renditions of Morrison's maternal theory, as I have argued throughout this book, affirms and confirms the truth and significance of Morrison's maternal theory. Morrison demonstrates the importance of this motherwork by describing the devastation, both personal and cultural, that arises when children are not preserved, nurtured, or do not receive cultural bearing. The absences therefore bespeak not a failure of the vision; rather they signify a narrative strategy—one that seeks to stress the crucial importance of mothering by showing the loss and suffering that occurs in its absence. The children's suffering—the anguish of Pecola, the loneliness of Sula, the alienation of Jadine and Milkman, and the desolation of Violet and Joe—testifies to the necessity of motherwork, in all of its dimensions, for personal well-being and cultural survival.

Motherless and unmothered children may also be found in *Love*. May is described as a motherless child: "[She] was the last daughter of an itinerant preacher who had to accept clothes from any congregation he could attract" (137). "A pretty, undercherished girl in an overmended coat" (137). May, as the text tells us, is "chosen" by Billy Boy because, "as anybody could see, [she] would neither disrupt nor rival the bond between father and son" (102). "Her whole life," L explains, "was making sure those Cosey men had what they wanted. The father more than the son; the father more than her own daughter. If I was a servant in that place, May was its slave" (102). Before her real death in 1976, May, "crazy-like-a-fox," struggled "to keep going, to protect what was hers . . . Husband dead; her crumbling hotel ruled by a rabid beach rat, ignored by the man for whom she had slaved, abandoned by her daughter to strange ideas, a running joke to neighbors—she had no place and nothing to command. So she recognized the war declared on her and fought it alone" (99–100).

Christine, May's daughter, is likewise "a motherless child." While Christine, unlike her own mother May, does have a biological mother, she is not loved, or more specifically protected or nurtured, by one. Christine comments: "Then there was her mother, who chose to send her away rather than confront him. Put her in a faraway school and discouraged summer vacations at home" (133). "Even when she returned, a sixteen-year-old, poised and ready to take her place in the family, they threw her away" (133). "Hating you," Christine tells Heed, "was the only thing my mother liked about me" (193). Heed, too, is a motherless child: sold, at the age of eleven, to Bill Cosey: "for two hundred dollars and a new pocketbook for Mama" (193). Or as L explains it, "that trash gave her up like they would a puppy" (105). Significantly, when Christine and Heed are reconciled at the conclusion of novel, their discussion, like that of Violet and Alice in *Jazz,* turns to their mothers:

> You know May wasn't much of a mother to me
> At least she didn't sell you
> No, she gave me away
> Maple Valley?
> Maple Valley. (184)

Junior is also a motherless child. Upon meeting Junior, Christine remarks that she had "the unnerving look of an underfed child. One you wanted to cuddle or slap for being needy" (23). She is named Junior, we are told, because while "her mother had meant to name her right away . . . [t]hree days had passed after the hard delivery before she could stay awake long enough to make a decision—during which time the baby's girl father called the newborn Junior" (55). Junior, similar to Christine, ran away from home at the age of eleven; the time, as I argued earlier, when daughters need their mothers the most to sustain them as they come into womanhood in a patriarchal culture. Indeed *Love,* as noted by Mary Mitchell in her review, "is dominated by women whose insides rattle. Junior's voracious appetite for food and sex speaks to that need to be filled up. Christine's search for a father's love [I would say it is a mother's love] leads her to look for it in the arms of a succession of sugar daddies, only to end up coveting the pureness of a childhood friend."

In this book, I have examined instances wherein motherhood, as a result of an individual or a community's loss of African American values, does not become a site of power for women or empowerment for children. In particular, I have considered how this inability or failure is signified metaphorically in images and experiences of failed reproduction. In *The Bluest Eye,* reproduction, in particular birth, signifies a black mother's inability to experience motherhood as a site of power and her subsequent failure to empower/nurture her daughter because of her assimilation in the values of the dominant culture—in particular its definitions of female beauty—and the resulting rejection of the black values that would empower her. In *Paradise,* reproduction signifies a black town's failure to grant women power in motherhood and allow them to nurture/empower their children because of the town's identification with the values of the dominant culture wherein power and ownership are valued over those of community and care. The bareness, abortions, miscarriages, sickly children, and dead babies in *Paradise* serve as metaphors for the denial and repression of the ancient properties and funk in the black town that would create community, make motherhood a site of power for women, and enable them to nurture/empower their young.

Failed reproduction in *Love* also signifies loss, though in this novel this loss is less about the ancient properties or the funk than about the loss or absence of self-love, a theme explored in chapter 6 of this book in my discussion of *Jazz.* Morrison argues that self-love depends on the self first being loved by another self. Informing Morrison's writing is her belief that mothering is essential for the emotional well being of children because it is the mother who first loves the child and gives to that child a loved sense of self. Before a child can love herself, she must experience her self being loved and learn that she is indeed valuable and deserving of affection. Unmothered children in Morrison's fiction thus do not journey from mother-love to self-love, and do not come to know their own selves. Every child in *Love,* as noted above, is motherless or unmothered. There is no mention of May's mother. Heed, Junior, and Christine all lose their mothers at the onset of adolescence: Heed by marriage, Junior in running away, and Christine by being sent away. As well, Billy Boy's mother dies when he is twelve. Moreover, as Jan Garden Castro notes in her review of the book: "The three women [May, Christine, and Heed] have all been psychologically and physically brutalized when they were children." Unmothered, and without the self-love and selfhood that mothering affords, the women in *Love* are rendered as vulnerable to and seduced by the charm of Bill Cosey as Pauline was by the movies in *The Bluest Eye.* They look to him, to paraphrase from *Beloved,* "to fill up their inside nothing." We are told of Junior: "As soon as she saw the stranger's portrait she knew she was home. She had dreamed him the first night, had ridden his shoulders through an orchard of green Granny applies heavy and thick on the boughs" (60). And Heed says of Bill Cosey, her husband, a fifty-two year old man who chose his granddaughter's best friend for a wife when she was just eleven: "Only Papa knew better, had picked her out of all he could have chosen. Knowing she had no schooling, no abilities, no proper raising, he chose her anyway while everybody else thought she could be run over" (72–73). "She was safe with him no matter what he muttered in his sleep" (79). The friendship of Christine and Heed, similar to that of Sula and Nel, develops in response to both of them feeling unloved and unwanted by their mothers. L describes Heed and Christine as "the kind of children who can't take back love or park it" (200). "When that's the case," L continues, "separation cuts to the bone. And if the breakup is plundered, too, squeezed for a glimpse of blood, shed for the child's own good, then it can ruin a mind" (200). "I blame May," L continues, "for the hate she put in them, but I have to fault Mr. Cosey for the theft" (200). Heed says to Christine, "He took all my childhood away from me, girl," and she responds: "He took all of you away from me" (194). "We could have been living our lives," Christine tells Heed, "instead of looking for Big Daddy everywhere" (189).

Heed, Christine, and Junior's search for a Big Daddy is, I want to suggest, motivated and sustained by the absence of maternal love in their lives. In chapter 6 I cited Deborah McDowell, who argued in her review of *Jazz* that "the memory of the lost mother is the motor force of *Jazz*" (1992: 3). I emphasized, in contrast, that more specifically the motor force of the text is the *search* for a surrogate mother. Similarly, Heed, Christine, and Junior, also without motherlove, do not develop self-love and hence go in search of a "Big Daddy" who can give them the love they can not give themselves. Heed and Junior, like Violet with Golden Grey, are captivated by Bill Cosey because, as L explains, "[he] was adept, you know, at spotting needy, wild women" (200). Even long dead, as reviewer Penny Hueston notes, "His legacy is being acted out by the damaged women he left behind."

Motherwork, in Morrison's first five novels, is represented as an act of prevention insofar as mothers, through preservation, nurturance, and cultural bearing, seek to empower children to survive and resist. With the last two, *Jazz* and *Paradise,* Morrison's concern becomes how to heal these wounds once inflicted. With *Love,* the concern is less with healing than with emphasizing how dangerous unloved women are to others and in particular to themselves. Heed, Junior, and Christine, being unloved as daughters, become desperate for love as women. This desperation causes them to tolerate, accept, even welcome, harm being done to them: Mr. Cosey's spanking of Heed, Christine's abuse at the hands of her many lovers, and Junior's "preference for being hurt" (153). As well, being unloved, while not causing the feud between Heed and Christine, did sustain and continue it.

In a recent interview Toni Morrison commented: "It's easy I suppose, to talk about the *oppressor.* But I'm not all that interested in it—or him. I'm interested in the impact that oppression has on *people.* Who survives? How? What are the strategies?" (as quoted in Weaver, emphasis in original). With her eighth novel, as Morrison reflects upon the damage that love can do, particularly forsaken, misused, ransomed, and distorted motherlove, she also looks to love for hope and in particular, redemption. L, reflecting upon the uses and misuses of love in the prologue and the epilogue, suggests that the good of love can be a counterforce to the bad. L tells us the legend of the "Police-heads," a metaphor for "bad" love, that come out of the ocean to "hunt desperate women and hardheaded, misraised children" (201). L recognizes that "it's trash, just another story made up to scare wicked females and correct unruly children. But it's all I have. I know I need something else. Something better. Like a story that shows how brazen women can take a good man down. I could hum to that" (10). But Love, "properly used," can, as L reminds us, "save you from the attention of

Police-heads" (201). And "she knows at least one woman who did this—[Celes-tial]" (201); the woman Morrison calls "unfettered and unencumbered . . . a free female" (O'Connor). A brazen woman, to use L's words, who is not damaged or destroyed by love, who can, in fact, again to use L's words, "take a good man down" (10). However, only a woman that has had good love as a child can defy and survive bad love as an adult. This, I want to suggest, is Morrison's maternal theory and the lesson of *Love*.

Notes

1. In 1986 little had been written on motherhood in feminist theory or in feminist literary theory. The major texts on motherhood were all published after 1986; 1989, in particular, was a watershed year for feminist scholarship on motherhood, seeing the release of groundbreaking works such as Sara Ruddick's *Maternal Thinking,* Marianne Hirsch's *Mother/Daughter Plot,* Paula Caplan's *Don't Blame Mother,* Valerie Walkerdine and Helen Lucey's *Democracy in the Kitchen,* and Miriam Johnson's *Strong Mothers, Weak Wives.* The notable exceptions were Adrienne Rich's classic *Of Woman Born* and Dorothy Dinnerstein's *The Mermaid and the Minotaur,* both published in 1976, and Nancy Chodorow's influential *The Reproduction of Mothering,* published in 1978. The first collection of feminist theory on motherhood, Joyce Trebilcot's *Mothering: Essays in Feminist Theory,* was published in 1984. As well, Sara Ruddick's landmark articles, "Preservative Love and Military Destruction: Reflections on Mothering and Peace and 'Maternal Thinking'" (in *Mothering: Essays in Feminist Theory,* ed. Joyce Trebilcot [Totowa, N.J.: Rowman and Allanheld]) were published in 1984 and Marianne Hirsch's important review article, "Mothers and Daughters," was published in 1980 (*Signs* 7, no.1 [Autumn 1981]: 200–22). However, early feminist theorists on motherhood, with the exceptions of Rich and Ruddick, generally analyzed motherhood in terms of the daughter's experience of being mothered and/or regarded motherhood as oppressive to women.

In the 1970s, the received view of motherhood was that it was the site and cause of women's oppression; see in particular: Jeffner Allen (1984), "Motherhood: The Annihilation of Women," in *Mothering: Essays in Feminist Theory* and Shulamith Firestone (1970), *The Dialectic of Sex.* As well, the mother and daughter relationship was seen as the way in which this female oppression was reproduced. Nancy Chodorow in *The Reproduction of Mothering* (1978) argued that female mothering constructs gendered identities that are both differentiated and hierarchical. The pre-Oedipal mother-daughter attachment, according to Chodorow, is more prolonged and intense than the mother-son relationship. Because the daughter and the mother are the same gender, the mother perceives and treats her daughter as identical to and continuous with her self. The sameness and continuity of the pre-Oedipal mother-daughter symbiosis engenders a feminine psychic structure that is less individuated and differentiated. The daughter's sense of self is relational; she experiences herself as connected to others. The relational sense of self which women acquire from the prolonged and intense pre-Oedipal attachment with their mothers, and bring to their own mothering, Chodorow goes on to argue, exacerbates female self-effacement and frustrates women's achievement of an authentic autonomous identity. Relationality, Chodorow concludes, is problematic for women because it hinders autonomy, psychological and otherwise; and since daughter-mother identification is the cause of this relationality in women, it is, in her words, "bad for mother and [daughter] alike." Chodorow, as Penelope Dixon noted in her feminist annotated bibliography on mothers and mothering, "was one of the first to write on the subject [of mothering] and subsequently has authored more books and articles on this subject than any other feminist writer" (4). Indeed, Chodorow's writings, particularly her now classic *The Reproduction of Mothering* (1978) has influenced the way a whole generation of scholars views motherhood. What is less acknowledged however, is how this influential writer, who is identified as a feminist, reinscribes the patriarchal narrative of mother-daughter estrangement even as she seeks to dismantle it.

The dominant view of the mother-daughter relation was that this relationship, particularly in the daughter's adolescent years, was one of antagonism and animosity. The daughter must differentiate herself from the mother if she is to assume an autonomous identity as an adult. The mother, in turn, is perceived and understood only in terms of her maternal identity. The mother represents for the daughter, according to the received narrative, the epitome of patriarchal oppression that she seeks to transcend as she comes to womanhood, and the daughter's failings, as interpreted by herself and the culture at large, are said to be the fault of the mother. This is the patriarchal narrative of the mother-daughter relationship. These cultural narratives shape the lives of mothers and daughters even as mothers and daughters live lives different from, and in resistance to, these assigned roles.

2. For a detailed discussion on how motherhood has been represented in feminist theory see Lauri Umansky's *Motherhood Reconceived* (1996) as well as the introduction to, and O'Reilly's chapter in, Abbey and O'Reilly *Redefining Motherhood* (1998) and O'Reilly and Abbey's introduction to *Mothers and Daughters: Connection, Empowerment, and Transformation* (2000). See also *From Motherhood to Mothering: The Legacy of Adrienne Rich's Of Woman Born*, edited by Andrea O'Reilly (State University of New York Press, 2004) and Andrea O'Reilly's *Reconceiving Maternity: Feminist Theory on Motherhood Since 1990* (forthcoming). Please also visit the website of *The Association for Research on Mothering and The Journal of the Association for Research on Mothering* website, *www.yorku.ca/crm,* for full information on feminist scholarship on motherhood.

3. For a discussion of my political mode of mothering please see "'Ain't That Love?': Antiracism and Racial Constructions of Motherhood" in *Everyday Acts Against Racism: Raising Children in a Multiracial World,* ed. Maureen T. Reddy (Seattle: Seal Press, 1996), 88–98. And "A Mom and her Son: Thoughts on Feminist Mothering," *Journal of the Association for Research on Mothering* 2, no. 1 (Spring/Summer 2000): 179–93, and "Mothers, Daughters, and Feminism Today: Empowerment, Agency, Narrative, and Motherline," *Canadian Woman's Studies* 18, nos. 2 & 3 (Summer/Fall 1998): 16–21.

4. See O'Reilly, "Mothers, Daughters, and Feminism Today: Empowerment, Agency, and Narrative" (1998), and "Introduction" to *Mothers and Daughters: Connection, Empowerment, and Transformation* (2000).

chapter one
A POLITICS OF THE HEART

1 Alice Walker (1983) defines womanist as "A black feminist or feminist of color. From the black folk expression of mothers to female children, 'You acting womanish,' i.e.,

like a woman. Usually referring to outrageous, audacious, courageous or willful behavior. . . . Womanist is to feminist as purple is to lavender."

2. "Childbearing and children are valued by members of this community and black women in The Flats," Stack continues, "unlike many other societies, . . . feel few if any restrictions about childbearing. Unmarried black women, young and old, are eligible to bear children, and frequently women bear their first children when they are quite young" (47). Many of these teenage mothers, however, do not raise their first born; this responsibility is left to the mother, aunt, or elder sister with whom the biological mother resides. The child thus may have both a "Mama," the woman "who raised him up," and the biological mother who birthed him. The mama, in Stack's terminology, is the "sponsor" of the child's personal kinship network; the network is thus matrilineal and matrifocal.

3. Johnson's argument is that contemporary African American culture is matrifocal; at no time does she suggest that black family or culture is matriarchal. Nonetheless, any discussion of matrifocality must locate itself in the infamous Moynihan report and the controversy it generated. The report described the black family as dysfunctional and argued that the mother was to blame for the purported pathologies of the race: "In essence, the negro community has . . . a matriarchal structure which . . . seriously retards the progress of the group as a whole" (75) (*The Moynihan Report: and the Politics of Controversy,* Lee Rainwater and William Yancey, eds. [1967]). Or as critic Michele Wallace put it: "The Moynihan Report said that the black man was not so much a victim of white institutional racism as he was of an abnormal family structure, its main feature being an employed black woman" (12). Swiftly and abruptly the report was condemned for its failure to take into account institutionalized racism to explain under/unemployment, family "breakdown," and so forth, not to mention the report's blame-the-victim rhetoric, and mother-blaming stance. For an excellent discussion of the Moynihan report in terms of the ideological constructions of black womanhood see Patricia Morton, *Disfigured Images: The Historical Assault on Afro-American Women* (1991), particularly chapter 9, "Rediscovering the Black Family: New and Old Images of Motherhood," 125–35. Morton argues that

> [T]he 1970's saw a veritable revolution in interpretation of the modern Afro-American family . . . [with] an emphasis on familial health. In contrast to the old equation of black deviance from white middle-class norms as pathologized and dysfunctional, the new black family studies increasingly emphasized Afro-American diversity—including familial and sexual departures from white norms—as a positive thing. (126)

The revisionist family scholarship set out to debunk the black matriarchy thesis by documenting the poverty and powerlessness experienced by black women. At the same time, the revisionist black family studies argued that it was precisely the strength and resiliency of black motherhood that enabled blacks to remain whole and intact in a racist world. Paradoxically, the new scholarship exposed black matriarchy as a myth while emphasizing the strength of black mothers. This paradox underscores the difference between matrifocality and matriarchy and points to the ideological impasse of the Moynihan report that linked strength with domination.

Scholars today often downplay the strengths of the black mother so as to appear that they are staying clear of the controversial black matriarchy thesis. This is evident in historical accounts of slavery, particularly the research of Herbert Gutman, *The Black Family in*

Slavery and Freedom, 1750–1925 (1976), where he emphasizes that the slave family remained, for the most part, intact, by which he means father-headed and nuclear. "It may be," Morton writes, "that matrifocality and strong slave women were too akin to the myth of the black matriarchy to be acceptable to contemporary historians" (133). Such a perspective keeps us locked in the Moynihan framework, pathologizing the very thing that keeps black families viable and resilient, namely black motherhood. Such a viewpoint also curtails honest and appreciative study of black women. For readings in revisionist black family studies refer to: Andrew Ballingsley, *Black Families in White America* (1968) and *Climbing Jacob's Ladder: The Enduring Legacy of African American Families* (1992); Robert Staples and Leanor Boulin Johnson, *Black Families at the Crossroads: Challenges and Prospects* (1993); Harriette Pipes McAdoo, ed., *Black Families* (1981), and *Family Ethnicity: Strength in Diversity* (1993).

4. Ladner continues:

> This sharp change in status occurs for a variety of reasons. Perhaps the most important value it has is that of demonstrating the procreative powers that the girls possess. Children are highly valued and a strong emphasis is placed on one's being able to give birth. The ultimate test of womanhood, then, is one's ability to bring forth life. This value underlying child bearing is much akin to the traditional way in which the same behaviour has been perceived in African culture. So strong is the tradition that women must bear children in most West African societies that barren females are often pitied and in some cases their husbands are free to have children by other women. The ability to have children also symbolizes (for these girls) maturity that they feel cannot be gained in any other way. (216)

For white middle-class culture, marriage, rather than motherhood, is what ushers girls into womanhood. The elaborate, ritualized—and I may add costly—customs of the wedding ceremony, bridal showers, bridal shows, wedding service and receptions, and so forth, bear testimony to the place of the wedding in that culture.

5. bell hooks continues:

> [The] libratory struggle has been seriously undermined by contemporary efforts to change that subversive homeplace into a site of patriarchal domination of black women by black men, where we abuse one another for not conforming to sexist norms. This shift in perspective, where homeplace is not viewed as a political site, has had a negative impact on the construction of black female identity and political consciousness. Masses of black women, many of whom were not formally educated, had in the past been able to play a vital role in black liberation struggle. In the contemporary situation, as the paradigms for domesticity in black life mirrored white bourgeois norms (where home is conceptualized as politically neutral space), black people began to overlook and devalue the importance of black female labor in teaching critical consciousness in domestic space. Many black women, irrespective of class status, have responded to this crisis of meaning by imitating leisure-class sexist notions of women's role, focusing their lives on meaningless compulsive consumerism. (47)

6. Joseph's research—a 1979–1980 survey—revealed that the majority of black daughters (94.5 percent) said that they respected their mothers.

Joseph's research identified different issues and trends in the Anglo-American mother-daughter relationship. She found a greater belief in romance amongst white mothers, as expressed in the commonly offered advice, "Marry for love." Joseph discovered further that "the ways in which the White daughters said they feared their mothers disclosed an area that was rarely, if ever, mentioned by the Black daughters. The response was, 'I fear I might be like her. I want to be independent of her'" (125). Here the Anglo-American daughters bespeak matrophobia first defined by Rich in *Of Woman Born* (1986). "White women were included" in the survey, but because of "the small number of respondents," Joseph writes, "it was not possible to conduct a comparative study between White subjects and Black ones" (125). Joseph discovered in her analysis that class was an important variable to the degree that working-class white mothers gave responses similar to the black mother's responses.

7. For a recent study of black feminist thought on the mother and son relationship, please see Andrea O'Reilly, "In Black and White: African American and Anglo-American Feminist Theory on the Mother and Son Relationship," in *Mothers and Sons: Feminism, Masculinity, and the Struggle to Raise our Sons,* ed. Andrea O'Reilly (2001).

8. I refer here to book-length studies of African American mothers and sons. Articles include: Audre Lorde, "Manchild: A Black Lesbian Feminist Response," *Sister Outsider* (1984), and O'Reilly, "In Black and White: African American and Anglo-American Feminist Theory on the Mother and Son Relationship," in *Mothers and Sons: Feminism, Masculinity, and the Struggle to Raise our Sons,* ed. Andrea O'Reilly (2001).

9. The conflicting demands of protection and nurturance first identified by Ruddick in *Maternal Thinking* (1989) become, in the instance of rearing black sons, an impasse, an irreconcilable contradiction. The women interviewed by King and Mitchell all spoke of this paradox in the mothering of black sons; while sons must go into the world to mature socially, psychologically, and otherwise, this same world threatens their very physical survival.

10. This again is the impasse of black mothers; one that is etched on the very bodies of black men, as Golden remarks of her own son: "The unscathed openness of Michael's demeanor was proof that he had been a protected, loved child. But this same quality was also suddenly a liability, one that he had to mask" (95). Nurturing sons to be confident and proud, mothers recognize that these same traits, because they may be misconstrued as insolence, obstinacy, and arrogance by other black youth, police, or whites generally, put their sons at risk. Golden realizes, as does King and Mitchell, that this paradox of mothering black sons necessitates a new mode of mothering, one fashioned specifically for black male children.

11. Their critique is typical of feminist thought in the 1970s. As one mother described motherhood: "I know that when my children are small they need me. But sometimes I think I'll go nuts if I don't get out of this house and meet some grown ups. I find I'm starting to talk like a three-year-old all the time now" (Meg Luxton, *More Than a Labour of Love* [Toronto: Women's Press, 1980], 87).

12. *Conversations with Toni Morrison* (1994), 188–217. In her early article, "What the Black Woman Thinks About Women's Lib," Morrison argued that "[the] black woman had nothing to fall back on: not maleness, not whiteness, not ladyhood, not anything. And out of that profound desolation of her reality she may very well have invented herself" (*New York Times Magazine,* 22 August 1971, 15).

13. "The One Out of Sequence" (1980), in *Conversations with Toni Morrison,* 67–83.

14. Rich emphasizes that she is not saying that "in order to write well, or think well, it is necessary to become unavailable to others, or to become a devouring ego. This had been the myth of the masculine artist and thinker; and I do not accept it" (43). She comments further: "There must be ways, and we will be finding out more and more about them, in which the energy of creation and the energy of relation can be unite" (43). I would suggest that Morrison, along with black women generally, have united the creation of relation with that of creativity.

15. Ruddick provides the following example to illustrate how these demands are intertwined: "A child leans out of a high-rise window to drop a balloon full of water on a passerby. She must be hauled in from the window (preservation) and taught not to endanger innocent people (training), and the method used must not endanger her self-respect or confidence (nurturance)" (23). As well, these demands are often in conflict as in the following situation: "If a child wants to walk to the store alone, do you worry about her safety or applaud her developing capacity to take care of herself?" (23).

16. A comment made by a mother in Meg Luxton's *More Than A Labour of Love,* 87.

17. One notable exception is Olga Silverstein and Beth Rashbaum's splendid book, *The Courage to Raise Good Men* (New York: Viking, 1994). They argue that mother-son connection is essential for the psychological health of men and emphasize that the mother's distancing from her son at adolescence, as mandated by psychological theory, is a betrayal of her son and is what sets him up for the macho masculinity he will assume in adulthood.

18. In her many interviews Morrison emphasizes the importance of storytelling. In an interview with Jane Bakerman (1977), Toni Morrison commented:

> Novels aren't dying! People crave narration. Magazines only sell because they have stories in them, not because somebody wants to read those ads! Aside from the little game shows, television is all narrative. People want to hear a story. They love it! That's the way they learn things. That's the way human beings organize their human knowledge—fairy tales, myths. All narration. And that's why the novel is so important! (Emphasis in original, Taylor-Guthrie, 1994, 35).

chapter two
DISCONNECTIONS FROM THE MOTHERLINE

1. He goes on to say: "The black man is attacked emotionally from childhood, living in two impossible worlds: the fairy tale world of lies when he is in contact with the white world and the equally incredible, grim world of black life" (113). Although insightful, this article is plagued by a highly problematic sexist bias.

2. "Text and Countertext in *The Bluest Eye,*" in *Toni Morrison,* ed. Henry Louis Gates Jr. and K. A. Appiah (New York: Amistad, 1993), 159–74. See also Elliot Butler-Evans's discussion in *Race, Gender, and Desire* (Philadelphia: Temple University Press, 1989). He argues that: "*The Bluest Eye* depicts the struggle between two warring factions. The Dick-and-Jane frame has as its referent not only the primer but the cultural values of the dominant society" (68).

3. "I was sitting back in my seat, and I had taken a big bite of that candy and it pulled a tooth right out of my mouth. I could have cried . . . I don't believe I'll ever get over that. There I was, five months pregnant, trying to look like Jean Harlow, and a front tooth gone. Everything went then" (98).

4. As quoted in Karen Carmean's *Toni Morrison's World of Fiction,* 1993. Richard O. Moore, dir., "The Writer in America," Perspective Films, 1978.

5. See also Patrick Bryce's Bjork's discussion in *The Novels of Toni Morrison: The Search for Self and Place Within the Community* (New York: Peter Lang, 1992), 44–48.

6. In the interview with Jane Bakerman (1977), "The Seams Can't Show: An Interview with Toni Morrison," Morrison comments:

When I wrote the section in *The Bluest Eye* about Pecola's mother, I thought I would have no trouble. First I wrote it out as an "I" story, but it didn't work because she, herself, didn't know a lot about things. Then I wrote it out as a "she" story, and that didn't work out very well because I couldn't get her thing into it. It was me, the author, sort of omnipotent, talking. I was never able to resolve that, so I used both. . . .(Taylor-Guthrie 1994: 37–38)

7. See also Trudier Harris, *From Mammies to Militants: Domestics in Black American Literature* (Philadelphia: Temple University Press, 1982), 35–69, for a discussion of Pauline and her domestic role. See Sue Jewell, *From Mammy to Miss America and Beyond: Cultural Images & the Shaping of US Social Policy* (New York: Routledge, 1993).

8. See bell hooks, "Homeplace: A Site of Resistance" and chapter 1 of above.

9. Cholly does attempt to rape her a second time.

10. *Don't Blame Mother: Mending the Mother-Daughter Relationship* (1989).

11. Morrison continues:

Hannah was not bitter, and she was not whining. She was reliable, and she was also a little off-centre. But she wasn't so off-centre that she frightened, just a little. I think she's the only person who never deliberately caused anybody any pain, although she does say something awful to Sula, but she never wanted to hurt anybody, she didn't have that ego or the vanity to want to impose herself on anybody. And I like that. It is genuinely maternal. (Koenen 1980, in Taylor-Guthrie 1994: 69)

12. In *Jazz,* a conversation overheard by Joe upsets the long-held conviction that children "do best" under their mothers' care and that children away from their mothers—cared for by others—are "at risk" and suffer from what is termed "maternal deprivation." In the hotel dining room, as he is serving coffee, Joe overhears a woman saying "the confoundest thing." "'I am bad for my children,' she said. 'I don't mean to be, but there is something in me that makes it so. I'm a good mother but they do better away from me; as long as they're by my side nothing good can come to them. The ones that leave seem to flower: the ones that stay have such a hard time. You can imagine how bad I feel knowing that, can't you?'" (125). Joe goes on to say that: "[He] had to sneak a look at her, it took strength to say that. Admit that" (125). What these novels tell us is that children are not always liked by their mothers and that mothers are not always good for their children. These sentiments cut at the core of our beliefs; and thus, as Joe recognizes, "[it takes] strength to say that, admit that." However, it also "takes strength" to listen to and acknowledge the truth of our mothers'

words. Ironically, when we limit our reading to a child-centered perspective we perpetuate the very myths of motherhood that Morrison seeks to deconstruct.

13. Sula does enter patriarchy with Nel at her side. But even their close bond does not withstand the normalizing pressures of patriarchy.

14. Morrison in Robert Stepto's (1976) interview (Taylor-Guthrie 1994: 27).

15. Morrison says in her interview with Robert Stepto: "In the process of finding themselves, black men are making themselves" (Taylor-Guthrie 1994: 26).

16. See Naomi Wolf's *Fire With Fire: The New Female Power and How It Will Change the 21st Century* (New York: Random House, 1993). Power feminism "calls for alliances based on economic self-interest and economic giving back rather than on a sentimental and workable fantasy of cosmic sisterhood" (53). I see Sula as the existentialist feminist and Jadine as the power feminist although there is some crossover. For a discussion of existentialist feminism see Josephine Donovan, *Feminist Theory: The Intellectual Traditions of American Feminism* (New York: Frederick Ungar Publishing Co, 1985); and Rosemarie Tong, *Feminist Thought: A Comprehensive Introduction* (Boulder: Westview Press, 1989).

17. Virginia Woolf wrote that in order for her to write she had to kill the Angel in the house or "she would have killed me." As Woolf kills the "Angel in the House," Sula kills, at least metaphorically, "the creator and sovereign . . . of the third floor"—Gilbert and Guber's mad woman in the attic.

18. See chapter 1 for a discussion of the Wall and female adolescence.

chapter three
RUPTURES/DISRUPTIONS OF THE MOTHERLINE

1. Johnson writes:

In my view the first step might be for women to rethink their relationship with their own mothers. Until women can understand and respect themselves as women without men, bringing men in, still unreconstructed, can hardly be of help. The question of women's own self-definition seems logically prior to the further inclusion of men. (66)

Johnson here is referring to Chodorow's so-called "co-parenting solution." This strategy, in Johnson's words, "solve[s] nothing" (8). "Indeed," as Johnson continues, "it will reinforce male dominance unless husband and wife are truly more equal" (8).

2. In chapter 5, I will argue that Ruth's culinary inability, along with her late nursing of her son, may be read as acts of resistance against patriarchal motherhood. The late nursing of her son, in particular, suggests an expression of the funk that she, as a "good" mother, has been required to repress.

3. See, for example, Barbara Offutt Mathieson, Ph.D., "Memory and Mother Love in Morrison's *Beloved*." Mathieson argues that "Morrison explores the dangers of retreat into the past by examining the destructiveness of prolonged mutual dependence of mother and child" (11). "Both maternal bonding and rememory are essential for human survival, yet either, if unrestrained," Mathieson continues, "devours the agent" (14). See also Barbara Schapiro, "The Bonds of Love and the Boundaries of Self in Toni Morrison's *Beloved*"; Jean Wyatt, "Giving Body to the Word: The Maternal Symbolic in Toni Morri-

son's *Beloved*"; Jennifer Fitzgerald, "Selfhood and Community: Psychoanalysis and Discourse in *Beloved*," in *Toni Morrison,* ed. Linden Peach (New York: St. Martins, 1995), 110–27; Jean Walton, "Re-Placing Race in (White) Psychoanalytic Discourse: Founding Narratives of Feminism."

4. In *"Quiet as it's kept"; Shame, Trauma, and Race in the Novels of Toni Morrison* (2000), J. Brooks Bouson counters this psychological reading of Beloved's attachment to Sethe to argue that "In describing Beloved's vast neediness, the novel . . . points to the awful emotional costs of slavery's disruption of the mother-child bond and the slave mother's forced abandonment of her children" (15).

5. Danger, devour, and destructiveness are some of the words used by the critics to describe Beloved and Sethe's relationship. Please see endnote 3.

6. Beloved is also, as Grewal observes in *Circles of Sorrow, Lines of Struggle* (1998), "reminiscent of Jung's archetype of the maiden, who is 'often described as not altogether human in the usual sense; she is either of unknown or peculiar origin, or she looks strange or undergoes strange experiences, from which one is forced to enter the maiden's extraordinary, myth-lie character'" (109).

7. In her review of *Jazz* Deborah A. McDowell speculates that Wild may be Beloved: "(Could she even be that 'devil child' [who takes] the shape of a pregnant woman" before vanishing at *Beloved*'s end?)" (1992: 3). The use of both trace and disappear in *Jazz* and *Beloved* supports such an interpretation: in *Beloved* we read: "Beloved and her memory "disappear": "By and by all trace is gone" (275). Significantly, Joe, the son of Wild, takes on the surname of Trace after his adoptive mother explains to him that his real parents "disappeared without a trace" (124). See the following chapter on *Jazz* for a discussion on Wild.

8. See Hirsch, *The Mother/Daughter Plot,* 197–98.

9. In *Toni Morrison and Womanist Discourse* (1999), Mori argues that "Sethe's mother's exploitation is symbolized by a circle and a cross branded on her rib. Mori goes on to argue,

> Although the circle at first indicates the enslavement and physical burden inflicted upon her body, she reverses the negative representation and uses it as a crucial identification by which daughter will remember her. Although she is executed, Sethe's mother possesses the potential fortitude to protect her daughter, repelling the confinement inscribed on her body. (136)

10. There is also no evidence of excessive relationality existing prior to the infanticide.

chapter four
RECONNECTIONS TO THE MOTHERLINE

1. What Christ does not examine, however, is how the spiritual quest is configured differently along racial lines. This difference is particularly apparent when naming is emphasized. Naming and renaming of self are central to African American history and literature, as slaves took the names of their masters under slavery and took on new names once freed to mark their new freed subjectivity.

2. As quoted by Wilfred Samuels and Clenora Hudson-Weems in *Toni Morrison,* 69.

3. Stephanie Demetrakopoulos, "The Interdependence of Men's and Women's Individuation," in *New Dimensions of Spirituality* (1987), writes:

I think men especially need women to keep in touch with, for grounding in, cyclical time. Women's bodies and their children mark time out in cycles and stages. Attempting to tack time in the narrowness of his all-male world, Henry Porter wallpapers his little room with calenders. He measures time by the killings he has done for the Days . . . (90)

4. In contrast, Macon, Pilate's brother, is disconnected from his motherline and is concerned only with progress and prosperity. He does not derive his self-definition from his history, nor does he synthesize the past with the present in his conception of time. Telling Milkman about his childhood, Macon reflects: "He had not said any of this for years. Had not even reminisced much about it recently" (51). In *Song,* time is specifically gendered. Men experience time in a linear manner while women experience time in a cyclical mode. At the conclusion of his quest, Milkman, as Carmean observes, "begins to perceive time as circular and mythic, [while] Guitar remains convinced of its linear and historic structure" (51). People, such as Morrison's flying men, who choose detachment over involvement, individualism over community, experience time in the way of the dominant culture. For such emotionally cut-off men, time is a line and not a circle. *Song* confirms, therefore, that not only is black cultural identity predicated upon community and history but that ancestral memory is predicated upon a communal consciousness. To paraphrase Morrison, "To know thy ancestor one must know thy neighbor."

Not only their sense of time differentiates Pilate and Macon; Pilate's home is organically created from the earth while Macon's household is built from the acquisition of property. In contrast to the women of Virginia who carried nothing in their hands (262), Macon always holds keys in his hands or pockets; they signify in this text the ownership of property and the attainment of prosperity. The keys also work as phallic icons, particularly as Macon believes that it was the two keys in his pocket that allowed him to "entertain thoughts of marrying the doctor's daughter." "Without those keys," Macon tells us, "he would have floated away at the doctor's first word . . . [o]r he would have melted like new wax under the heat of that pale eye" (22–23). The latter image is particular suggestive of impotence. Later Macon advises his son, "Let me tell you right now the one important thing you'll ever need to know: Own things. And let the things you own own other things. Then you'll own yourself and other people too" (55). Most disturbing is Macon's rendering of his own children and wife as property and his objectification of them as symbols of his affluence:

There were other children there. Barefoot, naked to the waist, dirty. But we stood apart, near the car, in white stockings, ribbons, and gloves. And when he talked to the men, he kept glancing at us, us and the car. . . . You see, he took us there so they could see us, envy us, envy him. . . . First he displayed us, then he splayed us. All our lives were like that: he would parade us like virgins through Babylon, then humiliate us like whores in Babylon. (217–18)

5. Please see chapter 3 for a detailed discussion of Jadine's quest.

6. Mbalia argues that Morrison makes Son a wife/woman killer to represent the need to sever Jadine's capitalist, class affiliations. I find this explanation highly problematic. It minimizes and trivializes the very real violence of the text. Her valorization of Son does not take into account his phallocentric and violent masculinity.

7. The architecture of Morrison's homes is significant. In this novel, the upstairs is clearly marked as white space. That is why Sydney is so outraged: "You know what I'm talking about, you was upstairs!" (162).

8. Jadine is a conventionally beautiful woman: tall, thin, light skinned, and fine featured. She fulfills all the requirements of what Naomi Wolf calls the beauty myth. Significantly, Son encounters and falls in love with Jadine as she is sleeping, reminiscent of the Sleeping Beauty fairy tale. What attracts Son to Jadine is not her talents, personality, intelligence, but her looks. I question whether he would have been attracted to Jadine had she been one of those "fat black ladies." Son longs for Jadine to embody authentic black womanhood, yet he is attracted to her precisely because she conforms to white definitions of beauty. The hypocrisy of Son's views is sexist, as well as racist.

9. That critic is Barbara Hill Rigney. She writes in *Voices of Toni Morrison:* "Son has murdered one wife, and he does beat Jadine, for all of which the night women forgive him, although, one hopes, Morrison does not" (96).

chapter five
MATERNAL INTERVENTIONS

1. Ogunyemi makes a similar point when he argues that the three families in *The Bluest Eye* are representations of types of African American families with Mrs. MacTeer being typical of the genteel, lower-middle-class blacks who, despite their outward religiosity, are not charitable enough to tolerate the less privileged. They undertake charity merely to maintain a facade of good-neighborliness, underscored in Mrs. MacTeer's constant grumbling against Pecola when Pecola was her ward (118).

2. We are told that M'Dear, the midwife, "ran her left [hand] over Aunt Jimmy's body. The backs of her long fingers she placed on the patient's cheek, then placed her palm on the forehead. She ran her fingers through the sick woman's hair, lightly scratching the scalp, and then looking at what at the fingernails revealed" (108).

3. Morrison's own father, she explained in an interview, "could get very aggressive about people who troubled us—throwing people out and so on . . ." (Bessie W. Jones and Audrey Vinson, [1985]), in Taylor-Guthrie 1994: 172. Mr. MacTeer, the father who protects, is contrasted to Cholly, the father who raped his daughter. The text tells us that "[h]aving no idea how to raise children, and having never watched any parent raise himself, he [Cholly] could not even comprehend what such a relationship should be" (126). "Abandoned in a junk heap by his mother, rejected for a crap game by his father" (126), Cholly becomes "Dangerously free" (125). He is one of Morrison's golden-eyed heroes; what she has called the "salt tasters."

4. Please see chapter 1 for a discussion of the ideology of sensitive mothering.

5. This evokes Morrison's description of her mother's soliloquies: "[She had the] habit of getting stuck like a record on some problem, going on for days and days and days and then singing in between . . . just like a saga" (Taylor-Guthrie 1994: 172).

6. In "Beyond Realism: The Fiction of Toni Morrison," Keith E. Byerman argues that the MacTeer family offers an alternative to the victimization experienced by both Cholly and Pauline. He writes: "The MacTeers make themselves into a family despite all the economic, psychological, and social forces opposing them" (60). However, Byerman goes on to emphasize that

> the MacTeers are not sentimentalized into the Dick-and-Jane family of the school reader. Morrison insists that it is in fact those who refuse such sentimentality who are the most heroic. The MacTeers live without illusion as much

as possible. The parents whip their children, complain about the burdens of life, and struggle only semi-successfully to acquire the necessities for survival. . . . But unlike the Breedloves and the light-skinned Geraldine and Maureen, they do not measure their human worth by the symbols of the dominant white culture. (60–61)

7. In addition to *The Empire of the Mother,* see Ruth Bloch's "American Feminine Ideals in Transition: The Rise of the Moral Mother," *Feminist Studies* 4, no. 2 (June 1978): 101–26; and Marlene Legates. "The Cult of Womanhood in Eighteenth-Century Thought," *Eighteenth-Century Studies* 10, no. 1 (Fall 1976): 21–39.

8. For perceptive analyses of slave motherhood as both ideology and experience see Barbara Bush, *Slave Women in Caribbean Society 1650–1838* (Bloomington: Indiana University Press, 1990); and Deborah Gray White, *Ain't I a Woman? Female Slaves in the Plantation South* (New York: W.W. Norton. 1985), Jacqueline Jones, *Labor of Love, Labor of Sorrow: Black Women, Work, and Family from Slavery to Present* (New York: Basic Books, 1985).

9. For a discussion on the complex relationship between ideologies of motherhood and the material practices of mothering see Andrea O'Reilly's "Talking Back in Mother Tongue: A Feminist Course on Mothering-Motherhood," in *Feminism and Education,* Vol. 2, ed. Paula T. Bourne (Toronto: CWSE Press, 1993), 221–38.

10. In the opening section of *Black Women Writing Autobiography* (1989), Braxton discusses the archetype of what she calls, "the outraged mother." In Afro-American literature and history, Braxton argues, the figure of the outraged mother appears repeatedly. "The archetypal outraged mother," Braxton writes, "travels alone through the darkness to impart a sense of identity and 'belonginess' to her child. She sacrifices and improvises to create the vehicles necessary for the survival of flesh and spirit. Implied in all of her actions and fueling her heroic ones is abuse of her people and her person" (21). Braxton then goes on to explore this archetype in Harriet Jacobs's *Incidents in the Life of A Slave Girl.* I argue that Morrison's *Beloved* continues the narrative of the archetypal outraged mother. It is Sethe's passionate love for her children that motivates her to flee Sweet Home and seek safety for her family.

11. It is interesting to note that Jacobs has not been accused of a "too thick" love though she clearly states that she, like Sethe, would choose infanticide over slavery for her children. She, of course, does not act upon her threat of infanticide. But this itself cannot account for the startling differences in critical opinion on Sethe and Harriet Jacobs. I think one explanation for the critics' discomfort with Sethe's passionate love is because her motherlove is so physically grounded in the nursing relationship.

12. In her article Wyatt writes: "Breaking the silence that has surrounded birth in Western narrative, Morrison provides a physically detailed account of childbirth, and— also new in Western cultural discourse—she gives labor its due as good work: Sethe and Amy 'did something together appropriately and well' (84)" (476). There are very few mother-centered narratives of birth: when birth is portrayed in literature the emphasis is on the child being born and the point-of-view is usually that of a male narrator. As Kathryn Allen Rabuzzi notes in her book *Motherself: A Mythic Analysis of Motherhood,* "Being born is everywhere celebrated in myth and ritual; giving birth is quite another matter. Often it is simply ignored" (71).

13. Not only is the content of the narrative different, so too is the form—the way the story is told. The journey is not developed linearly and chronologically; rather, it is told in fragments, the storyline is dropped and then picked up later by someone else. The beginning of the tale is told from Sethe's perspective (30–35); while the remaining part of the story is told by Denver to Beloved (76–85). This nonlinear and fragmented structure of time passing has been described by the French theorist, Julia Kristeva, as "Woman's Time" and has been identified with the maternal. Thus, in both theme and form, Sethe rewrites the traditional genre of the male quest to create a specifically maternal one.

14. In *Motherself, A Mythic Analysis of Motherhood,* Kathryn Allen Rabuzzi develops a particular quest pattern which she calls "the way of the mother." The "way of the mother" is radically different from the traditional heroic quest because the selfhood that is to be obtained is one that is not individuated and autonomous, as in the male quest, but one that consists of "a binary-unity." A selfhood that is "simultaneously two and one at the same time, its parts consisting of mother and child in varying relationships to each other" (11). This gynocentric relational experience of selfhood is called the "motherself" or "motherselfhood" as opposed to "heroselfhood." I would suggest that Sethe's sense of self is that of the "motherself."

15. I find Demetrakopoulos's article highly problematic. Her perspective privileges the masculine values of separateness and individuation over the feminine values of connectedness and relatedness. She continues the patriarchal devaluation of Nature. She also positions a man, Paul D., as the hero who rescues Sethe from the enemy, which for Demetrakopoulos, is Sethe's own Self as mother. She writes: "Her idea that her children are her best parts, her best self (ultimately her only self) becomes such a central motif in Sethe's characterization that her dilemma is resolved by Paul D.'s telling her, 'You your best thing, Sethe, you are' (273)" (54). And later: "When Sethe finally connects with Paul D., she moves towards individuation, becomes connected with her own animus and, thus, assumes a position from which she can escape the deadly toils of nature" (54). And "Paul D. gives Sethe the animus quality of initiative to escape from the mother/family matrix into individuation that celebrates the self as 'her best thing'" (57).

16. Marsha Darling, "Ties that Bind, An Interview with Toni Morrison," *Women's Review of Books* 5, no. 6 (1988): 4–6.

17. For a thorough and perceptive analysis of Paul D's character see Samuels and Hudson-Weems: 123–34.

18. Davies juxtaposes this woman's reading to that of her academic friends. Davies writes: "At the same time, my academic feminist critic friends uniformly marveled at its narrative 'mastery' and all the rich implications for literary analysis" (46).

19. There are many articles on Sethe's motherlove but none, to my knowledge, on her sexuality.

20. Although there have been several feminist readings of *Beloved* and the novel itself invites such questioning through statements such as "the last of the Sweet Home men was there to catch her if she sank" (18), Sethe's relationship with Paul D. has not been considered or critiqued. It would seem that the scholarly community thinks it is quite all right for Sethe to fall for a man but not all right for her to live for her children.

21. Although this is a normal and modest ambition, it is for Sethe a radical act because slave motherlove is denied and prohibited under slavery.

22. This is not to suggest that the white middle-class women enjoyed any real power: only that their position as mother of the children was naturally assumed.

23. Sethe kills her child so she will not have to die: she injures her to keep her from harm: "[I] carried, pushed, dragged them through the veil, out, away, over there where no one could hurt them. Over there. Outside this place, where they would be safe" (163). She was carrying her children to the "timeless place" where they all would be together and reunited with Sethe's own mother: "[My] plan was to take us all to the side other where my own ma'am is" (203).

24. Significantly, the word *claim* is used here by schoolteacher.

25. The notable exception is Pauline Breedlove in *The Bluest Eye*.

26. The quotation reads:

Eva knew there was time for nothing in this world than the time it took to get there and cover her daughter's body with her own. She lifted her heavy frame up on her good leg, and with fists and arms smashed the window pane. Using her stump as support on the window sill, her good leg as a lever, she threw herself out of the window. Cut and bleeding she crawled the air trying to aim her body toward the flaming, dancing figure. She missed and came crashing down some twelve feet from Hannah's smoke. Stunned but still conscious, Eva dragged herself, toward her firstborn. . . . (75–76)

27. From Mervyn Rothstein's article "Toni Morrison in Her New Novel Defends Women," *New York Times,* 26 Aug. 1987: C17.

28. Toni Morrison, *Beloved* (New York: Plume, 1987), 162.

29. Harris goes on to say that Eva "never considers rehabilitation for her son," but this is the 1920s when rehabilitation for black man was not on the social or medical agenda; witness the poor treatment Shadrack receives when he is hospital.

30. In *Fiction and Folklore* Trudier Harris writes: "Also, in killing Plum and trying to save Hannah, Eva exhibits a preference for the woman centered consciousness that pervades most of the novel. Perhaps, Plum, in his addiction, is too sharp a reminder of the ineffectuality of Boyboy as husband and father. Perhaps Eva sees history about to repeat itself in him. Her contemplation of 'no-count' males, then, is further motivation for Eva to end a seemingly useless life" (75). I disagree. This passage shows Eva's love for her son and her own anguish at having to kill her beloved child.

31. Barbara Hill Rigney writes in *Voices of Toni Morrison:* "The return to the mother, erotic as this return always is in all of Morrison's novels, is also always associated with castration, death, oblivion, but also paradoxically—with enlightenment, revelation, transcendence." Rigney refers to Kristeva's concept of "a non Oedipal incest" that "opens the eyes of a subject who is nourished by the mother . . . neither animal, god, nor man, he is Dionysus, born a second time for having had the mother" (94).

chapter six

MATERNAL HEALING

1. This is similar to the mother-daughter relationship of Pauline and Pecola in Morrison's first novel, *The Bluest Eye*. Pecola longs for blue eyes because in her world blue eyes

signify beauty and desirability; those with blue eyes are the loved and chosen ones. When Pecola accidently drops the berry cobbler in the kitchen of her mother's employers, Mrs. Breedlove slaps and scolds her daughter with "words that were hotter and darker than the smoking berries" (87); while the upset "pink and yellow" Fisher girl is comforted and soothed with "words of honey." The lesson that Violet and Pecola learn is that they are not the beloved child; another, white and/or male, child has claimed their mothers' hearts. (In Violet's case, the mother in her late childhood is the grandmother.)

2. In a 1985 conversation with Gloria Naylor (in *Conversations with Toni Morrison*), Toni Morrison described her writing as a process of reclamation which brings back to life the dead girl:

[B]it by bit I had been rescuing her from the grave of time and inattention. Her fingernails maybe in the first book; face and legs, perhaps, the second time. Little by little bringing her back into living life. So that now she comes running when called—walks freely around the house, sits down in a chair; looks at me, listens to . . . anybody she wants to. She cannot lie. Doesn't know greed or vengeance. Will not fawn or pontificate. . . . She is here now, alive. I have seen, named and claimed her—and oh what company she keeps. (Taylor-Guthrie 1994: 217)

3. Female friendship is a central theme in Morrison's fiction, particularly in *Sula*. In *Jazz* laughter brings Violet comfort and insight. "Violet learned then what she had forgotten until this moment: that laughter is serious. More complicated, more serious than tears" (113).

4. In her popular book on the Wild Woman archetype, *Women Who Run With Wolves* (1992), Clarrisa Pinkola Estes explains that wild, as an archetype, means "to live a natural life" (8). As an archetype the Wild Woman is the "Innate instinctual Self" (6). The Wild Woman, Estes explains

is the female soul . . . she is the source of the feminine. . . . She is the Life/Death/Life force. She is the incubator. She is intuition. . . . She encourages humans to remain multilingual: fluent in the languages of dreams, passions, and poetry. She whispers from night dreams. . . . She is the source, the light, the night, the dark, and daybreak. She is the smell of good mud. . . . The birds which tell us secrets belong to her. (13)

5. See Luce Irigarary, "Plato's Hysteria," in *Speculum of the Other Woman* (1985), 243–364.

6. In contemporary Western society, fathers are not physically or emotionally available to their sons; there is no father present to teach the son what it means to be a male; no elder male about to initiate the son into adult manhood. Bly writes: "When women, even women with the best intentions, bring up a boy alone, he may in some way have no male face, or he may have no face at all" (17). Thus, the son must "cut his soul away from his mother-bound soul" to discover his masculinity and be healed (165). On his journey to manhood, the son must confront his father, undergo male initiation by his elders, and seek guidance from various mentors, whom Bly calls male mothers. With their assistance the son is able to free himself from his mother's apron strings. For an excellent critique of Bly see the articles in *Women Respond to the Men's Movement,* ed. Kay Leigh Hagan (San Francisco; Harper Collins, 1992).

7. In this passage (1992, 180–84), we move back and forth between the search for Wild and the stalking of Dorcas. The question that ends the section, "But where is she?" (184), refers simultaneously to both Dorcas and Wild.

8. "International Symposium on Toni Morrison's *Paradise*," February 24, 1999; coordinated by Dr. Andrea O'Reilly and hosted by MacLaughlin College, York University, Toronto, Ontario, Canada.

Works Cited

Abbey, Sharon, and Andrea O'Reilly. *Redefining Motherhood: Changing Identities and Patterns.* Toronto: Second Story, 1998.

Abel, Elizabeth, Barbara Christian, and Helene Moglen, eds. *Female Subject in Black and White: Race, Psychoanalysis, Feminism.* Berkeley: University of California Press, 1997.

Allen, Jeffner. "Motherhood: The Annihilation of Women" in *Mothering: Essays in Feminist Theory.* Totowa, N.J.: Rowman and Allanheld, 1983.

Allen, Paula Gunn. *The Sacred Hoop.* Boston: Beacon, 1986.

Arcana, Judith Pilders. *Our Mothers' Daughters.* Berkeley: Shameless Hussy, 1979.

Arden, Jann. "Good Mother," *Living Under June.* CD 31454 0789 2 (1994, A & M Records, a division of PolyGramGroup Canada Inc.).

Arnup, Katherine. *Lesbian Parenting: Living with Pride and Prejudice.* Charlottetown, P. E. I.: Gynergy, 1995.

———, Andrea Levesque, and Ruth Roach Pierson, eds. *Delivering Motherhood: Maternal Ideologies and Practices in the 19th and 20th Centuries.* London and New York: Routledge, 1990.

Association for Research on Mothering and The Journal of the Association for Research on Mothering website: *www.yorku.ca/crm*

Awkward, Michael. "Roadblocks and Relatives: Critical Revision in Toni Morrison's *The Bluest Eye.*" *Critical Essays on Toni Morrison.* Ed. Nellie Y. McKay. Boston: G. K. Hall, 1988.

———. "The Evil of Fulfillment: Scapegoating and Narration in *The Bluest Eye.*" *Toni Morrison Critical Perspectives, Past and Present.* Ed. Henry Louis Gates Jr. and K. A. Appiah. New York: Amistad, 1993.

Badinter, Elizabeth. *Motherlove: Myth and Reality.* New York: Macmillan, 1981.

Baker, Houston. *Workings of the Spirit: The Poetics of Afro-American Women's Writings.* Chicago: University of Chicago Press, 1991.

Ballingsley, Andrew. *Black Families in White America.* Englewood, Cliffs, N.J.: Prentice-Hall, 1968.

———, ed. *Climbing Jacob's Ladder: The Enduring Legacy of African American Families.* New York: Simon and Schuster, 1992.

Bart, Pauline. "Review of Nancy Chodorow's *The Reproduction of Mothering.*" *Mothering Essays in Feminist Theory.* Ed. Joyce Trebilcot. Totowa, N.J.: Rowman and Allanheld, 1983.

Bassin, Donna, Margaret Honey, and Meryle Mahrer Kaplan, eds. *Representations of Motherhood.* New Haven: Yale University Press, 1994.

Bassoff, Evelyn. *Mothering Ourselves: Helping and Healing for Adult Daughters.* New York: Penguin, 1991.

Belenky, Mary Field, Blythe McVicker Clinchy, Nancy Rule Goldberger, and Jill Mattuck Tarule, eds. *Women's Ways of Knowing: The Development of Self, Voice, and Mind.* New York: Basic, 1986.

Bell, Roseann, P. Parker, and B. Guy-Schetfall, eds. *Sturdy Black Bridges: Visions of Black Women in Literature.* New York: Anchor/Doubleday, 1979.

Bell-Scott, Patricia et al., eds. *Double Stitch: Black Women Write About Mothers and Daughters.* Boston: Beacon, 1993.

Benjamin, Jessica. *The Bonds of Love: Psychoanalysis, Feminism, and the Problem of Domination.* New York: Pantheon, 1988.

Bernard, Candance, et al. "'She Who Learns Teaches': Othermothering in the Academy." *Journal of The Association for Research on Mothering* 2: 2 (Fall/Winter 2000): 66–84.

Bernard, Jessie. *The Future of Motherhood.* New York: Dial, 1974.

Bernard, Wanda Thomas, and Candace Bernard. "Passing the Torch: A Mother and Daughter Reflect on their Experiences Across Generations." *Canadian Woman Studies* 18: 2 & 3 (Summer/Fall 1998). Toronto: Inanna Publications and Education Inc, 1998.

Birns, Beverly, and Dale F. Hall. *The Different Faces of Motherhood.* New York and London: Plenum, 1988.

Bjork, Patrick Bryce. *The Novels of Toni Morrison: The Search for Self and Place Within the Community.* New York: Peter Lang, 1992.

Black Mother, Black Daughter. Dirs. Sylvia Hamilton and Claire Prieta. NFB Film, Atlantic Studio, 1990.

Blakely, Mar Kay. *American Mom: Motherhood, Politics, and Humble Pie.* Chapel Hill: Alonquin Books, 1994.

Bloch, Ruth H. "American Feminine Ideals in Transition: The Rise of the Moral Mother, 1785–1815." *Feminist Studies* 4: 2 (1978): 101–26.

Bloom, Harold. *The Anxiety of Influence: A Theory of Poetry.* New York: Oxford University Press, 1973.

Bly, Robert. *Iron John.* New York: Vintage, 1990.

Bordo, Susan. *Unbearable Weight: Feminism, Western Culture, and the Body.* Berkeley: University of California Press, 1993.

Boultan, Mary Georgia. *On Being a Mother: A Study of Women with Pre-School Children.* London: Tavistock, 1983.

Bouson, Brooks J. *Quiet as It's Kept: Shame, Trauma, and Race in the Novels of Toni Morrison.* Albany: State University of New York Press, 2000.

Brand, Dionne. *At the Full and Change of the Moon*. Toronto: Alfred A. Knopf Canada, 1999.

———. *In Another Place, Not Here*. Toronto: Vintage Canada, 1997, c1996.

———. *No Burden To Carry: Narratives of Black Women in Ontario, 1920s to 1950s*. Toronto: Women's Press, 1991.

Brandt, Di. *Wild Mother Dancing: Maternal Narrative in Canadian Literature*. Winnipeg: University of Manitoba Press, 1993.

Braxton, Joanne M. *Black Women Writing Autobiography: A Tradition Within a Tradition*. Philadelphia: Temple University Press, 1989.

Brown, Miekl, and Carol Gilligan. *Meeting at the Crossroads: Women's Psychology and Girls' Development*. Cambridge: Harvard University Press, 1992.

Bush, Barbara. *Slave Women in Caribbean Society 1650–1838*. Bloomington: Indiana University Press, 1990.

Butler-Evans, Elliott. *Race, Gender, and Desire: Narrative Strategies in the Fiction of Toni Morrison and Alice Walker*. Philadephia: Temple University Press, 1989.

Byerman, Keith. "Intense Behaviors: The Use of the Grotesque in *The Bluest Eye* and *Eva's Man*." *CLA* 5 (1982): 447–57.

Bynum, Victoria E. *Unruly Women: The Politics of Social and Sexual Control in the Old South*. Chapel Hill: University of North Carolina Press, 1992.

Canadian Women's Studies Vol. 18, Nos 2 & 3, Summer/Fall, 1998. York University, Toronto: Inanna Publications and Education, 1998.

Caplan, Paula J. *Don't Blame Mother: Mending the Mother-Daughter Relationship*. New York: Harper and Row, 1989.

Carby, Hazel V. *Reconstructing Womanhood: The Emergence of the Afro-American Woman Novelist*. New York: Oxford University Press, 1987.

Carmean, Karen. *Toni Morrison's World of Fiction*. Troy, New York: Whitston, 1993.

Castro, Jan Garden. "Love." *St, Louis Today*. October 25, 2003. *www.stltoday.com*

Chodorow, Nancy. *The Reproduction of Mothering: Psychoanalysis and the Sociology of Gender*. Berkeley: University of California Press, 1978.

Christ, Carol. *Diving Deep and Surfacing: Women Writers on Spiritual Quest*. Boston: Beacon Press, 1980.

Christian, Barbara. *Black Feminist Criticism: Perspectives on Black Women Writers*. New York: Pergamon, 1985.

———. *Black Women Novelists: The Development of a Tradition 1892–1976*. Westport, Conn.: Greenwood, 1980.

Collins, Patricia Hill. "Shifting the Center: Race, Class, and Feminist Theorizing About Motherhood." *Mothering: Ideology, Experience, and Agency*. Ed. Evelyn Nakano Glenn, Grace Chang, and Linda Rennie Forcey. New York: Routledge, 1994. 45–65.

———. "The Meaning of Motherhood in Black Culture and Black Mother-Daughter Relationships." *Double Stitch: Black Women Write About Mothers and Daughters*. Ed. Patricia Bell-Scott et al. New York: HarperPerennial, 1993. 42–60.

———. *Black Feminist Thought: Knowledge, Consciousness, and the Politics of Empowerment*. New York: Routledge, 1991.

Cooper, Baba. "The Radical Potential in Lesbian Mothering of Daughters." *Politics of the Heart: A Lesbian Parenting Anthology*. Ed. Sandra Pollack and Jeanne Vaughn. Ithaca, N.Y.: Firebrand Books, 1987.

Cosslett, Tess. *Women Writing Childbirth: Modern Discourses of Motherhood*. Manchester, England: Manchester University Press, 1994.

Dally, Ann. *The Invention of Motherhood: The Consequences of an Ideal*. London: Burnett, 1982.

Daly, Brenda O., and Maureen T. Reddy, eds. *Narrating Mothers: Theorizing Maternal Subjectivities*. Knoxville: University of Tennessee Press, 1991.

Darling, Marsha Jean. "Ties that Bind, Interview with Toni Morrison." *Women's Review of Books* 5: 6 (1988): 4–6.

Davidson, Cathy N., and E. M. Broner, eds. *The Lost Tradition: Mothers and Daughters in Literature*. New York: Frederick Ungar, 1980.

Davies, Carole Boyce. "Mother Right/Write Revisited: *Beloved* and *Dessa Rose* and the Construction of Motherhood in Black Women's Fiction." *Narrating Mothers Theorizing Maternal Subjectivities*. Ed. Brenda O. Daly and Maureen T. Reddy. Knoxville: University of Tennessee Press, 1991.

———. "Mothering and Healing in Recent Black Women's Fiction." *Sage* 2: 1 (1995): 41–43.

Davis, Angela. *Women, Race, & Class*. New York: Random House, 1981.

Davis, Cynthia A. "Self, Society, and Myth in Toni Morrison's Fiction." *Toni Morrison*. Ed. Harold Bloom. New York: Chelsea, 1990. 7–25.

———. *Women, Culture, and Politics*. New York: Vintage, 1984.

Debold, Elizabeth, Marie Wilson, and Idelisse Malave. *Mother Daughter Revolution: From Good Girls to Great Women*. New York: Addison-Wesley, 1993.

DeLancey, Dayle, "Motherlove is a Killer: *Sula, Beloved,* and the Deadly Trinity of Motherlove." *Sage* 8: 2 (1990): 15–18.

de Lauretis, Teresa, ed. *Feminist Studies, Critical Studies*. Bloomington: Indiana University Press, 1986.

———. *Technologies of Gender: Essays on Theory Film and Fiction*. Bloomington: Indiana University Press, 1987.

———. "The Female Body and Heterosexual Presumption." *Semiotica* 67: 3/4 (1987): 259–79.

Demetrakopoulos, Stephanie. "The Nursing Mother and Feminine Metaphysics: An Essay on Embodiment." *Soundings* LXV: 4 (Winter 1982): 430–43.

———, and Karla Holloway. *New Dimensions in Spirituality: A Biracial and Bicultural Reading of the Novels of Toni Morrison*. New York: Greenwood, 1987.

———. "Maternal Bonds as Devourers of Individuation." *African American Review* 26: 1 (Spring 1992): 52–58.

Denard, Carolyn. "The Convergence of Feminism and Ethnicity in the Fiction of Toni Morrison." *Critical Essays on Toni Morrison.* Ed. Nellie Y. McKay. Boston: G. K. Hall, 1988.

de Waal, Mieke. "Teenage Daughters on their Mothers." *Daughtering & Mothering: Female Subjectivity Reanalysed.* Eds. Jannake van Mens-Verhulst, Karlein Schreurs, and Liesbeth Woertman. New York: Routledge, 1993. 35–43.

de Weever, Jacqueline. "The Inverted World of Toni Morrison's *The Bluest Eye* and *Sula.*" *CLA* 22 (1979): 402–14.

———. *Mythmaking and Metaphor in Black Women's Fiction.* New York: St. Martin's, 1991.

Dickerson, Vanessa. "The Naked Father in Toni Morrison's *The Bluest Eye.*" *Refiguring the Father: New Feminist Readings of Patriarchy.* Ed. Patrcia Yaeger and Beth Kowaleski-Wallace. Carbondale: Southern Illinois University Press, 1989.

Dinnerstein, Dorothy. *The Mermaid and the Minotaur: Sexual Arrangements and the Human Malaise.* New York: Harper Colophon, 1976.

DiQuinzio, Patrice. *The Impossibility of Motherhood.* New York: Routledge, 1999.

Dixon, Christa, K. *Negro Spirituals From Bible to Folksong.* Philadelphia: Fortress, 1976.

Donovan, Josephine. *Feminist Theory: The Intellectual Traditions of American Feminism.* New York: Frederick Ungar, 1985.

Dragu, Margaret, Sarah Sheard, and Susan Swan, eds. *Mothers Talk Back: Momz Radio.* Toronto: Coach House, 1991.

Eagleton, Terry. *Literary Theory.* Minneapolis: University of Minnesota Press, 1983.

Edelman, Hope. *Motherless Daughters: The Legacy of Loss.* New York: Delta, 1994.

Edwards, Arlene. "Community Mothering: The Relationship Between Mothering and the Community Work of Black Women." *Journal of The Association for Research on Mothering* 2: 2 (Fall/Winter 2000): 66–84.

Eisenstein, Hester. "The Cultural Meaning of Mothering III: The Construction of Gender Identity." *Contemporary Feminist Thought.* Boston: G. K. Hall, 1983: 87–95.

Eisenstein, Hester, and Alice Jardine, eds. *The Future of Difference.* New Brunswick and London: Rutgers University Press, 1987.

Erickson, Peter. "Images of Nurturance in *Tar Baby.*" *Toni Morrison: Critical Perspectives, Past and Present.* Ed. Henry Louis Gates Jr. and K. A. Appiah. New York: Amistad, 1993. 293–307.

Estes, Clarrisa Pinkola. *Women Who Run with the Wolves.* New York: Ballantine, 1992.

Eyer, Dianne. *Mother-Infant Bonding: A Scientific Fiction.* New Haven: Yale University Press, 1992.

Faderman, Lillian. *Surpassing the Love of Men: Romantic Friendship and Love Between Women from the Renaissance to the Present.* New York: William Morrow, 1981.

Feminist Studies. Special Issue: Towards a Feminist Theory of Motherhood 4: 2 (Summer 1978).

Ferguson, Ann. *Blood at the Root: Motherhood, Sexuality, & Male Dominance.* London: Pandora, 1989.

Flax, Jane. "The Conflict Between Nurturance and Autonomy in Mother/Daughter Relationships and within Feminism." *Feminist Studies* 4: 1 (1978): 171–89.

———. *Thinking Fragments: Psychoanalysis, Feminism, & Post-Modernism in the Contemporary West.* Berkeley: University of California Press, 1990.

Forcey, Linda. *Mothers of Sons: Toward an Understanding of Responsibility.* New York: Praeger, 1987.

Friday, Nancy. *My Mother My Self: The Daughter's Search for Identity.* New York: Dell, 1977.

Friedland, Ronnie, and Carol Kort, eds. *The Mother's Book: Shared Experiences.* Boston: Houghton Mifflin, 1981.

Frontiers: A Journal of Women Studies. Special Issue: Mothers and Daughters 3: 2 (Summer 1978).

Furman, Jan. *Toni Morrison's Fiction.* Columbia: University of South Carolina Press, 1996.

Fuss, Diana. *Essentially Speaking: Feminism, Nature, and Difference.* New York: Routledge, 1990.

Garner, Shirley, Claire Kahane, and Madelon Sprengnether, eds. *The (M)other Tongue: Essays in Feminist Psychoanalytic Interpretation.* Ithaca and London: Cornell University Press, 1985.

Gates, Henry Louis, Jr., ed. *Black Literature and Literary Theory.* New York: Methuen, 1984.

———, ed. *Reading Black, Reading Feminist.* New York: Meridian Books, 1990.

———, and K. A. Appiah, eds. *Toni Morrison: Critical Perspectives, Past and Present.* New York: Amistad, 1993.

Gibson, Donald. "Text and Countertext in The Bluest Eye." *Toni Morrison Critical Perspectives, Past and Present.* Ed. Henry Louis Gates and K. A. Appiah. New York: Amistad, 1993.

Gibson, Priscilla. "Developmental Mothering in an African American Community: From Grandmothers to New Mothers Again." *Journal of The Association for Research on Mothering* 2: 2 (Fall/Winter 2000): 31–41.

Giddings, Paula. *When and Where I Enter: The Impact of Black Women on Race and Sex in America.* New York: Bantam, 1984.

Gieve, Katherine, Ed. *Balancing Acts.* London: Virago, 1989.

Gilbert, Sandra M., and Susan Gubar, eds. *The Norton Anthology of Literature.* New York: W. W. Norton, 1985.

———. *The Madwoman in the Attic: The Woman Writer and the Nineteenth-Century Literary Imagination.* New Haven: Yale University Press, 1979.

Gilligan, Carol. *In A Different Voice: Psychological Theory and Women's Development.* Cambridge: Harvard University Press, 1982.

Giovanni, Nikki. "Nikki-Rosa." *Black Judgment.* Detroit: Broadside, 1968. 10.

Glenn, Evelyn Nakano, Grace Chung, and Linda Rennie Forcey. *Mothering: Ideology, Experience, and Agency.* New York: Routledge, 1994.

Glickman, Rose. *Daughters of Feminists: Young Women with Feminist Mothers Talk About Their Lives.* New York: St Martin's, 1993.

Golden, Marita. *Saving Our Sons: Raising Black Children in a Turbulent World.* New York: Doubleday, 1995.

Gordon, Tuula. *Feminist Mothers.* New York: New York University Press, 1990.

Grant, Robert. "Absence into Presence: The Thematics of Toni Morrison's *Sula.*" *Critical Essays on Toni Morrison.* Ed. Nellie Y. McKay. Boston: G. K. Hall, 1988. 90–103.

Grewal, Gurleen. *Circles of Sorrow, Lines of Sorrow.* Baton Rouge: Louisiana State University Press, 1998

Grosz, Elizabeth. *Sexual Subversions.* Sydney: Allen and Unwin, 1989.

———. *Jacques Lacan: A Feminist Introduction.* New York: Routledge, 1990.

Gutman, Herbert. *The Black Family in Slavery and Freedom: 1750–1925.* New York: Vintage, 1976.

Hagan, Karen Leigh. *Women Respond to the Men's Movement.* San Francisco: Harper Collins, 1992.

Hamilton, Sylvia. *Black Mother, Black Daughter* (videorecording). National Film Board of Canada, 1989.

Harding, Wendy, and Jacky Martin. *A World of Difference: An Inter-Cultural Study of Toni Morrison's Novels.* Westport, Conn.: Greenwood, 1994.

Harper, Frances E. W. *Iola Leroy.* 1893. Boston: Beacon, 1987.

Harris, Claire. *Drawing Down a Daughter.* Fredericton, N. B.: Goose Lane, 1992.

Harris, Joel Chandler. *Tar Baby: Tales of Brer Rabbit.* London: Creation, 2000.

Harris, Trudier. *From Mammies to Militants: Domestics in Black American Literature.* Philadelphia: Temple University Press, 1982.

———. *Fiction and Folklore: The Novels of Toni Morrison.* Knoxville: University of Tennessee Press, 1991.

Hayes, Sharon. *The Cultural Contradictions of Mothering.* New Haven: Yale University Press, 1986.

Heilbrun, Carolyn. *Writing a Woman's Life.* New York: Ballantine Books, 1988.

Heinze, Denise. *The Dilemma of "Double-Consciousness" in Toni Morrison's Novels.* Athens: The University of Georgia Press, 1993.

Henderson, Mae Gwendolyn. "Speaking in Tongues: Dialogics, Dialectics, and Black Women's Literary Tradition." *Reading Black, Reading Feminist.* Ed. Henry Louis Gates Jr. Toronto: Meridian, 1990. 116–42.

Herton, Calvin. *The Sexual Mountain and Black Women Writers: Adventures in Sex, Literature, and Real Life.* New York: Anchor Books, Doubleday, 1987.

Hine, Darlene Clark, ed. *Black Women in United States History.* 16 vols. Brooklyn: Carlson, 1990.

Hirsch, Marianne. *The Mother/Daughter Plot: Narrative, Psychoanalysis, Feminism.* Bloomington: Indiana University Press, 1989.

———. "Mothers and Daughters." *Signs* 7: 1 (Autumn 1981): 200–22.

Hite, Shere. *The Hite Report on the Family.* New York: Grove, 1994.

Hoffert, Sylvia D. *Private Matters: American Attitudes toward Childrearing and Infant Nature in the Urban North, 1800–1860.* Urbana and Chicago: University of Illinois Press, 1989.

Holloway, Karla. *Moorings & Metaphors: Figures of Culture and Gender in Black Women's Literature.* New Brunswick: Rutgers University Press, 1992.

———, and Stephanie Demetrakopoulos. *New Dimensions in Spirituality: A Biracial and Bicultural Reading of the Novels of Toni Morrison.* New York: Greenwood, 1987.

Holman, Hugh, C. *A Handbook to Literature.* Fourth Edition. Indianapolis: Bobbs-Merrill, 1980.

Homans, Margaret. "'Her Very Own Howl': The Ambiguities of Representation in Recent Women's Fiction." *Signs* 9: 2 (1983): 186–205.

hooks, bell. "Homeplace: A Site of Resistance." *Yearning: Race, Gender, and Cultural Politics.* Boston: South End, 1990. 41–49.

———. *Talking Back: Thinking Feminist, Thinking Black.* Toronto: Between the Lines, 1988.

———. "Revolutionary Parenting." *Feminist Theory: From Margin to Center.* Boston: South End, 1984.

———. *Arn't I a Woman?: Black Women and Feminism.* Boston: South End, 1981.

Horwitz, Deborah. "Nameless Ghosts: Possession and Dispossession in *Beloved.*" *Studies in American Fiction* 17: 2 (1989): 157–67.

House, Elizabeth. "The Sweet Life in Toni Morrison's Fiction." *American Literature* 56 (1984): 181–202.

———. "Toni Morrison's Ghost: The Beloved Who is Not Beloved." *Studies in American Fiction* 18: 1 (1990): 17–26.

Hovet, Grace Ann, and Babara Lounsberry. "Flying as Symbol and Legend in Toni Morrison's *The Bluest Eye, Sula,* and *Song of Solomon.*" *CLA* 27 (1983): 119–40.

Hoy, Suellan. *Chasing Dirt: The American Pursuit of Cleanliness.* New York: Oxford University Press, 1995.

Hueston, Penny. "Love." *Pinnacle Gardens.* October 18, 2003. *www.theag.com*

Hughes, Langston. "Mother to Son." *The Collected Poems of Langston Hughes.* Ed. Arnold Rampersad. New York: Alfred A. Knopf, 1994. 30.

Hull, Gloria, Patricia Bell-Scott, and Barbara Smith, eds. *All the Women Are White, All the Blacks Are Male, But Some of Us Are Brave: Black Women Studies.* New York: The Feminist Press, 1982.

Hurston, Zora Neale. *Mules and Men.* 1935. Bloomington, Indiana University Press, 1978.

———. *Spunk: The selected Short Stories of Zora Neale Hurston.* Berkeley: Turtle Island Foundation, 1985.

————. *Tell My Horse: Voodoo and Life in Haiti and Jamaica.* 1938. New York: Harper and Row, 1990.

Hypatia. Special Issue: Motherhood and Sexuality 1: 2 (Fall 1986).

Ireland, Mardy. *Reconceiving Women: Separating Motherhood from Female Identity.* New York: Guilford Press, 1993.

Irigarary. Luce. "One Doesn't Stir Without the Other." *Signs* 7: 1 (1981): 61–65.

————. "Plato's Hysteria." *Speculum of the Other Woman.* Trans. Gillian C. Gill. Ithaca: Cornell University Press, 1985. 243–64.

Jackson, Marni. *The Mother Zone: Love, Sex, & Laundry in the Modern Family.* Toronto: Macfarlane Walter and Ross, 1992.

Jacobs, Harriet A. *Incidents in the Life of a Slave Girl Written by Herself.* 1861. Cambridge: Harvard University Press, 1987.

James, Stanlie M. "Mothering: A Possible Black Feminist Link to Social Transformation?" *Theorizing Black Feminism: The Visionary Pragmatism of Black Women.* Ed. Stanlie James and A. P. Busia. New York: Routledge, 1999. 44–54.

Jenkins, Nina. "Black Women and the Meaning of Motherhood." *Redefining Motherhood: Changing Patterns and Identities.* Ed. Sharon Abbey and Andrea O'Reilly. Toronto: Second Story, 1998.

Jewell, Sue. *From Mammy to Miss America and Beyond: Cultural Images & the Shaping of US Social Policy.* New York: Routledge, 1993.

Johnson, Elizabeth. "Mothers at Work: Representations of Maternal Practice in Literature" in *Mothers and Daughters: Connection, Empowerment, and Transformation.* Eds. Andrea O'Reilly and Sharon Abbey. New York: Rowman and Littlefield, 2000.

Johnson, Miriam. *Strong Mothers, Weak Wives: The Search for Gender Equality.* Berkeley: University of California Press, 1990.

Jones, Jacqueline. *Labor of Love, Labor of Sorrow: Black Women, Work, and Family, from Slavery to the Present.* New York: Vintage, 1985.

Jordon, Judith. "The Relational Self: A Model of Women's Development." *Daughtering & Mothering: Female Subjectivity Reanalysed.* Ed. Jannake van Mens-Verhulst, Karlein Schreurs, and Liesbeth Woertman. New York: Routledge, 1993. 135–44.

Joseph, Gloria I., and Jill Lewis, eds. *Common Differences: Conflicts in Black and White Feminist Perspectives.* Boston: South End, 1981.

————. "Mothers and Daughters: Traditional and New Perspectives." *Sage* 1: 2 (1984): 17–21.

Kaplan, Ann. *Motherhood and Representation: The Mother in Popular Culture and Melodrama.* New York: Routledge, 1992.

Kaplan, Elaine Bell. *Not Our Kind of Girl: Unraveling the Myths of Black Teenage Motherhood.* Berkeley: University of California Press, 1997.

Kaplan, Meryle Mahrer. *Mothers' Images of Motherhood.* New York: Routledge, 1992.

Kendrick, Dolores. *The Women of Plums: Poems in the Voices of Slave Women.* New York: William Morrow, 1989.

Kincaid, Jamaica. *Annie John.* New York: Plume, 1983.

King, Joyce Elaine, and Carolyn Ann Mitchell. *Black Mothers to Sons: Juxtaposing African American Literature with Social Practice.* New York: Peter Lang, 1995.

Kinsey, David R. *The Sword and the Flute: Kali and Krisna, Dark Visions of the Terrible and the Sublime in Hindu Mythology.* Berkeley: University of California Press, 1975.

Kitzinger, Sheila. *Women as Mothers.* Glasgow: William Collins Sons, 1978.

Koenen, Anne. "'The One Out of Sequence': An Interview with Toni Morrison." *History and Tradition in Afro-American Culture.* Ed. Gunter H. Lenz. Frankfurt, Germany: Campus, 1984. 207–21.

Kristeva, Julia. "Women's Time." Trans. Alice Jardine. *Signs* 7: 1 (1981): 13–35.

———. *Revolution in Poetic Language.* Trans. Margaret Walker. New York: Columbia University Press, 1984.

Kubitschek, Missy Dehn. *Claiming the Heritage: African-American Women Novelists and History.* Jackson: University Press of Mississippi, 1991.

Kuwabong, Dannabang. "Reading the Gospel of Bakes: Daughters' Representations of Mothers in the Poetry of Claire Harris and Lorna Goodison." *Canadian Woman Studies* 18. 2 & 3 (Summer/Fall 1998): 132–38.

Ladner, Joyce. *Tomorrow's Tomorrow: The Black Woman.* New York: Doubleday, 1971.

Lawson, Erica. "Black Women's Mothering in a Historical and Contemporary Perspective: Understanding the Past, Forging the Future." *Journal of The Association for Research on Mothering* 2: 2 (Fall/Winter 2000): 21–30.

Lazarre, Jane. *The Mother Knot.* Boston: Beacon, 1986.

Lee, Claudette, and Ethel Wilson. "Masculinity, Matriarchy, and Myth: A Black Feminist Perspective" in *Mothers and Sons: Feminism, Masculinity, and the Struggle to Raise Our Sons.* Ed. Andrea O'Reilly. New York: Routledge, 2001.

Lee, Dorothy H. "*Song of Solomon:* To Ride the Air." *Black American Literature Forum* 16 (Summer 1982): 64–70.

Legates, Marlene. "The Cult of Womanhood in Eighteenth-Century Thought." *Eighteenth-Century Studies* 10: 1 (1976): 21–39.

Leira, Halldis, and Madelien Krips. "Revealing Cultural Myths on Motherhood." *Daughtering & Mothering: Female Subjectivity Reanalysed.* Ed. Jannake van Mens-Verhulst, Karlein Schreurs, and Liesbeth Woertman. New York: Routledge, 1993.

Lerner, Gerda, ed. *Black Women in White America: A Documentary History.* New York: Pantheon, 1972.

Levine, Lawrence. *Black Culture, Black Consciousness: Afro-American Folk Thought From Slavery to Freedom.* New York: Oxford University Press, 1977.

Livingston, John. *Birds of the Eastern Forest: 2.* Toronto: McClelland and Stewart, 1977.

Loewenberg, Bert James, and Ruth Bogin, eds. *Black Women in Nineteenth-Century American Life: Their Words, Their Thoughts, Their Feelings.* University Park and London: The Pennsylvania State University Press, 1976.

Logan, Onnie Lee. *Motherwit: An Alabama's Midwife's Story*. New York: E. P. Dutton, 1989.

Lorde, Audre. "Manchild: A Black Lesbian Feminist Response." *Sister Outsider*. Trumansburg, N.Y.: The Crossing, 1984.

Loth, Heinrich. *Women in Ancient Africa*. Trans. Shelia Marnie. Westport, Conn.: Lawrence Hill, 1987.

Louis, Genevie, and Eva Margolis. *The Motherhood Report: How Women Feel about Being Mothers*. New York: Macmillan, 1987.

Lounsberry, Barbara, and Grace Ann Hovat. "Principles of Perception in Toni Morrison's *Sula*." *Black American Literature Forum* 13 (1979).

Lowinsky, Naomi Ruth. *The Motherline: Every Woman's Journey to Find Her Female Roots*. Formerly titled, *Stories from the Motherline: Reclaiming the Mother-Daughter Bond, Finding Our Feminine Souls*. Los Angeles: Jeremy P. Tarcher, 1992.

Luxton, Meg. *More Than a Labour of Love: Three Generations of Women's Work in the Home*. Toronto: Women's Educational Press, 1980.

Mann, Judy. *The Difference: Growing Up Female in America*. New York: Warner Books, 1994.

Margolis, Maxine. *Mothers and Such: Views of American Women and Why They Changed*. Berkeley: University of California Press, 1984.

Marks, Elaine, and Isabelle de Courtivron, eds. *New French Feminisms: An Anthology*. Amherst: University of Massachusetts Press, 1980.

Mason, Theodore O., Jr. "The Novelist as Conservator: Stories and Comprehension in Toni Morrison's *Song of Solomon*." *Toni Morrison*. Ed. Harold Bloom. New York: Chelsea, 1990. 564–81.

Mathieson, Barbara Offutt. "Memory and Mother Love in Morrison's *Beloved*." *American Imago* 47: 1 (1990): 1–21.

Matus, Jill. *Toni Morrison*. Manchester: Manchester University Press, 1998.

Mbalia, Doreatha Drummond. *Toni Morrison's Developing Class Consciousness*. Selinsgrove: Susquenhanna Press, 1991.

McAdoo, Harriette Pipes, ed. *Black Families*. Beverly Hills: Sage, 1981.

——— , ed. *Family Ethnicity: Strength in Diversity*. Beverly Hills: Sage, 1993.

McDowell, Deborah. "'The Self and Other': Reading Toni Morrison's *Sula* as the Black Female Text." *Critical Essays on Toni Morrison*. Ed. Nellie Y. McKay. Boston: G. K. Hall, 1988. 77–84.

——— . "Harlem Nocturne." *The Women's Review of Books* 9: 9 (1992): 1–5.

McKinney-Whetstone, Diane. "The Nature of Love" Interview with Toni Morrison. *Essence*. October 2003. *www.essence.com*

McMahon, Martha. *Engendering Motherhood: Identity and Self-transformation in Women's Lives*. New York: Guilford Press, 1995.

McMillen, Sally G. *Motherhood in the Old South: Pregnancy, Childbirth, and Infant Rearing*. Baton Rouge and London: Louisiana State University Press, 1990.

Middleton, Victoria. "*Sula:* An Experimental Life." *CLA* 28: 4 (1983): 367–81.

Miller, Jean Baker. *Toward a New Psychology of Women.* Boston: Beacon, 1986.

Miner, Madonne M. "Lady No Longer Sings the Blues: Rape, Madness, and Silence in *The Bluest Eye.*" *Conjuring Black Women, Fiction, and Literary Tradition.* Ed. Majorie Pryse and Hortense J. Spillers. Bloomington: Indiana University Press, 1985. 176–91.

Minh-ha, Trinh T. *Woman Native Other.* Bloomington: Indiana University Press, 1989.

Minturn, Leigh, and William Lambert. *Mothers of Six Cultures: Antecedents of Child Rearing.* New York: John Wiley and Sons, 1964.

Mitchell, Mary. "Morrison lite." *Chicago Sun-Times.* October 26, 2002. *www.suntimes.com*

Mobley, Marilyn Sanders. "Narrative Dilemmas: Jadine as Cultural Orphan in *Tar Baby.*" *Toni Morrison: Critical Perspectives, Past and Present.* Ed. Henry Louis Gates Jr. and K. A. Appiah. New York: Amistad, 1993. 284–92.

Mogadime, Dolina. "A Daughter's Praise Poem for Her Mother: Historicizing Community Activism and Racial Uplift Among Women." *Canadian Women's Studies* 18: 2,3 (Fall 1998): 86–91.

Morgan, Robin. "Every Mother's Son." *Lesbians Raising Sons: An anthology.* Ed. Jess Wells. Los Angeles: Alyson Books, 1997.

Mori, Aoi. *Toni Morrison and Womanist Discourse.* New York: Peter Lang, 1999.

Morrison, Toni. *The Bluest Eye.* New York: Washington Square, 1970.

———. *Sula.* New York: New American Library, 1973.

———. *Song of Solomon.* New York: New American Library, 1977.

———. *Tar Baby.* New York: Plume, 1981.

———. "Rootedness: The Ancestor as Foundation." *Black Women Writers (1950–1980).* Ed. Mari Evans. New York: Doubleday, 1984. 339–45.

———. *Beloved.* New York: Plume, 1987.

———. *Jazz.* New York: Alfred A. Knopf, 1992.

———. *Paradise.* New York: Alfred A. Knopf, 1998.

———. "A Knowing So Deep." *Essence* (May 1985): 250.

———. "The Site of Memory." *Inventing the Truth: The Art and Craft of Memoir.* Ed. William Zinsser. Boston: Houghton Mifflin, 1987. 103–24.

———. "'Unspeakable Things Unspoken': The Afro-American Presence in American Literature." *Michigan Quarterly* 28 (Winter 1989): 1–34.

———. "What the Black Woman Thinks About Women's Lib." *New York Times Magazine,* 22 August 1971: 14, 15, 63, 64, 66.

———. *Love.* New York: Knopf, 2003.

Morton, Patricia. *Disfigured Images: The Historical Assault on Afro-American Women.* Westport, Conn.: Greenwood, 1991.

Nakano, Glenn Evelyn, Grace Chang, and Linda Rennie Forcey. *Ideology, Experience, and Agency.* New York: Routledge, 1994.

Naylor, Gloria. "A Conversation: Gloria Naylor and Toni Morrison." *Conversations with Toni Morrison*. Ed. Danille Taylor-Guthrie. Jackson: University Press of Mississippi, 1994.

Neumann, Erich. *The Great Mother*. Trans. Ralph Manheim. Princeton: Princeton University Press, 1983.

Neverdon-Morton, Cynthia. *Afro-American Women of the South and the Advancement of the Race, 1895–1925*. Knoxville: University of Tennessee Press, 1989.

News from Princeton University. Office of Communications, Princeton University, October 22, 2003. *www.princeton.edu*

Nurse, Donna Bailey. "Morrison's jazz". *Toronto Star*. November 30, 2003. *www.torontostar.ca*

Oakley, Ann. *Social Support and Motherhood: The Natural History of a Research Project*. Oxford, UK: Blackwell, 1992.

O'Barr, Jean F., Deborah Pope, and Mary Wyer, eds. *Ties That Bind: Essays on Mothering and Patriarchy*. Chicago: University of Chicago Press, 1990.

O'Brien, Mary. *The Politics of Reproduction*. Boston: Routledge, 1981.

O'Connor, Anne-Marie. "*Love* and the outlaw women: Toni Morrison's latest explores the relationship between the sexes and segregation's end." *Los Angeles Times*. October 15, 2003. *http://blackvocies.com/features/books/news/bv-books-morrison*

O'Daly, Brenda, and Maureen T. Reddy, eds. *Narrating Mothers: Theorizing Maternal Subjectivities*. Knoxville: University of Tennessee Press, 1991.

O'Donnell, Lydia N. *The Unheralded Majority: Contemporary Women as Mothers*. Lexington: D. C. Heath, 1985.

Ogunyemi, Chikwenye Okonjo. "Order and Disorder in Toni Morrison's *The Bluest Eye*." *Critique* 19 (1977): 112–20.

———. "*Sula:* 'A Nigger Joke.'" *Black American Literature Forum* 13 (1979): 130–34.

O'Reilly, Andrea. *Reconceiving Maternity: Feminist Theory on Motherhood Since 1990*. (forthcoming).

———, ed. *From Motherhood to Mothering: The Legacy of Adrienne Rich's Of Woman Born*. Albany: State University of New York Press, 2004.

———. "Introduction." *Mothers and Daughters: Connection, Empowerment, and Transformation*. Ed. Andrea O'Reilly and Sharon Abbey. Lanham, Md.: Rowman and Littlefield, 2000.

———, ed. *Mothers and Sons: Feminism, Masculinity, and the Struggle to Raise our Sons*. New York: Routledge, 2001.

———. "'I come from a long line of uppity irate black women': African American Feminism on Motherhood, the Motherline, and the Mother-Daughter Relationship." *Mothers and Daughters: Connection, Empowerment, and Transformation*. Ed. Andrea O'Reilly and Sharon Abbey. Lanham, Md.: Rowman and Littlefield, 2000. 143–59.

———. "A Mom and her Son: Thoughts on Feminist Mothering" *Journal of the Association for Research on Mothering* 2: 1 (Spring/Summer 2000): 179–93.

———. "Across the Divide: Contemporary Anglo-American Feminist Theory on the Mother-Daughter." *Redefining Motherhood: Changing Identities and Patterns.* Ed. Sharon Abbey and Andrea O'Reilly. Toronto: Second Story, 1998.

———. "Mothers, Daughters, and Feminism Today: Empowerment, Agency, Narrative, and Motherline." *Canadian Woman's Studies* 18: 2,3 (Summer/Fall 1998): 16–21.

———. "'Ain't That Love?': Anti-Racism and Racial Constructions of Motherhood." *Everyday Acts Against Racism: Raising Children in a Multiracial World.* Ed. Maureen Reddy. Seattle: Seal Press, 1996. 88–98.

———. "Talking Back in Mother Tongue: A Feminist Course on Mothering-Mother-hood." *Feminism and Education* Vol. 2. Ed. Paula T. Bourne. Toronto: CWSE Press, 1994. 221–38.

———, and Sharon Abbey, eds. *Mothers and Daughters: Connection, Empowerment, and Transformation.* Lanham, Md: Rowman and Littlefield, 2000.

Otten, Terry. *The Crime of Innocence in the Fiction of Toni Morrison.* Columbia: University of Missouri Press, 1989.

Payne, Karen, ed. *Between Ourselves: Letters Between Mothers and Daughters.* Boston: Houghton Mifflin, 1983.

Page, Philip. *Dangerous Freedom: Fusion and Fragmentation in Toni Morrison's Novels.* Jackson: University Press of Mississippi, 1995.

Peach, Linden. *Toni Morrison.* New York: St. Martin's, 1995.

Pearlman, Mickey, ed. *Mother Puzzles: Daughters and Mothers in Contemporary American Fiction.* New York: Greenwood, 1989.

Perry, Ruth, and Martine Watson Brownley, eds. *Mothering the Mind: Twelve Studies of Writers and their Silent Partners.* New York: Holmes and Meier, 1984.

Pettis, Joyce. "Difficult Survival : Mothers and Daughters in *The Bluest Eye.*" *Sage* 4: 2 (1987): 26–29.

Philip, M. Nourbese. *A Genealogy of Resistance: And Other Essays.* Toronto: Mercury, 1997.

Pipher, Mary. *Reviving Ophelia: Saving the Selves of Adolescent Girls.* New York: G. P. Putnam's Sons, 1994.

Pollack, Sandra, and Jeanne Vaughn. *Politics of the Heart: A Lesbian Parenting Anthology.* Ithaca, N.Y.: Firebrand, 1987.

Portales, Marco. "Toni Morrison's *The Bluest Eye:* Shirley Temple and Cholly." *Centennial Review* 30 (1986): 496–506.

Pratt, Annis. *Archetypal Patterns of Women's Fiction.* Brighton, England: Harvester, 1982.

Pryse, Marjorie, and Hortense J. Spillers, eds. *Conjuring: Black Women, Fiction, and Literary Tradition.* Bloomington: Indiana University Press, 1985.

Rabuzzi, Kathryn Allen. *Motherself: A Mythic Analysis of Motherhood.* Bloomington: Indiana University Press, 1988.

Rainwater, Lee, and William L. Yancey, eds. *The Moynihan Report and the Politics of Controversy.* Cambridge: M.I.T., 1967.

Raymond, Janice. "Female Friendships: Contra Chodorow and Dinnerstein." *Hypatia Special Issue: Motherhood and Sexuality* 1: 2 (1986): 34–48.

Reddy, Maureen T. *Crossing the Color Line: Parenting, Race, and Culture.* New Brunswick: Rutgers, 1994.

Reddy, Maureen, Martha Roth, Amy Sheldon, eds. *Mother Journeys: Feminists Write about Mothering.* Minneapolis: Spinsters Ink, 1994.

Reyes, Angelita. "Ancient Properties in the New World: The Paradox of the 'Other' in Toni Morrison's *Tar Baby.*" *Black Scholar* 17 (1986): 19–25.

Rich, Adrienne. *On Lies, Secrets, and Silence.* New York: W.W. Norton, 1979.

———. *Of Woman Born: Motherhood as Experience and Institution.* New York: W.W. Norton, 1986.

Rigney, Barbara Hill. "Hagar's Mirror: Self and Identity in Morrison's Fiction." *Toni Morrison.* Ed. Linden Peach. New York: St. Martin's, 1998.

———. *The Voices of Toni Morrison.* Columbus: Ohio State University Press, 1991.

Rodgers-Rose, La Frances, ed. *The Black Woman.* Beverly Hills: Sage, 1980.

Ross, Val. "Giving a human face to 'chaos.'" *The Globe and Mail* 5 May, 1995, C1+.

Rossiter, Amy. *From Private to Public: A Feminist Exploration of Early Mothering.* Toronto: Women's Press, 1988.

Rothman, Barbara Katz. *Recreating Motherhood: Ideology and Technology in a Patriarchal Society.* New York: W. W. Norton, 1989.

Rothstein, Mervyn. "Toni Morrison in Her New Novel Defends Women." *New York Times* 26 Aug. 1987: C17+.

Rubin, Merle. "Toni Morrison's story of love, its many forms." *The Washington Times.* November 2, 2003. *www.washtimes.com*

Ruddick, Sara. "Preservative Love and Military Destruction: Reflections on Mothering and Peace and 'Maternal Thinking'" in *Mothering: Essays in Feminist Theory.* Ed. Joyce Trebilcott. Totowa, N.J.: Rowman and Allanheld, 1984.

———. *Maternal Thinking: Toward a Politics of Peace.* New York: Ballantine, 1989.

Russell, Sandi. "It's OK to Say OK, An Interview Essay," 1986. *Critical Essays on Toni Morrison.* Ed. Nellie Y. McKay. Boston: G. K. Hall, 1988. 43–47.

Ryan, Mary P. *The Empire of the Mother: American Writing about Domesticity 1830–1860.* New York: Harrington Park Press, 1985.

Sage. Special Issues: Mothers and Daughters 1: 2 (Fall 1984) and 4: 2 (Fall 1987).

Saint-Martin, Lori. *Le nom de la mère : mères, filles et écriture dans la littérature québécoise au féminine.* Montréal : Editions Nota bene, 1999.

Samuels, Wifred, and Clenora Hudson-Weems. *Toni Morrison.* Boston: Twayne, 1990.

Scarry, Elaine. *The Body in Pain: The Making and Unmaking of the World.* New York: Oxford University Press, 1985.

Schapiro, Barbara. "The Bonds of Love and the Boundaries of Self in Toni Morrison's *Beloved.*" *Contemporary Literature* 32: 2 (1991): 194–210.

Segal, Lynne. *Is the Future Female? Troubled Thoughts on Contemporary Feminism.* London: Virago, 1987.

Shannon, Anna. "'We Was Girls Together': A Study of Toni Morrison's *Sula.*" *Midwestern Miscellany* 10 (1982): 9–22.

Shields, Carol. *The Stone Diaries.* Toronto: Vintage, 1993.

Showalter, Elaine. "Feminist Criticism in the Wilderness." *The New Feminist Criticism.* New York: Pantheon, 1985.

Silverman, Kaja. *The Subject of Semiotics.* New York: Oxford University Press, 1983.

Silverstein, Olga, and Beth Rashbaum. *The Courage to Raise Good Men.* New York: Viking, 1994.

Sistren. *Lionheart Gal: Life Stories of Jamaican Women.* Toronto: Sister Vision, 1987.

Sjoo, Monica, and Barbara Mor. *The Great Cosmic Mother.* New York: HarperCollins, 1991.

Skerrett, Joseph, Jr. "Recitation to the Griot: Storytelling and Learning in Toni Morrison's *Song of Solomon.*" *Conjuring: Black Women, Fiction, and Tradition.* Ed. Marjories Pryse and Hortense Spillers. Bloomington: Indiana University Press, 1985. 192–202.

Smith, Barbara, ed. *Home Girls: A Black Feminist Anthology.* New York: Kitchen Table-Women of Color Press, 1983.

Smith, Babette. *Mothers and Sons.* St. Leonards, N.S.W., Australia: Allen and Unwin, 1995.

Smith, Valerie. "The Quest for and Discovery of Identity in Toni Morrison's *Song of Solomon.*" *The Southern Review* 21: 3 (July 1983).

Sokoloff, Janice. "Intimations of Matriarchal Age Notes on the Mythical Eva in Toni Morrison's *Sula.*" *Journal of Black Studies* 16: 4 (1986): 429–34.

Spelman, Elizabeth. *Inessential Woman: Problems of Exclusion in Feminist Thought.* Boston: Beacon, 1988.

Sprengnether, Madelon. *The Spectral Mother.* Ithaca: Cornell University Press, 1990.

Stack, Carol B. *All Our Kin: Strategies for Survival in a Black Community.* New York: Harper and Row, 1974.

———, and Linda Burton. "Kinscripts: Reflections on Family, Generation, and Culture." *Mothering: Ideology, Experience, and Agency.* Ed. Evelyn Nakano Glenn, Grace Chang, and Linda Rennie Forcey. New York: Routledge, 1994.

Staples, Robert, and Leanor Boulin Johnson. *Black Families at the Crossroads: Challenges and Prospects.* San Francisco: Jossey-Bass, 1993.

Steady, Filomina Chioma, ed. *The Black Woman Cross-Culturally.* Cambridge, Mass.: Schenkman, 1981.

Steele, Cassie Premo. "Drawing Strengths from Our Other Mothers: Tapping the Roots of Black History." *Journal of The Association for Research on Mothering* 2: 2 (Fall/Winter 2000): 7–17.

Sutton, Terri. "Love among the ruined: Morrison explores a family dynamic and the toll betrayal takes on hearts." *JSOnline Milwaukee Journal Sentinel* October 25, 2003. *www.jsonline.com/enter/books/reviews/oct03/179731.asp*

Taylor-Guthrie, Danille. *Conversations with Toni Morrison*. Jackson: University Press of Mississippi, 1994.

Terborg-Penn, Rosalyn, Sharon Harley, and Andrea Benton Rushing, eds. *Women in Africa and the African Diaspora*. Washington, D.C.: Howard University Press, 1987.

Theriot, Nancy M. *The Biosocial Construction of Femininity, Mothers and Daughters in Nineteenth-Century America*. Lexington: University Press of Kentucky, 1996.

Thurer, Shari. *The Myths of Motherhood: How Culture Reinvents the Good Mother*. New York: Penguin, 1994.

Todd, Janet. *Women's Friendship in Literature*. New York: Columbia University Press, 1980.

Tong, Rosemarie. *Feminist Thought: A Comprehensive Introduction*. Boulder: Westview, 1989.

Traylor, Eleanor W. "The Fabulous World of Toni Morrison: *Tar Baby*." *Critical Essays on Toni Morrison*. Ed. Nellie Mckay. Boston: G.K. Hall, 1988. 135–49.

Trebilcot, Joyce, ed. *Mothering: Essays in Feminist Theory*. Totowa, N.J.: Rowman and Allanheld, 1984.

Treichler, Paula. "Feminism, Medicine, and the Meaning of Childbirth." *Body/Politics, Women and the Discourse of Science*. Ed. Mary Jacobus, Eveyln Fox Keller, and Sally Shuttleworth. New York: Routledge, 1989.

Truth, Sojourner. "Ain't I A Woman?" *The Norton Anthology of Literature*. Ed. Sandra M. Gilbert and Susan Gubar. New York: W. W. Norton, 1985. 253.

Tune, Anne Ruth. *The Politics of Motherhood*. Ann Arbor: University of Michigan Press, 1989.

Turnage, Barbara. "The Global Self-Esteem of an African-American Adolescent Female and Her Relationship with Her Mother." *Mothers and Daughters: Connection, Empowerment, and Transformation*. Ed. Andrea O'Reilly and Sharon Abbey. Lanham, Md.: Rowman and Littlefield, 2001. 175–87.

Umansky, Lauri. *Motherhood Reconceived: Feminism and the Legacies of the Sixties*. New York: New York University Press, 1996.

Van Mens-Verhulst, Janneke, Karlein Schreurs, and Liesbeth Woertman, eds. *Daughtering and Mothering: Female Subjectivity Reanalysed*. New York: Routledge, 1993.

Wachtel, Eleanor. "Interview with Toni Morrison." CBC FM Radio, 18 July 1993.

Wade-Gayles, Gloria. *Pushed Back to Strength: A Black Woman's Journey Home*. Boston: Beacon, 1993.

———. *No Crystal Stair: Visions of Race and Sex in Black Women's Fiction*. New York: Pilgrim Press, 1984.

Walker, Alice. "In Search of Our Mothers' Gardens." *In Search of Our Mothers' Gardens*. San Diego: Harcourt Brace Jovanovich, 1983.

———. *The Temple of My Familiar*. New York: Pocket Books, 1989.

———. *Possessing the Secret of Joy*. New York: Harcourt Brace Jovanovich, 1992.

Walker, Barbara. *The Women's Encyclopedia of Myths and Secrets*. New York: HarperCollins, 1983.

Walkerdine, Valerie, and Helen Lucey. *Democracy in the Kitchen: Regulating Mothers and Socializing Daughters*. London: Virago, 1989.

Wall, Cheryl A., ed. *Changing Our Own Words: Essays on Criticism, Theory, and Writing by Black Women*. New Brunswick and London: Rutgers University Press, 1989.

Wallace, Michele. *Black Macho and the Myth of the Superwoman*. New York: Verso, 1990.

Walton, Jean. "Re-Placing Race in (White) Psychoanalytic Discourse: Founding Narratives of Feminism." *Female Subject in Black and White: Race, Psychoanalysis, Feminism*. Ed. Elizabeth Abel, Barbara Christian, Helene Moglen. Berkeley: University of California Press, 1997. 223–51.

Wane, Njoki Nathani. "Reflections on the Mutuality of Mothering: Women, Children, and Othermothering." *Journal of The Association for Research on Mothering* 2: 2 (Fall/Winter 2000): 105–16.

Ware, Vron. *Beyond the Pale: White Women, Racism, and History*. London: Verso, 1992.

Washington, Mary Helen, ed. *Invented Lives: Narratives of Black Women 1860–1960*. New York: Anchor, Doubleday, 1988.

——, ed. *Black-eyed Susans, Midnight Birds: Stories by and about Black Women*. New York: Anchor, Doubleday, 1990.

——, ed. *Memory of Kin: Stories About Family by Black Writers*. New York: Doubleday, 1991.

——. "I Sign My Mother's Name: Alice Walker, Dorothy West, Paule Marshall." *Mothering the Mind: Twelve Studies of Writers and Their Silent Partners*. Ed. Ruth Perry and Martine Watson Brownley. New York: Holmes and Meier, 1984.

Washington, Valora. "The Black Mother in the United States: History, Theory, Research, and Issues." *The Different Faces of Motherhood*. Ed. Beverly Birns and Dale F. Hay. New York: Plenum, 1988. 185–213.

Wearing, Betsy. *The Ideology of Motherhood*. Sydney: George Allen and Unwin, 1984.

Weaver, Tereak. "Morrison's new Love: A master probes deep emotional places." *The Atlanta Journal-Constitution*. October 26, 2003. *www.ajc.com*

Weigle, Marta. *Creation and Procreation: Feminist Reflections on Mythologies of Cosmogony and Parturition*. Philadelphia: University of Pennsylvania Press, 1989.

Wells, Jess, ed. *Lesbians Raising Sons: An anthology*. Los Angeles: Alyson Books, 1997.

Werner, Craig. "The Briar Patch as Modernist Myth: Morrison, Barthes, and Tar Baby As-Is." *Critical Essays on Toni Morrison*. Ed. Nellie McKay. Boston: G. K. Hall, 1988. 150–67.

Westkott, Marcia. "Mothers and Daughters in the World of the Father." *Frontiers* 3: 2 (1978): 16–21.

White, Deborah Gray. *Ar'n't I A Woman? Female Slaves in the Plantation South*. New York: W. W. Norton, 1985.

Williams, Sherley Anne. "Some Implications of Womanist Theory." *Reading Black Reading Feminist: A Critical Anthology.* Ed. Henry Louis Gates Jr. New York: Meridian, 1990. 68–75.

Willis, Susan. "Eruptions of Funk: Historicizing Toni Morrison." *Black Literature and Literary Theory.* Ed. Henry L. Gates Jr. New York: Methuen, 1984. 263–83.

———. "I Shop, Therefore I Am: Is There a Place for Afro-American Culture in Commodity Culture?" In *Changing Our Own Words: Essays on Criticism, Theory, and Writing by Black Women.* Ed. Cheryl Wall. New Brunswick: Rutgers University Press, 1989. 173–95.

Wilson, Harriet. *Our Nig: Or, Sketches from the Life of a Free Black.* 1859. New York: Random House, 1983.

Wilt, Judith. *Abortion, Choice, and Contemporary Fiction: The Armageddon of the Maternal Instinct.* Chicago: University of Chicago Press, 1990.

Winters, Wendy Glasgow. *African American Mothers and Urban Schools: The Power of Participation.* New York: Lexington, 1993.

Wolf, Naomi. *Fire With Fire: The New Female Power and How It Will Change the 21st Century.* New York: Random House, 1993.

Woloch, Nancy. *Women and the American Experience.* New York: Alfred A. Knopf, 1984.

Women's Studies Quarterly. Special Issue: Teaching About Mothering 11: 4 (Winter 1983).

Wong, Shelley. "Transgression as Poesis in *The Bluest Eye.*" *Callaloo* 13 (Summer 1990): 471–81.

Woolf, Virginia. *A Room of One's Own.* 1929. New York: Granada, 1977.

Wright, Sarah. *This Child's Gonna Live.* 1969. New York: The Feminist Press, 1986.

Wyatt, Jean. "Giving Body to the Word: The Maternal Symbolic in Toni Morrison's *Beloved.*" *PMLA* 108: 3 (1993): 474–88.

Wylie, Philip. *A Generation of Vipers.* New York: Reinhart and Company, 1942.

Index

217

Printed in Great Britain
by Amazon